INNOVATION IN PATIENT CARE

AN ACTION RESEARCH STUDY OF CHANGE IN A PSYCHIATRIC HOSPITAL

Edited by
DAVID TOWELL and CLIVE HARRIES

CROOM HELM LONDON

© 1979 Crown Copyright
Croom Helm Ltd, 2-10 St John's Road, London SW11

British Library Cataloguing in Publication Data

Innovation in patient care.
    1. Psychiatric hospital care – Great Britain
    2. Aged – Hospital care – Great Britain
    I. Title   II. Towell, David   III. Harries, Clive
    IV. Fulbourn Hospital Innovation Project
    362.2'1'0941   RC450.G7

ISBN 0–85664–692–X

Printed and bound in Great Britain

CONTENTS

TABLES AND FIGURES

Tables

Figures

ACKNOWLEDGEMENTS

In reporting on the development of the Fulbourn Hospital Innovation Project between 1972 and 1977, this book represents the work of very many individuals and in some small measure the efforts of a whole institution. All the contributors would like to acknowledge their immense debt to other participants in this project, from and with whom we still have so much to learn. Particular thanks are due to the many colleagues who have helped to stimulate the ideas and sustain the commitment which this work has involved. The project is also heavily indebted to the Department of Health and Social Security and the King Edward's Hospital Fund for London who provided external support and financed the experimental creation of the new role of social research adviser at Fulbourn. The first two incumbents of this role, David Towell and Clive Harries, wish to express gratitude to their secretaries, Susan Finch and Pam Mills, who gave invaluable assistance throughout the development of this project, and similarly to Olga Patchett and Avril Deighton, who shared with the editors the task of producing this book. Finally, thanks are due to *Nursing Times* and *Health and Social Service Journal* for permission to reproduce in Chapters 3 and 4 material first published in these journals.

INTRODUCTION: DEVELOPING INNOVATION FROM WITHIN

David Towell and Clive Harries

Constant change is here to stay has become a popular maxim. It is a statement about common experiences. It also provides some guide to how these experiences are being understood. One meaning is that since change is now endemic, we had better get used to it; possibly even thrive on it. Underlying this however, there are, we suspect, more ambivalent responses. Is change something we can control; or is change controlling us? Is it change for a purpose; or change for its own sake? And indeed, has all this change actually led to any *real* change?

These dilemmas have a special significance for many people concerned with the health and welfare services. The attempts in recent years to bring about improvements have been followed by disillusion and considerable doubts about the efficacy of change imposed from the 'top downwards'. At the same time, the 'Cinderellas' of these services — provision for the mentally ill, mentally handicapped, and growing numbers of the elderly — have typically continued in the traditions inherited from past deprivation, despite recurrent public concern about the quality of care available to these groups of clients. Indeed there is considerable evidence that over a long period, these services have had few resources and received low priority within medicine. Against this heritage, the major advances of the 1950s and 1960s have still left many aspects of such provision and care a long way behind what in the late 1970s can be regarded as tolerable, let alone desirable. Greater public awareness of these deficiencies may contribute to the political struggle for priority to be given to these services. However with the public expenditure constraints that seem likely to operate for the next few years, it is essential that the very best use is made of available resources if improved care is to be achieved. All this appears particularly relevant to the large institutions, often a nineteenth-century legacy still determining the main features of many of these services, but usually characterised in both popular discourse and social scientific literature as highly resistant to change.

One response to these problems has been the search for further solutions on a national scale. In the case of the National Health Service as a whole, the Royal Commission is having to consider the need for more radical changes. In the case of large institutions, the Secretary of State for Social Services has established a high level working group to study the main difficulties reported in recent mental hospital enquiries with a view to making new recommendations.

Whatever the value of these central initiatives, we should like to invite attention to an alternative, and perhaps complementary approach to change. We start by recognising that whatever its deficiencies, the NHS continues to command widespread public support. The post-war period has seen extensive developments in treatment and care, including in the less favoured services. No one who has examined even the most deprived of our institutions is likely to doubt that considerable resources of commitment and skill are to be found in those who work there.

Our own observations suggest that these staff in the 'front line' often have good ideas about how improvements in care can be accomplished: if it is possible to start from the problems these staff experience and work from there, much can be achieved. Aware of the limitations of change for its own sake, we recognise that some systematic examination of these problems together with adequate reflection and conceptualisation is necessary to provide the basis and motivation for informed change. We also believe that managers have crucial roles to play in providing the leadership required to facilitate and encourage genuine participation in such initiatives.

Accordingly we take seriously the view that substantial change is possible from the 'bottom up' in the health and welfare services if only the potential contribution of staff at all levels can be more fully realised. Our central theme then is that of *developing innovation from within*.

Exploring this theme has been a collaborative venture which we have shared with many colleagues. It has required from all of us some willingness to engage with new experiences and seek better ways of understanding. In the course of this work we have come to formulate questions from fresh perspectives and with different emphases. In learning from our own experiences, we have striven to rethink old concepts and examine their wider relevance.

Thus we have come to see that innovation is likely to entail putting aside what one thinks one knows and accepting the uncertainty which follows, in the effort to think critically about what is usually taken for granted. If this process can be supported, it becomes possible to create alternatives, try experiments, and make choices. In turn this implies encouragement for diversity, as skills and resources are mobilised in relation to the problems being confronted. Perhaps most important, change then can be understood as a continuous activity which needs to be achieved through the exercise of greater autonomy by those involved. In an organisational context, this approach also draws attention to the wider conditions required to foster innovation and make these processes self-sustaining.

In what follows, we describe and analyse how these ideas were developed, realised and tested in the particular context of an action research study of change in a psychiatric hospital.

The Hospital Innovation Project

The origins of this study can be located in both the problems facing the psychiatric services in the early 1970s and some particular circumstances which came together to make an initiative of this kind seem possible. At national level there was recurrent concern with the deficiencies in psychiatric care and growing interest in how social research could be effectively applied to health service issues. At Fulbourn Hospital, leading staff were starting to consider how the hospital's progressive reputation could be sustained in new conditions which might require different approaches to change. A young sociologist was completing a detailed study of psychiatric nursing practice and seeking ways of developing this work further. The report of a Hospital Advisory Service team, which visited during the summer of 1971, included the recommendation that the availability of advice on research might be a valuable support to staff members undertaking projects of relevance to current problems facing this hospital.

These influences were the starting point for a five year experiment designed to develop new approaches to encouraging improvements in psychiatric care — an experiment which has become known as the Hospital Innovation Project (HIP). Central to this work has been the attempt to involve staff members in more or less systematic investigations of problems emerging in their own work, as a basis for staff groups themselves making informed innovations in hospital organisation and practice. The Project as a whole can be regarded therefore as an exploration of how far this aim could be practically realised and established in the Fulbourn setting. Its wider importance has been in suggesting how institutions — with their traditional image of resisting necessary changes, but even more than in the past now faced both internally and externally with the need for innovation — can use the contribution of staff to meet more effectively the developing needs of the communities they serve.

With support from research funds for the pilot stage of this experiment, a key feature of the Project was the creation in 1972 of a new role at Fulbourn, that of social research adviser. This role was intended to provide a service in the hospital such that any group of staff could seek help in identifying, investigating and tackling problems arising in their day-to-day work. As the availability of this service became known and with encouragement from some senior staff, a variety of problems were raised for attention and several of these received more detailed examination. Thus over the first two years many projects were initiated in various parts of the hospital, directly involving a large number of staff from different professions, and leading to a range of substantive innovations in aspects of the hospital's work. Moreover by 1974 there was evidence that the cumulative impact of these endeavours was contributing to more general developments in the organisation and management of the hospital and to a wider climate conducive to informed change.

Although not of course the only stimulus to change in this period, these benefits were judged of sufficient value by staff at Fulbourn for them to want HIP to continue after this pilot stage. Following an intermediate phase in which some features of this approach were sustained through the dislocations of NHS reorganisation, it proved possible to re-establish the role of social research adviser towards the end of 1975 with the help of further external funding. In 1978, costs of this post are being met wholly from the hospital's own budget and with continuing support from senior staff, further projects are being undertaken on problems of current relevance. These later stages of this work have provided the opportunity to use the experience of the first stage to seek further improvements in services based on the hospital in the very different conditions which have prevailed more widely since 1974. Lessons from HIP are also being applied and tested elsewhere through a wider programme of work on the development of the 'Cinderella' services.

From the beginning of this Project, participants have been committed to monitoring these experiences carefully so as to learn as much as possible from this experiment. In its sixth year this work is still progressing and we continue to learn more about change in psychiatric care in the face of new demands and in different situations. Indeed there is clearly a sense in which innovation is always unfinished and such work should become in some form an enduring facet of hospital life. With the opportunity to reflect on this first five years however, we believe it is now worth reporting on our experiences more widely. This book represents the work then of some two hundred people more or less directly involved in the activities which comprised the Hospital Innovation Project at Fulbourn between 1972 and 1977. We were privileged to have the opportunity of sharing in this work throughout this period as the first two incumbents of the social research adviser role and as participants in the Steering Committee which has managed HIP. On behalf of the individuals, groups and organisations concerned therefore, we have accepted responsibility for editing this account.

Social Science Perspectives

Most of those involved or interested in this Project would identify themselves primarily as practitioners concerned with how improvements in care can be achieved. At the same time, the potential value of some conceptual framework which assists in the struggle to understand better the complex problems these efforts encounter would be widely recognised. In our own case, the attempt to develop and also to analyse and evaluate HIP, has looked particularly to the social sciences. We have drawn on three main strands of work, which can be briefly summarised.

Of central importance has been the distinctive contribution to applied social research represented in the work of the Tavistock Institute of Human Relations. Between 1971 and 1976, David Towell was one of a small group of staff at the Institute engaged in a wider programme of action research in health care systems, focussed on problems of long-term care. Building on earlier Tavistock studies (notably, Menzies, 1960; Sofer, 1961; and Miller and Rice, 1967) this programme has led to the evolution of a more or less common *social systems approach* to projects of this kind. Four elements in this approach can be distinguished.

Fundamental is the commitment to action research. In collaboration with the people concerned, all these projects have aimed both to contribute to the resolution of practical problems and to increase understanding of the issues being studied. Through close working relationships it has been possible not only to conduct research on health care, but also to become involved in implementing change and confronting the difficulties that arise in trying to use such research. Accordingly the research worker's own experiences, particularly as change proceeds, have provided the means for further learning about these issues.

To complement this research strategy, a theoretical stance has been developed which gives initial orientation to any new work and provides the basis for generating more precise hypotheses during the process of field research. The starting point here is an interest in discovering how the various participants in a health care setting themselves 'define the situations' in which they are involved. This setting can be viewed as an 'arena' (see Strauss et al, 1963) in which professional, non-professional and client groups meet, each with their own perspectives and purposes, to 'negotiate' the courses of action to be followed. The main outcomes to these negotiations can be seen in the enduring patterns of work and forms of organisation which characterise particular situations. These processes of interaction can in turn be understood as both reflecting and being influenced by such factors as the previous division of labour and distribution of power among the groups involved and the resources available for the tasks in question.

In analysing the structure of health care organisations, it has then been found useful to adopt what may be described as an 'open systems' model (see Miller, 1976a). Essentially this heuristic device invites attention to the inter-relatedness of various aspects of the internal functioning of organisations with each other and with factors in the organisations' environment. A key aspect of the relationship between any organisation and its environment is the nature of its 'throughput'. In the case of hospitals for example, the primary throughput is usually patients, who may be successfully treated and returned to normal roles in society. The activities through which this is achieved can typically be differentiated into a number of sets, each with their own contribution to the overall task. Again to take the hospital example; ward nursing, occupational therapy, and social work support, might all be so distinguished. Suggestions for alternative forms of organisation can be derived through considering different ways in which boundaries might be drawn round sets of activities in order to carry out this task. Organisational design also requires identifying how transactions across these internal boundaries, and between the total system and its environment, can best be managed. Each of these steps is well illustrated by the analysis of different patterns of care in residential institutions for the disabled, provided by Miller and Gwynne (1972).

A further element of this approach seeks to complement such analysis with insights drawn from psychodynamic interpretations of group and organisational processes (see Bion, 1961; Higgin and Bridger, 1964). Participants bring to organisations more than just the role-related aspects of their selves; they are present as people whose current attitudes and actions may reflect, not necessarily consciously, the precipitate of many previous experiences. For example in the case of nursing, the distinctive features of the task of caring, particularly the extent of the patient's dependency, are likely to generate considerable anxieties: the way these are dealt with will be an important determinant of nurse-patient interaction. These dynamic processes enter into inter-group relationships too, as can be seen sometimes in the conflicts which arise between the different professions caring for the same patients. Over time, the whole functioning of an institution may be shaped to support a particular set of defences against anxiety, as Menzies (1960) has demonstrated in her study of general nursing. In thus helping to illuminate irrational aspects of the way organisations work, difficulties in achieving social change can also be better understood, since it can be anticipated that innovations which threaten established defences will themselves increase anxiety among those likely to be affected.

Supplementing this Tavistock approach, we have found helpful a growing body of other research in social psychiatry and medical sociology. Much of the best known of this research is American (for example the classic mental hospital studies of Stanton and Schwartz, 1954; Greenblatt et al, 1957; Caudill, 1958; Goffman, 1961; and Strauss et al, 1964); but there have also been significant British contributions, particularly in developing the concept of therapeutic communities (for example, Jones, 1952; Clark, 1964; Jones, 1968) and more recently in systematic studies of residential care (Wing and Brown, 1970; King et al, 1971). This second strand of work is more fully reviewed elsewhere (see Towell, 1975), but in short its main importance here is in suggesting a variety of working hypotheses about how therapeutic processes and outcomes are influenced by the social organisation of health services. For example of particular relevance among research of this genre was David Towell's earlier study of psychiatric nursing at Fulbourn, which shows how hospital organisation, the prevailing approaches to treat-ment, and patterns of staff training, all interact in shaping patient care on different kinds of ward.

Other work in the health field has reflected the increasing application of social science based approaches in efforts to secure organisational and service development. Of some importance because of its influence on the reorganisation of the NHS as a whole, is the ongoing work of the Brunel University team (see Rowbottom, 1973). In the genesis of HIP however, we learnt more from smaller scale experiments. For example, Dykens et al (1964) analyse the distinctive characteristics of mental hospitals pertinent to the design of change strategies and show the importance of genuine collaboration with staff in determining the productivity of any attempts at innovation. Pantall and Elliot (1965, 1967) demonstrate something of the range of problems on which applied research can aid hospital management. The 'Hospital Internal Communications' Project (see Revans, 1972; Wieland and Leigh, 1971) suggests many lessons for any subsequent attempts to improve patient care through involving staff in research on their own activities.

These experiments in the health service can also be seen as part of the third significant strand of work on which we have drawn: a range of studies concerned more generally with the utilisation of social science and the processes by which innovation occurs in organisations. These have of course been continuing foci for Tavistock work (see most recently, Lawrence and Robinson, 1975), but the arguments of the Heyworth Committee (1965) on the 'need for social scientists to work at the points where problems first emerge' has given rise to wider pre-occupation with these issues, best represented in Britain by the programme of the 'Centre for Utilisation of Social Science Research' at Loughborough (for example, Cherns, 1968; Ford and Plumb, 1970; and Clark, 1972a). Similar work has developed on a larger scale in the United States (for example Havelock, 1969, 1970). Combining insights from this body of research (particularly Clark, 1972b; Zaltman et al, 1973) we have developed an analytical framework for examining the relationship between strategies of applied social research and the processes by which innovations are created and implemented in different organisations: attending here to such variables as the roles and approaches adopted by social scientists involved in this work, and the organisational conditions which may facilitate or hinder change.

This third strand of work has been closely linked with the development of methodologies for evaluation. In health, but more particularly in education and community action, the considerable difficulties in assessing social change programmes and the deficiencies in some of the larger attempts to achieve this (see for example Marris and Rein, 1972; Town, 1973) have given rise to extensive debate. In evaluating innovations, some proponents have favoured what might be described as 'before and after' assessments based essentially on experimental designs; others have argued for 'illuminative evaluation' (see Parlett and Hamilton, 1972) focussing rather on the processes by which change occurs and more influenced by social anthropological approaches to field research. We think it possible however to suggest an intermediate evaluation strategy, which combines a concern with understanding the complex processes involved in the interaction between an innovatory project and its host institution with appropriate attention to evidence on the nature and benefits of particular changes.

Using This Book

In applying these social science perspectives to the development of HIP we have increasingly come to realise the importance of individuals and groups using their own authority to achieve innovations, and correspondingly accepting the responsibility for assessing their own work and communicating their experiences to others. Evaluation in this sense has involved participants in critically reviewing current practices; seeking to explore and understand the possibility of change; and applying their own values in coming to some assessment of whether particular changes are beneficial. It follows from this last point that all the Fulbourn work was the subject of multiple evaluations depending on the perspectives through which change was seen by people in many different roles, inside and outside the hospital.

In our editorial role, we have sought through this book to give expression to the full range of contributions which HIP mobilised. While providing a co-ordinating framework, we have encouraged the many contributors to write in their own way about the aspects of this work which interested them most. The resultant diversity we have accepted as reflecting the pluralism of contemporary psychiatry and one of its potential strengths. It also means that different parts of the book may vary in significance for a similarly diverse readership.

The staff involved in the Project and the social scientists who assisted, have sought to share their experiences through honest accounts which attend openly to difficulties and disappointments as well as what were judged to be successes. We have all been aware that although many of the ideas informing HIP might be seen as simple, some measure of the problems to be overcome in practice is provided by the rarity with which the necessary conditions for a simple experiment of this kind are actually established.

Accordingly, we hope that this study in depth of how innovation was and was not achieved in one psychiatric hospital will prove of much wider value. Consistent with the approach of the Project itself however, we shall not be offering any blueprints for change or rules to be passively followed. Rather we invite interested readers to examine critically their own experiences in the light of those reported here. Used in this way, the book may become a tool through which people can increase understanding of their own professional roles and work situation with a view to informed action.

The book is organised as follows.

Building on this Introduction, Chapter 1 explores further the problems of change confronting the 'Cinderella' services in the early 1970s and the particular history of Fulbourn Hospital as an institution trying to adapt to the challenges and opportunities presented by new patterns of post-war psychiatry. Against this background, a fuller account is provided of the ways in which the Hospital Innovation Project developed at Fulbourn between 1972 and 1977. The main contribution of HIP has been through the wide variety of projects undertaken during this period. From descriptions prepared by the staff directly involved in these projects, it is possible to examine in more detail the range of problems tackled, the methods employed, the difficulties encountered and the precise nature of the innovations which these staff were able to achieve. Chapters 2, 3 and 4 therefore each present two studies concerned with important issues arising in these efforts.

In Chapter 2, the theme is that of how the experiences of patients in hospital can be made of greater therapeutic value through attention to changing the ward social environment, with examples from both short-stay and long-stay situations. The related theme of Chapter 3 is the potential that exists for improving the care of the elderly, especially where effective collaboration can be developed between health and social services. Chapter 4 addresses the kinds of changes in management and training required to support such innovations in treatment and care, particularly drawing on examples from nursing.

Chapter 5 then begins the more systematic analysis and evaluation of Project experience. Comparative examination of all the projects initiated by the end of 1975 provides the basis for understanding the social processes through which innovation in various aspects of hospital performance was or was not brought about. This chapter also describes what has been learnt about the new role of social research adviser as a means of fostering informed change.

This analysis is continued in Chapter 6, where an attempt is made to identify the wider conditions required to facilitate innovation in psychiatric care — presented in the form of a 'model organisation' for this task. A series of working hypotheses direct particular attention to the importance of multi-disciplinary collaboration between the professions involved in treatment and supportive management arrangements in the institution as a whole. The contribution which HIP has made to the development of this form of organisation at Fulbourn is examined and the subsequent impact of NHS reorganisation at hospital level is explored.

In Chapter 7, the assessment of HIP is given further depth through contributions representing senior and junior staff at Fulbourn and others who have taken an interest in this work. From these various perspectives, it is possible to understand more fully the relationship between hospital leadership and the experiences of 'grass roots' participants. Chapter 8 then shows how the various themes emerging from this analysis might have much wider relevance. An external view of HIP is presented, which locates this Project in the context of a diverse range of other work concerned with 'development' — whether of people, organisations or communities. Examination of these different experiences points to the central importance of autonomy in more fully realising the potential of individuals and groups. Significant inferences follow for the role of management and the kind of support required, particularly in changing health care systems.

In the Conclusion, further attention is invited to how what has been learnt from HIP might find application elsewhere. The magnitude of the problems facing the caring services is recognised. Nevertheless recent experiences of using the HIP approach in different situations indicate that scope exists for new initiatives. General lessons are drawn for future strategies of service development and some implications of this approach for other key issues facing the health and welfare services are suggested.

The book is addressed then to practitioners and managers in these services; students in the health and social work professions; social scientists interested in institutional change; and more widely to people considering how organisations can develop and use better the potential contributions of their members.

It should be particularly relevant to all those concerned with tackling the dilemmas confronting the psychiatric and other traditionally deprived services. Writing at a time when there is much disquiet about the quality of these 'Cinderella' services, we shall regard the effort invested in this work as worthwhile if the experiences reported here and the lessons learnt help others seeking to improve patient care and stimulate further efforts towards this end.

Fulbourn Hospital, Cambridge   David Towell and Clive Harries
March 1978

1 CHALLENGE AND CHANGE IN THE CINDERELLA SERVICES

Clive Harries, David H. Clark and David Towell

The quest to develop better health and welfare services for the more disadvantaged groups in our society poses a great challenge in contemporary circumstances. Whatever the need for change, the problems in achieving this can often seem substantial. Moreover these problems are typically rooted in a long history which has continuing relevance for the strategies required to tackle current dilemmas.

In the case of the psychiatric services, each of these points has particular force. At both a national and a local level, close examination is likely to suggest distinctive opportunities and constraints which shape new responses to the difficulties involved in improving care. Thus the origins and significance of the Hospital Innovation Project can best be understood through attention to its social and historical setting. Three contributions from different perspectives seek to identify key influences in the background and development of this Project.

Clive Harries begins by exploring the dilemmas of institutional psychiatry in the context of national changes in provision and expectations over the past twenty years, drawing particularly on his own more recent experiences while working with the Hospital Advisory Service. Relevant features in the special history of Fulbourn Hospital are then examined by David Clark, who as medical superintendent (1953-71) and consultant psychiatrist himself played a central role in the progress made at this hospital over the same period. The third contribution describes how HIP was designed in the light of these antecedents, and provides an overview of how the Project developed in practice. Here David Towell writes from his perspective as social scientist making the new role of social research adviser.

The National Context

Clive Harries

The National Health Service in the United Kingdom has succeeded in making some notable achievements since its institution in 1948. Even in the areas of care which perhaps capture least popular interest, least professional attention, and least publicity for their advances — such as the psychiatric services – there is evidence that the National Health Service has been able to raise the basic minimum standard of care in a way that has not been possible in some other western countries.

Nevertheless, despite considerable progress, many parts of the health services have found it extremely difficult to institute change. Yet there is a demand for change originating from both outside and inside the service. The general public have come to expect a higher standard of treatment, and the media raise questions regarding care standards. Within the service, the professions themselves have increasingly articulated the need for changing and improving the services of which they are part.

The usual view is that change in national institutions comes from the central government. Five year plans are initiated by ministers. Reorganisations are decreed by Parliament and implemented by the Secretary of State. Legislative changes are preceded by expert royal commissions, and other changes too have been preceded by expert groups giving advice directly to the relevant government department. Over the years, therefore, this essentially centralised way of working has, not unnaturally, led many health service organisations to look 'upwards' to what is now the DHSS for guidance regarding changes.

This orientation has undoubtedly been encouraged by enquiries which put the psychiatric and mental handicap services on the agenda for public attention. Reports have made a number of institutions almost household names – such as Ely, Farleigh, Whittingham. Attention has been drawn to the many deficiencies, and the difficulties that some services experience in trying to adapt and change have been highlighted. More recently, the St Augustine's enquiry (SETRHA, 1976) has illuminated some of the difficulties afresh. This documented well the difficulties of a psychiatric hospital trying to cope with criticism regarding care standards made by members of its own staff, which, if responded to positively, might have provided a stimulus for improving care from within the organisation. It also described the dilemmas posed for all staff in determining issues of responsibility and accountability in treatment and care. It clearly recognised that a multi-professional approach to solving care problems was necessary. The report also noted that there had been difficulty in implementing the advice of the Hospital Advisory Service which had visited the hospital some two years earlier. Chances of improving care originating both from inside and outside the organisation had been missed.

New expectations in care, apart from guidance originating from the DHSS, have often been seen as originating from medical staff. In the

days of the medical superintendent, the introduction of change by him
was to an extent easier. He had authority over the whole institution;
and the nursing staff were usually responsible to him, enabling rapid
compliance with any new developments. Although the post of medical
superintendent has largely disappeared, consultant medical staff are
often now looked to as a source of change. Yet in reality many patients
receive little medical time – indeed it may be as little as twelve minutes
in a year for some long stay or psychogeriatric patients (Morgan, 1967).
This is compounded by the fact that with the move into the community there is an increasing demand for psychiatrists to apportion
more of their available time to demands outside the hospital. It is not
difficult to see, therefore, that any organisation that depends solely on
medical staff for initiating change may see few alterations. This would
be true even if the relationship between medical and other professional
staff had remained unchanged over the last decade. As it is, other
professions have legitimately developed their independent organisations.
This can be seen most dramatically in the case of the Seebohm
reorganisation of social services. Nurses too have developed the Salmon
system of organisation which has not only defined areas of administrative responsibility for nursing officers more clearly, but has also
permitted and encouraged nurses to develop independently their own
policies and procedures regarding issues of importance to them. In
encouraging nurses to manage themselves more purposefully, the
difficulties of collective decision making between professions have been
highlighted. Thus the medical administrative route to change, whatever
its former advantages and disadvantages, has become increasingly
weakened.

A further factor which needs consideration, whether in terms of
cause or effect, is that it has been difficult to recruit quality staff to
the Cinderella services in many areas. In psychiatry those in post have
been stretched by growing demands on their services, and by developments in the community. Also the development of small psychiatric
units in general hospitals has reduced the commitment to large
psychiatric hospitals.

Efforts to raise care standards have brought psychiatric hospitals
more clearly into a field of conflict. In particular, the development of
the 'open' hospital, with all its advantages both for short-term and more
disabled patients, has also opened the hospital to the ambivalence and
conflict in public views (reflected often in the stance of many other
non-psychiatric health care professions) regarding those who are said
to be mentally ill. As a result of this openness and of more attention

from the media, the results of past financial and professional neglect and the continuing deficiencies are now more visible for those who wish to see, as well as those who would rather not see.

The problem of the shortage of cash and staff for the Cinderella services, despite repeated attempts on the part of ministers and secretaries of state to channel greater proportions of regional budgets to these deprived areas, has been such as to give the people in these services the feeling that their work is less important and less valued by politicians, the general public and also professionals in other parts of the Health Service. This has been reinforced by their feeling that they are made a 'dumping ground' by society at large as well as by other better staffed and financed parts of the Health Service.

It is suggested then that the tradition of change from the top along with the disbursement of finances from the top, has led to people in the service looking to central government for guidance for change; even perhaps made them dependent on central government for this stimulus. Yet, this may have served to mask the fact that there has always been considerable scope at local level for initiative in making change; particularly change in the organisation of services, changes in attitudes and changes in practice. These changes in care in psychiatry, mental handicap and geriatrics are often the unrecognised but precious equivalents of technological change in general medicine. Some of the Cinderella services were able to grasp this initiative. Others were not, and saw the solution to all problems only in terms of more hard cash.

The series of crises in the late 1950s arising particularly in the mental handicap field, raised questions about the adequacy of services, the standards of management, treatment and care, the hidden nature of many problems, and how these complex difficulties originated. In direct response to these problems, the Hospital Advisory Service was established, and was later extended to the fields of general psychiatry and geriatrics.

The Advisory Service itself represented a departure from traditional practices. Its teams were formed from members of different professions who could draw on wide experience from the field elsewhere, and who could provide advice at local level, although perhaps without much subsequent support for bringing about changes following their departure. Furthermore, the reports of the teams were sent directly to the Secretary of State, so maintaining these services close to political awareness and by-passing the extensive DHSS bureaucratic channels.

Annual reports of the independent Advisory Service consistently pointed to the poor conditions existing in the psychiatric, mental

handicap and geriatric fields of care. Such conditions were hardly
surprising when one report (HAS, 1970, p.23) stated, 'I have heard
comments to the effect that services for the elderly should take second
place, that the needs of the chronic patient are far less important than
the needs of the acute patient and that less money should be spent on
that part of the service.' The same report pin-pointed more specific
needs – that of the importance of human relationships in the hospital
service and the need for professionals from different disciplines to work
together on problems. Certainly the Hospital Advisory Service
encountered many hospitals which suffered from problems arising from
a rigid hierarchical organisation which found adaptation difficult with
little change being invited from within. Many such hospitals also
attracted relatively little attention in terms of priority of action from
their (then) Regional Hospital Boards. Within these hospitals, large
wards, few staff, many patients, an absence of team work, and general
lack of purpose regarding care were often prevalent. Reasons abounded
for *not* doing things, rather than trying to use local initiative and find
ways to do things.

A Hospital Advisory Service team (of which I was a member) visited
Fulbourn Hospital late in 1971. In appearance Fulbourn was a typical
nineteenth-century asylum, with a castellated water tower rising above
the trees. Extensions to the 100-year-old building had been made
through the decades in different styles and there was a scatter of
relatively new buildings in the grounds, with large playing fields in
front. There were some 22 wards, many of them housing patients of
both sexes, some well upgraded, and accommodating at the time about
690 patients, with an establishment of 230 nursing staff.

The hospital seemed different from many visited: it had lively
treatment units, good morale, few problems with recruitment of
nurses and doctors, and a good local and national reputation. But it
appeared to have something else – an enquiring self-questioning
atmosphere. Also there seemed to be more potential for staff to make
grass roots decisions, which was beginning to receive the support of
managers who were encouraging a decentralised form of working. It
seemed possible, therefore, to try a new approach to encouraging
change. At that time a sociologist (David Towell) was studying the
training and practice of psychiatric nursing in the hospital, and staff at
different levels had consulted him on occasions over problems they
were experiencing and had made informed changes after studying these
problems using his help. It seemed possible that if this approach could
be extended, and a consultative service made more freely available, the

potential of staff at grass roots level might be more effectively harnessed. This might have the benefit of providing a new and rational method of bringing about organisational change, as well as increasing the perceptiveness of people providing the patient centred care.

The Advisory Service team recommended that behavioural science resources should be made available to staff in the hospital to facilitate change. The hospital welcomed this, and ways of implementing the recommendation were explored. This proved to be the beginning of the Hospital Innovation Project.

Fulbourn Hospital as a Setting for Change

David H. Clark

The Hospital Innovation Project grew naturally from the work of Fulbourn Hospital and flourished there. It is of importance in assessing HIP and its relevance elsewhere, therefore, to understand Fulbourn Hospital, its history, its idiosyncrasies, its strengths and its weaknesses. Why was Fulbourn so suitable in the 1970s for such a study to develop? The answer probably lies partly in the uneventful first century of Fulbourn's existence, partly in its response to the ferment of social psychiatry in Britain in the 1950s and partly to the ideas of administrative therapy and social therapy which we had developed and explored at Fulbourn during the 1960s.

Fulbourn Hospital was opened in 1858 as the Cambridgeshire and Isle of Ely Pauper Lunatic Asylum. It was one of the Victorian County Asylums — not one of the pioneers, but one of those built after the 1845 Asylums Act. Its peak population (1954) was 950 people; in 1976 it contained 580 patients. It was still the only in-patient psychiatric accommodation for a population (1976) of about 450,000 living mostly in small towns and scattered small villages (including the Fen district of intensive market gardening) and including the ancient University City of Cambridge (100,000 population).

Fulbourn's first century was uniformly humdrum. It pioneered no advances, it was the site of no notable scandals. Its staff were mediocre; none of its superintendents was either eminent or scandalous. The patients were East Anglian peasants, as were most of the staff, placid in both psychosis and professional life. The 1920s and 1930s, which saw some ferment in British psychiatry, passed Fulbourn by. The same three medical gentlemen ran Fulbourn from 1923 to 1945. In 1951, the medical superintendent of Fulbourn had been in the hospital since 1923, the matron since 1926, the chief male nurse since 1934 and the

group secretary had lived on the estate since 1910 when his father came
to work on the staff. The nursing staff, mostly locally recruited,
married one another and lived on the hospital estate.
World War II overcrowded the hospital; many staff went to the
Services and did not return. Not much money was spent on repairs in
the immediate post war years; by the early 1950s Fulbourn Hospital –
like the majority of psychiatric hospitals in England then – was
overcrowded, understaffed, shabby and dilapidated, with a general air
of dispirited acceptance of low standards and little hope of
improvement.
There was, however, a considerable wish for change, outside and
inside the hospital. In 1948 Fulbourn became part of the National
Health Service and in 1951 it gained its own Hospital Management
Committee. They and the Regional Board wanted to see change. Within
the hospital the younger consultants and the abler nurses, especially
men returned from war service, wanted to improve things. The medical
superintendency fell vacant in 1953; they sought a young man and
appointed me. It was my good fortune to come at a time when Britain
was full of ideas for improving psychiatric hospitals – open doors,
sheltered workshops, industrial therapy, halfway houses, rehabilitation,
etc.
The 1950s were the time of the beginnings of social psychiatry in
which Britain, and especially British mental hospitals, led the world.
This was linked with the ideas of the therapeutic community and the
work of Maxwell Jones at Belmont, but was also rooted in the older
British traditions of humane hospital management, the ideas of the
'moral management' and 'no restraint' eras of the early nineteenth
century with which the names of Tuke and Conolly were attached. It
was aided by the willingness of the developing National Health Service
to put money into helping psychiatric hospitals and by the changing
public attitudes which culminated in the Mental Health Act of 1959.
The lead in the changes were taken by better known hospitals like
Dingleton, Mapperley and Warlingham Park, but Fulbourn followed
briskly. There was the open door movement; in 1951 all ward doors in
Fulbourn were locked, by 1958 all were open. There was a great
development of organised work in psychiatric hospitals with sheltered
workshops and industrial therapy; Fulbourn Hospital opened its first
sheltered workshop ('Fulbourn Industries') in 1956. Many long stay
patients were discharged, sometimes to special accommodation; a
halfway house was opened in Cambridge in 1958. Therapeutic
communities were attempted; the first therapeutic community at

Fulbourn started in 1958.

The story of this surge of enthusiasm has many strands, but a few are important for HIP. These initiatives involved all kinds of people — all grades and types of staff, many of the patients. A new sports field was laid out by the Estate Officer and the work carried out by patients supervised by ward orderlies and nurses. An open day and flower show involved the engineers, the garden staff, the lay administration and the nurses. The activities were well publicised, especially in the local newspaper, which caused a rise in morale and self esteem, both for individual people and for the hospital as a whole. People began to feel pride in the hospital and confidence in its ability to innovate. The depth of previous demoralisation gave force to the surge of enthusiasm.

Thus an atmosphere of change — and the excitement of change — developed at Fulbourn Hospital in the late 1950s. The people — the nurses, the long stay residents — saw for themselves the advantage of change. Nearly all the changes in the 1950s were for the better and many brought manifest and undoubted advantage. The unlocking of the doors reduced tension and violence markedly. Emptying the wards by day relieved some of the squalid congestion. The workshops brought money into the hospital, so that the patients' living standards rose. Vigorous recruitment brought new staff into the hospital. Rehabiliation reduced patient numbers and relieved the overcrowding. Change was worthwhile.

At first the change was brought about in the traditional manner. I heard of a good idea; I convinced the Management Committee, my consultant colleagues, the senior nurses, I got the facilities (paint, workshops, staff, money) and implemented the change by the exercise of the authority vested in me. The only choice that lower grade staff or patients had was to go along with reforms or to block them by passive resistance. It was in this way that the 'work for all' drive of 1954-6 was operated, the 'open door' drive of 1956-8 and the 'active rehabilitation' push of 1960-2.

Gradually, however, I began to see the value of projects that the nurses and patients themselves developed. I began to see myself as a facilitator rather than as a direct innovator. Patients started small gardens; nurses redecorated their wards; ward groups raised money by cooking and bought themselves ward ornaments.

The first therapeutic community was started by the initiative of the ward doctor and ward sister; I only played a protective part in the change process. Through the 1960s this pattern of 'change from below' became steadily more the Fulbourn style. Wards and units started projects and involved others; new ideas, especially for rehabilitation, cropped up all over. In 1962-3 I had a year's leave at the Center for Advanced Studies in Behavioral Sciences at Stanford, California; I used it to study what had happened at Fulbourn during the previous nine years. I wrote the book *Administrative Therapy* which brought together a number of ideas that had developed at Fulbourn. It was in part a plea to young doctors working in mental hospitals to interest themselves in the way their patients lived (rather than focussing on the patients' internal psychopathology and its correction by drugs or individual psychotherapy). It did, however, take as its central thesis that administration, the process of management within the hospital, was a potent tool of therapy, of producing beneficial change in the patients. Although mostly discussing the malignant effects of traditional administration (as demonstrated by the sociologists – Goffman, Belknap, Dunham, etc.) it also explored better ways of helping the hospital to change and foreshadowed some of the notions of 'change from below' which were later central to HIP.

A feature of the Fulbourn change process was built-in monitoring. Although some Fulbourn figures and statistics were gathered and published as part of the programme of public education, opinion change and even propaganda, there was also a self critical gathering of information from the start. The material gathered was considered and discussed, published in the annual reports of the hospital and also in learned journals. Thinking about what you were doing, writing about it, and publishing your results became established as a prestigious and personally rewarding Fulbourn activity.

The charge nurse of the male disturbed ward described how they had opened the ward doors (Pattemore, 1957); a ward sister related how a therapeutic community became established (Mungovan, 1968); and a ward doctor described the first therapeutic community (Clark, Hooper and Oram, 1962).

Research was no new idea for Fulbourn Hospital. Like any institution or landscape feature near to Cambridge it had been always available as a place where eager university academics could quarry material for their studies. The staff had always known that gentlemen from the university would come collecting the oddest things; urine, blood, pieces of brains, psychological test results, questionnaires; they did no harm (though perhaps no good) and research was regarded as prestigious but harmless. But in all this the hospital and the patients were just passive material for the researchers. In the late 1950s, however, for the first time, research workers began looking at the way the hospital functioned, going into the wards, asking people what they were doing, making notes, collecting figures.

In 1957 Douglas Hooper began his sociological research into the process of change at Fulbourn Hospital and he was followed by Edmund Oram (1960-3), Kenneth Myers (1966-9) and David Towell (1967-70). Fortunately for the good name of research within the hospital, these were all men of good sense and considerable awareness of areas of sensitivity. Then, as the years went by, the staff began to see the results of co-operation. The research workers were able to feed back useful information about what they were doing or what had happened to the patients. Douglas Hooper helped Adrian Ward change its pattern of work (Hooper, 1962). Eddie Oram found out how well the discharged chronic patients were getting on (Clark and Oram, 1966). Ken Myers proved that Hereward House was doing a better job than the control ward in another hospital (Myers and Clark, 1972). David Towell helped the student nurses to understand what was happening to them as they became psychiatric nurses (Towell, 1975). Gradually most staff came to feel that research could be positively helpful to the tasks of running and planning the hospital. Even the most sceptical admitted that research workers might do more good than harm.

During the 1960s innovative thinking in Fulbourn was more concentrated within wards and small units rather than on the hospital as a whole. This was the period in which I and my colleagues explored the therapeutic community method, applying it to the disturbed wards and to the admission units. Those who worked in therapeutic communities have always had an ambivalent attitude towards research. Many of the pioneers were impatient romantics, for whom numbers were merely one of the things to throw into the eyes of powerful people (such as governing bodies) to dazzle them. On the other hand, much of the original basic support came from the work of the social scientists working at institutions – especially painstaking number gatherers such as Ivan Belknap, Morris Schwartz, Warren Dunham and others who did the original ground work. This ambivalence was clearest demonstrated at Belmont Hospital in the 1950s where Maxwell Jones, having brilliantly pioneered a radically new form of social milieu and treatment, called in Rapoport and his social science research team, as he put it, 'to tell us what we are doing'.

At Fulbourn there had been a continual attempt to keep the 'two cultures' in contact and Myers' studies of Hereward House (Clark and Myers, 1970; Myers and Clark, 1972) showed this most clearly. Having spent some years making changes on the wards, Myers spent three years studying Hereward House from an 'objective' stance to see how its results compared with those of a control ward.

Thus, when the Hospital Advisory Service, with Clive Harries as a member, came to Fulbourn Hospital in 1971, they found a situation ready for what was to become HIP. Fulbourn Hospital was ripe soil for the seed of HIP to fall on. Not only was it a lively hospital, interested in social psychiatry and full of stimulating change, but it had some unusual characteristics – a belief that change should come from below, a concern with the relationship between social organisation and patient care, a tradition of examining critically what was being done and good experience of research workers as valuable helpful people.

The Development of the Hospital Innovation Project
David Towell

Against this background of the national problems facing the Cinderella services and the distinctive post war history of Fulbourn Hospital, the origins and development of HIP can now be more fully traced. At the time of the HAS visit, I had just completed the research for my Ph.D. at Cambridge on *Understanding Psychiatric Nursing*. This involved more than three years work at Fulbourn during which I carried out detailed studies of the roles of nurses and their relationships with patients on different kinds of ward. Also during this period I assisted groups of staff in a number of small research projects concerned with topical problems in the hospital. As a result of these experiences I was interested in the prospect of further collaboration with staff and particuarly keen that the investment in my Ph.D. should be of some real practical benefit to the institution which had welcomed my presence in an academic research role.

In this situation, the HAS recommendation described by Clive Harries provided an important stimulus to the generation of this new Project; with encouragement from leading members of Fulbourn's staff, I set out to explore the prospects of funding. It was then that I joined the Tavistock Institute of Human Relations, and began what was to become a close working relationship with Eric Miller, who agreed to act as consultant to this initiative. We approached the Department of Health and Social Security, who expressed interest and gave us the opportunity to undertake some exploratory work (in the winter of 1971-2) before submitting a comprehensive proposal. The Department subsequently agreed to support a two year pilot experiment from April 1972.

During this preparatory period we were able to consider how the basic ideas presented in the Introduction could be implemented and make more detailed plans for the first stage of the Project. At the same time we tried to maintain a flexible strategy so as to be able to respond to problems and opportunities that were to arise. Through my own previous knowledge of Fulbourn, this planning took account of the hospital's recent history and the several assets which David Clark has described. It also drew on our *social science perspectives* and a review of other work of this genre. In particular, further mention should be made of the reports just being published (Wieland and Leigh, 1971; Revans, 1972) on the Hospital Internal Communications Project, which had reflected some similar aims but was perceived then as less than successful.

Thus, beginning with the notion of involving staff in systematic investigations of problems arising in their own work, we had first to consider how staff might engage in such investigations and how these could be focussed on important areas of hospital activity which would justify this use of resources. Second, we were concerned with how pertinent staff could be involved so as to encourage the implementation of any innovations arising from these investigations. Third, on the assumption that problems affecting patient care in hospitals are not usually the province of a single professional group, we needed to find ways in which staff from different professions could work together in tackling these problems. Fourth, we had to consider, if this Project turned out to be useful, how the approach we were developing could be made an enduring aspect of the hospital's work with less reliance on an external research institution. And fifth, we already had in mind the question of how what was learnt from this experiment might be disseminated more widely.

Arising from these and related considerations, the main features of our initial plans took shape. Central to these plans was the intention to create the new role of social research adviser to the hospital, which I was to fill on a substantial part-time base for the pilot stage of the Project. This role was to provide a service to staff members through which they could seek help:

in identifying and clarifying problems arising in their day-to-day work; designing and carrying out investigations relevant to these problems; and
working through the implications of such investigations with a view to bringing about improvements in hospital organisation and practice.

Much of my own subsequent learning about HIP arose from my struggle to work out through experience how various tensions implicit in this role could best be resolved, so that I could contribute effectively to these objectives.

In launching the Project at Fulbourn in April 1972, Eric Miller and I regarded the three main priorities as being to establish an effective Steering Committee for this work; to disseminate widely amongst the hospital's staff information about the availability of the social research adviser's services; and to begin work on a range of projects of relevance to the problems then facing the hospital.

These immediate tasks were largely achieved in the first six months. A Steering Committee comprising the chairman of the division of psychiatry which included Fulbourn (David Clark), the hospital secretary (David Storr), the principal nursing officer (Maurice Fenn) and the senior nursing officer (the newly appointed Clive Harries) came together initially to represent the hospital in discussions with us, as we sought funds for this work from DHSS. Subsequently, as the Project began, this committee assumed responsibility for setting priorities among the project ideas raised with the social research adviser, relating project work to the management of the hospital, and exercising leadership in encouraging productive innovations. It also provided the hospital-wide sanction required for this work.

Meetings between the Steering Committee and this Tavistock team (of two) quickly became valuable forums for the review of project work and the examination of issues arising in the development of the Project as a whole, with a gradual emergence of common understandings about how this work might best be pursued. In addition, the Steering Committee reported on initial developments in the Project to the Hospital Management Committee and thereby gained further support for this work. Both this support and the Steering Committee's encouragement later proved of considerable importance to the autonomous development of this Project as part of the hospital's ongoing activities: particularly in the efforts to institutionalise this work after the pilot stage of the Project had ended.

Steering Committee members also played a key role in the early stages of the Project in disseminating information about the presence of the new service amongst hospital staff members. This presence was given concrete form by the hospital's provision of an office for the adviser, where I was readily available for discussions with interested staff. A service was provided then so that any group of staff at Fulbourn could, through their representatives, spontaneously seek the adviser's help on problems of concern to them; but with the Steering Committee being able to define priorities in the uses of my time for the hospital as a whole.

Even during the exploratory period I had begun some work in my new role; it was not long before my services were in growing demand and after some months were being fully utilised. A variety of problems were raised by different groups of staff, many of which became the focus for more detailed study. A typical pattern was for representatives to approach the adviser about an issue in which they were interested. Then followed wider discussions with the staff group concerned. These discussions usually led to the establishment of some kind of project committee which could give sanction for any further work to be undertaken and which involved the main staff affected by these problems. Project committees were able to consider with my help the appropriate resources to allocate to an investigation of the problems identified and also to accept responsibility for making use of what emerged from these investigations.

Over the first two years, more than 20 major and minor projects were initiated at different levels and different areas of the hospital, in which staff members set out with the adviser's assistance to examine problems of concern to them in their work. Altogether these projects involved 40 staff directly in some form of investigation, a further 40 as members of project committees, and a larger number to the extent of receiving feedback and being concerned with the use of work undertaken. While nurses were most represented in this work, several project committees were multi-disciplinary, involving doctors, occupational therapists, psychologists, social workers, and in some cases administrative and service staff. Commonly, the investigative part of these projects was carried out either by the members of the staff groups themselves, or by trainees attached to the staff group for the duration of the project. Occasionally I myself made a research contribution. These investigations varied from quite small scale activities — for example a survey on the use of volunteers within the hospital carried out by two cadet nurses — to other more substantial investments of energy. For example, a review of the rehabilitative needs of every long-stay patient was carried out by teams of staff from all the wards involved. Participation in this work provided extensive on-the-job training for staff members. The outcomes to projects were mixed, but particular initiatives led to a variety of identifiable innovations in organisation, policy, procedures, training processes and directly in patient care. (A summary of each major project is attached at Appendix A.)

Some of this work also seemed of rather wider relevance, and staff members began to publish accounts of their projects in the professional journals. Other opportunities to encourage diffusion of what was being learned were also taken. In November 1973, following an invitation from the King's Fund Centre, participants in the Project presented a one day conference on 'Developing the Hospital from Within' to an influential audience of other health service staff. This (and the further publicity which followed) stimulated a succession of visitors to Fulbourn, interested in discovering more about aspects of the work being done there. The Report of the Hospital Advisory Service for 1973 explicitly commended this approach to other staff concerned to foster change in NHS institutions. Arising from these activities, opportunities arose to explore the application of HIP in a number of new situations, each providing further illumination of the strategies and conditions necessary for wider dissemination.

At Fulbourn this approach to innovation in the many particular projects was contributing to a number of more general developments in the organisation and culture of the hospital. In each case these developments had their antecedents in the recent history of the hospital as David Clark has described but there was evidence that previous assets were reinforced and complemented by HIP. There was some strengthening of the pattern of organisation based on the concept of multi-disciplinary clinical teams taking responsibility for particular sets of treatment services. There was movement towards greater decentralisation in the control of these services so that groups of staff actually providing patient care had more autonomy in their areas. Senior managers were assuming more of a sponsoring and facilitative role in encouraging these trends. And all this was accompanied by the generation of what can be described as a climate for self-innovation, in which certain ideas about the desirability and means of achieving informed change were becoming quite widely shared by staff members.

In sum, by 1974 there was some optimism at Fulbourn that this experiment was encouraging the development of an adaptive form of organisation, better able to harness the contribution and commitment of staff at all levels in responding to the changing demands involved in delivering high standards of patient care. Senior staff judged these benefits to be of sufficient value in relation to the costs involved for them to want this approach to innovation to continue after the pilot stage (which had been funded until March 1974). With support from the Hospital Management Committee, the Steering Committee therefore sought funds to enable the hospital to establish the full-time role of social research adviser.

From the experiences of both success and failure in the previous two years, the Tavistock team had learnt a great deal about this role and some opportunities had already been taken to test the feasibility of it being performed by a staff member (notably through the sustained contribution by Clive Harries to a project on psycho-geriatric care). On this basis, we were able to assist in the design of this next stage of the Project and identify the arrangements which would be required to support my successor.

Funds were initially sought from the East Anglian Regional Hospital Board: but although receiving some encouragement, in the general upheaval of reorganisation this application ended unproductively. Moreover the financial situation of the new Health Authorities was such that these efforts were unsuccessful for the whole of the following year. In this hiatus, DHSS provided some further limited support for the Tavistock team to work with Fulbourn staff in developing alternative ways of sustaining (at least in the interim) the innovative approach within the hospital.

Of particular importance here was the creation of an 'innovations forum' through which a cross-section of staff members met on a peer group basis to provide mutual support and advice on project work; at the same time constituting a panel of resources which could be drawn on by staff groups for more extensive assistance in the process of innovation. Clive Harries acted as convenor of this forum, which thus became a transitional mechanism for my withdrawal and his gradual accession to the social research adviser role. In this way it also proved possible to sustain some elements of HIP for more than a year, although at a rather lower level of activity than that achieved during the pilot stage.

By the autumn of 1975 however, the Steering Committee had succeeded in obtaining the support of the King Edward's Hospital Fund for the Project; enabling the hospital to establish the full-time role of social research adviser until April 1977, by which time savings from the hospital's own budget were being used to continue this work.

However all these later developments have occurred in a wider context very different from that prevailing when HIP began. The reorganisation of the NHS in 1974 meant the incorporation of Fulbourn into a teaching district dominated by its general hospital, and loss of the Hospital Management Committee which had previously helped to give the psychiatric services their identity. Successive staff changes at senior level proved disruptive of effective management in the hospital. The new managers were faced with financial stringency, inflation and conflict.

From my role as adviser to the Steering Committee in these last three years, it has seemed that all this has served to undermine the achievements of the pilot stage, represented in the organisational conditions we saw as necessary to support HIP; and possibly even put at risk Fulbourn's much longer reputation for administrative therapy and social psychiatry. Over this period project work has appeared less thriving. Although significant new projects have begun, particularly relating to services in the community, these developments have been patchy and the resources represented by HIP do not seem to have been used in tackling some major problems confronting the hospital. At the same time HIP has provided some resilience against the more damaging effects of imposed structural change and staff relocation. Moreover its development since 1974 has given us a unique means to monitor and understand further the impact of reorganisation at hospital level.

In 1977 therefore, HIP still seemed precarious and its future development uncertain. However there has been some encouraging recent evidence that with the emergence of an effective Hospital Management Team and a period of stability among senior staff, Fulbourn is struggling to regain the autonomy necessary to develop the psychiatric services further. If so, HIP will provide extensive experience on which to draw, perhaps best represented throughout this ebb and flow, by the continuing project work. It is to the more detailed examination of these projects that this overview of the development of HIP now leads.

2 CREATING ENVIRONMENTS FOR SOCIAL THERAPY

David Towell, John Burgess, Lalchan Bhim and Clive Harries

In all the main projects undertaken as part of the Hospital Innovation Project, groups of staff have made sustained efforts to improve the services being offered. Understanding the achievements of these projects can begin most appropriately from the accounts provided by some of those centrally engaged in this work. Each of these accounts seeks to describe in some depth the nature of the problems being examined; what was done and by whom; what was the outcome of this activity; and what was learnt of more general relevance.

Here two projects are reported; these share a concern with increasing the therapeutic value of patients' experiences in hospital by changing the social environment — but in the very different situations of a busy acute admission ward and a long-stay rehabilitation ward. In the former case, staff were particularly interested in tackling the problems arising in their efforts to move from traditional medical orientations towards a more social psychiatric approach to treatment. In the latter, the focus was on finding ways of reducing the culture of 'chronicity' affecting patients who had spent many years in hospital.

The admission ward project was the first major initiative in the pilot stage of HIP. The account of this project examines from the social research adviser's perspective, the critical early steps in work which was to extend from March 1972 until September 1973. David Towell shows how an exploratory piece of research enabled him to reconceptualise the presenting problem of whether nurses should wear uniform, within an analysis of more fundamental issues relating to staff roles and the articulation of different approaches to treatment. This analysis then provided the basis for subsequent work with staff as a whole, in which they gradually took on the task of examining more systematically the evolving social organisation of the ward and the implications of new developments for patient care.

The work on the long-stay ward arose from nursing staff concern with how they could be more helpful to the residents there. The experience of this project between April 1975 and September 1976 is described by the ward's charge nurse, John Burgess, a staff nurse,

Lalchan Bhim, and the social research adviser in this period, Clive Harries. Their account shows how through interviewing patients about their lives in hospital, staff were able to modify their perceptions of patients and came to understand them more as individuals. With continuing support, learning through this simple research technique provided the basis for changes in staff roles which in turn encouraged complementary changes among patients: over time helping to undermine some aspects of past chronicity.

In both these projects, there is evidence that attention to ward organisation, staff roles and training processes, are important in developing new approaches to treatment and care.

Developing New Approaches to Treatment in an Admission Ward
David Towell

Early in 1972 I was invited by the staff of one of the three admission wards at Fulbourn to help them in an examination of problems they were then experiencing. Thus began the first project in which I was to play my new role as social research adviser. It was therefore a particularly significant learning opportunity for me as I struggled to find appropriate ways of working with staff on these problems through a dialogue which was to develop over the following eighteen months. In this account I draw on my experiences to describe the initial phases of this working relationship and to explore how the first substantial innovation — the establishment of 'counselling groups' for the ward's staff — was achieved.

This ward was one which I had studied four years previously in my own research for *Understanding Psychiatric Nursing*. At that time the approach to treatment was distinctly 'medical' — relying heavily on drugs and electro-convulsive therapy, the management of the ward was centralised and hierarchical, and the overall pattern of activities had led me to characterise the ward as being organised for the 'medical servicing' of patients. Correspondingly, the behaviour of patients was largely interpreted through diagnostic categories, and nursing staff experienced considerable difficulties in mobilising the 'personal relationships' aspect of their role.

In the period since that earlier study there seemed to have been considerable stability in the dominant features of this pattern. Some six months before I was invited back to the ward however, the previous senior registrar was replaced by a doctor with particular interests in therapeutic community work and community psychiatry, and a long serving ward sister was replaced by a much younger successor keen to increase the contribution and skills of her nursing staff. Returning after four years I was impressed by the changes in social organisation, staff roles and treatment culture on the ward which the leadership of these two new staff had apparently been generating. I was also aware of a desire, at least among some staff, to continue these efforts at innovation.

Perhaps most striking were the changes being made in the roles of nursing staff. Nurses as a whole and junior nurses in particular appeared to have much greater involvement in the processes of treatment. For example, doctors and nurses engaged together in seeing and assessing patients and sometimes families over the course of the patient's career through the ward. Participation in consultant rounds had widened; making nurses parties to the clinical discussion and allowing them to hear the views of other staff with some of whom there had been traditionally rather little contact. Most radically, the 'allocation' of patients to particular nurses had created new expectations for nurses to meet, and given greater organisation to their therapeutic endeavours.

There had also been changes in the roles of more senior staff. The new ward sister had brought to the ward a different leadership style which encouraged a wider sharing of responsibility. Some restructuring of medical roles had also led to more decentralised ways of working. More generally, these changes seemed to represent movement towards a pattern of ward organisation characterised by wide participation in formal meetings and informal discussions, and increasing recognition of the potential contribution of all staff members to the processes of administration and treatment.

Further evidence of the ward moving away from the 'medical servicing' pattern towards a social psychiatric approach to treatment was to be found in the increased use of group methods (including daily 'community meetings') on the ward; the new emphasis being given to assessing patient behaviour in its social context (reflected particularly in 'family therapy'); and the start of efforts to create closer links between the ward and extra-hospital services (general practitioners and social workers).

Initiation of the Project

As was to emerge in my subsequent work with the ward, these developments were raising substantial problems for the staff involved. For example there had been some months of inconclusive debate about whether nursing staff should cease to wear uniform, and it was this issue which formed the basis for my invitation to the ward. Some staff apparently felt that I might be able to assist them in a systematic study of the change out of uniform and thus help resolve some of the conflicts which existed about the effects of this change.

Following an approach from the nursing officer responsible for the ward, I agreed to attend the ward's weekly administrative meeting (where most staff were present) for fuller discussion of this idea. At this meeting I outlined the main components of my new role, emphasising the theme of helping staff themselves to identify, examine and resolve problems arising in their work. In subsequent discussion I sensed that initial ambivalence about my involvement in the ward gradually gave way to a fairly positive commitment from the meeting to my suggestion that this project might begin with me undertaking a short exploratory study. It was agreed that over the following four weeks I should discuss with ward members their views about the uniform question against the background of the way the ward had changed since my previous study there; then report back to this weekly meeting before decisions were taken about any further steps.

With this contract established, I spent the next three weeks visiting the ward almost daily for a few hours at a time, observing activities and attending various meetings. I also interviewed all the nurses, some other staff, and a small cross-section of patients.

Conceptualisation and Redefinition of Problems

This exploratory study provided me with the opportunity to increase my familiarity with the changes taking place on the ward and to locate the difficulties about nursing uniform within a fuller understanding of current problems.

As I was later to report back, my interviews with nurses and the arguments for and against wearing uniform suggested that the issues involved in this question were quite complex. A number of what might be regarded as practical points were raised, the most often mentioned (particularly by those preferring to wear uniform) being that of the extra costs incurred in wearing one's own clothes to work. Further discussion suggested however that attitudes to uniform were embedded within wider sets of views about the nurse's role. For example, among those who were against mufti, a common argument was that patients looked up to and had more confidence in staff if they were wearing uniform. This argument in turn often seemed linked to the idea that it was the nurse's job to do something directly to solve the patient's problems, and some people commented on their feeling of inadequacy when they were unable to do this. Thus it was suggested that nurses should wear uniform so that patients would readily be able to identify who to go to for special help. It could also be inferred that some nurses regarded the uniform as a source of protection and security without which they would find it more difficult to approach patients. By contrast nurses who would have preferred to be in mufti most often argued that in one's own clothes it was possible to relate to patients more 'personally', 'informally' or 'naturally' as well as to be more comfortable.

The ways in which these attitudes were linked to wider views on the nurse's role were perhaps most clearly indicated where pairs of nurses used similar arguments about the effects of wearing uniform but came to opposite conclusions about its desirability. For example, while one woman thought both nurses and doctors should wear uniform, 'As in a general hospital, so that patients will have confidence in us,' another argued that the trouble with uniform was that, 'It makes patients expect you to do things for them, as in a general hospital, but that isn't the nurse's job here'. Similarly, while one man described uniform as being 'the source of the nurse's authority', another complained that 'this air of authority is a barrier to relationships with patients'.

Some parallel differences were also evident in the discussions with patients. Among those who preferred to see nurses in uniform, a common view seemed to be that the hospital was, or perhaps ought to be, a 'warm and friendly' place in which one was 'looked after' while staff, particularly one's own doctor, 'helped to sort out your problems'. Some patients who did not mind whether nurses wore uniforms or not, seemed more inclined to the view that other patients as well as staff could be of help and that it was the person rather than the role which was of importance.

These interviews also provided the opportunity to examine more closely the perhaps more fundamental divergencies in orientation towards the nurse's role and the nature of treatment on this kind of ward, which seemed to be emerging during this period of change. Again, as I was later to report back, it seemed probable that the introduction of innovations was itself bringing new problems for staff as their roles were extended and the demands on them increased. This was perhaps particularly true of the greater involvement of nurses in the treatment process where the 'allocation' of patients had given nurses more specific responsibilities in some cases extending to patients outside hospital.

The first question here was whether the expectations generated by these new arrangements were clear either to the nurses who had to carry them out, or to their medical partners in the treatment teams. There were also doubts about whether adequate attention had been given to the implications of the wide differences in training and experience of the nurses taking on these responsibilities. And even where staff had lower expectations of less experienced nurses, there was still the problem that patients might make demands on the nurse with which she felt as yet unable to cope.

A related set of questions about which there was some uncertainty concerned how much time nurses were actually spending working with patients allocated to them, what was done in that time, and what contribution this made to treatment. In the interviews, nurses of varying experience described a number of different aims for their activities with patients, from 'getting to know them', 'listening to their problems', 'giving advice' and 'gaining information' to 'working with patients to put the particular policies decided for each of them into practice'. My tentative impression from these interviews was that in regard at least to this latter aim and in dealing with interpersonal problems, there was an absence in the ward culture of common perspectives or agreed strategies which might guide nurses in their direct work with patients. This problem in turn seemed part of wider difficulties relating to the approaches to treatment being developed on the ward.

For the purposes of analysis, it seemed possible to describe much of what happened on the ward in terms of the influence of two different approaches to treatment. On the one hand there was the new philosophy of social psychiatry, while on the other there was the longer established, more medically dominated orientation. I suggested that the difference between these approaches might be illustrated by examining what answers they gave to the questions, 'What gets patients well?' and, 'What is the nurse's role in this process?'

In the medical approach, staff apparently got patients better through taking decisions, often in the patient's absence: then doing things to and for the patient to implement these decisions. The nurse's role became to encourage a patient to have confidence in herself and the doctor's treatment, to carry out staff decisions, and to collect information from and about the patient to influence later decisions.

In the social psychiatric approach, which was less well defined but possibly most clearly represented by the 'community meetings', patients were regarded as more active participants in their own treatment, perhaps getting better through learning experiences in which they shared problems with other patients and drew on the contributions of staff members. The nurse's role was to work with patients, express

feelings openly and help patients to develop confidence in themselves.
The central problem here could be expressed in terms of how these
two approaches could be appropriately articulated in an admission ward
setting. How could staff act efficiently to give patients the medical
treatment they required, recognising their different needs, while at the
same time developing a social structure and culture in which patients'
experiences would maximally encourage growth and successful coping?

There was considerable evidence from my observations on the ward
that although this problem was being worked on, these two approaches
co-existed on the ward at that time in a state of partial competition.
This competition was reflected among other things in conflicts over
the priority for different activities, considerable overload on the key
role of ward sister, and difficulties in day-to-day ward organisation.

Reporting Back

On the basis of the contract I had established earlier with ward staff as
a whole, it was this general understanding of developments on the ward
which I sought to report back: first verbally at the administrative
meeting, and then in response to their request, in the form of a written
working note which was circulated to all staff on the ward. This note
drew attention to the difficulties which could be anticipated in
trying to bring about innovations on such a ward. It went on to
emphasis the tentative nature of my observations but expressed the
hope that these would prove helpful to staff: first in providing an
agenda for discussion through which issues facing the ward might be
better understood; second, in suggesting issues which would repay
more detailed study by staff themselves.

I was gradually to learn that for staff to make use of this kind of
written contribution was a much more problematic process than I had
at that stage anticipated. Even getting worthwhile discussion of these
observations at the weekly meeting was quite difficult in a situation
where immediate issues tended to dominate the agenda and there was
little continuity from one week to the next. However, through discussion at these meetings and further work with individual staff
members over the following weeks, there was growing evidence of some
reconceptualisation of the problems facing the ward and recognition
that the uniform question was to some extent a displacement from
more fundamental issues. Staff decided therefore that decisions about
wearing mufti should be postponed (and in fact nine months later the
ward had developed to the stage when the change into mufti could be
made with general agreement). Instead, more urgent attention was

required to clarify expectations about the nurse's role in the new ward situation and provide the appropriate training for nurses to be able to meet these expectations, focussing on how they could be given adequate support in this area. Accordingly, an experiment in 'group counselling' for staff was decided upon by the weekly meeting.

Innovation in Staff Training

The form this experiment might take had gradually emerged in my discussions with key members of the ward's staff. It appeared that the main needs which had been identified could at least in part be met through the use of group methods to enhance the experiential learning of nurses. It was agreed that 'counselling groups' should be established to provide nurses (and subsequently other staff) with the opportunity to talk about their direct experiences with patients and learn from the reflections of other staff on these experiences. In addition staff would be able to raise for discussion problems they were encountering in understanding the ward culture and their role in the ward team. Each group was to consist of a few staff meeting weekly with a more experienced member of the ward team who was to take a non-directive leadership role, somewhat akin to social work supervision. Over a period it was intended that these groups should contribute to clarifying the expectations on staff members, providing support for them in their new roles, and developing some shared perspectives to guide them in their direct work with patients.

At the beginning, the ward's senior registrar, social worker, and sister agreed to make their time available to act as counsellors. I suggested that these three staff might in turn meet regularly with me in a group, which would similarly provide opportunities for the counsellors to enhance their counselling through learning from each other. This meeting was also to be used for monitoring the progress of this experiment, considering improvements to the initial design, and seeking to understand more about the development of the ward and the contribution staff could make to social therapy.

Through my participation in this group over more than six months I was able to support the counsellors in working through the main difficulties encountered in establishing this innovation in staff training. Fundamental to these difficulties appeared to be the absence in existing patterns of nurse training of any attempt to help people learn from their own experiences with patients. This seemed to be compounded in the case of some middle-ranking staff by a reluctance to accept that learning could be a continuing process which does not end arbitrarily when one becomes 'qualified'. Both these difficulties were reflected in wavering attendances at the counselling groups over the first few months and the initial pressures to take up more directive roles experienced by the counsellors.

However, in parallel with other efforts to strengthen the social psychiatric approach on the ward, this innovation through stages became institutionalised as a permanent aspect of ward life. First, the membership widened so that all staff passing through the ward were able to participate in the groups. Second, the leadership of these groups was extended by the psychologist and occupational therapist, as well as other experienced nurses, becoming counsellors. Third, a new senior registrar took over my role in the counsellors' group. Four years later this approach to staff training on the ward was still being employed, and some efforts had been made to introduce this innovation elsewhere, including within a nearby general hospital.

Further Work on Basic Issues

While progress was being made on this and other specific innovations, I continued to work with the ward's staff as a whole on the fundamental issues identified in my working note. The main forum for this work was the weekly administrative meeting. Here from examination of the items raised for discussion, I sought to help staff clarify the tasks and roles being performed on the ward: at the same time contributing to the longer term elucidation of the pattern of organisation most appropriate to the approaches to treatment they were trying to develop. For more than a year in fact, my regular attendance at this meeting represented a sustained commitment to sharing with staff the very real difficulties this involved.

Some of these difficulties arose from the nature of this weekly meeting itself. As the one occasion in the week when all staff met together, there was a strong tendency for immediate items (crises with patients, inter-personal difficulties between staff) to swamp the agenda. The lack of continuity between meetings both in content and to some extent in staff attendance (particularly because of the shift system) also made it an unproductive setting in which to do work on medium term issues of ward policy and organisation. My agreement to write the first working note after my verbal feedback to this meeting was itself partly conditioned by the need to find some way of keeping these issues on the ward agenda.

A number of ways of overcoming these difficulties were introduced over the next year as staff became more aware of the limitations they imposed. In particular, some three months after I had initially suggested it, staff instigated a series of occasional review meetings to provide a forum in which a longer term and more detached examination of issues facing the ward could be attempted. In the first of these meetings, there was considerable discussion of what further steps needed to be taken to strengthen the social psychiatric approach on the ward and examination of what this approach implied for particular staff roles. Arising from this discussion, staff decided that more attention needed to be given to the psycho-social assessment of patients at the time of their referral for admission. As a result the ward social worker was commissioned to undertake, with my assistance, a small study of what different staff believed should be included in this assessment. A summary of the main points emerging from this meeting was prepared for circulation on the ward by an experienced nurse and a junior doctor, again with my assistance.

In subsequent meetings this pattern became more firmly established so that six months later, the contributions reflected in my preparation of the first working note had been almost entirely taken over by staff members themselves. Thus nominated staff members were undertaking the analysis of issues and writing up emergent points for further examination (although with some tendency for writing papers to be mistaken for doing something about the problems identified). And individuals or groups of staff were attempting to investigate more systematically the evidence which might illuminate these issues.

As with the work on patient assessment, these investigations were usually on a small scale: one example being the collection of data on trends in the use of electro-convulsive therapy on the ward; another being a study of the distribution of admissions to the ward from different parts of the catchment area. Towards the end of this first year, however, a larger exercise (involving a number of ward staff in interviewing patients and the subsequent analysis of these interviews by a project committee) sought to increase understanding of the patients' experiences of hospitalisation; contributing significant new insights to an assessment of the changes which had occurred.

Emergent Changes

In reviewing progress on the ward over this first year, staff were able to identify several ways in which the process of developing a more social psychiatric approach to treatment had continued and some of the earlier problems of innovation had been successfully tackled. There was evidence, for example, of greater shared understanding of the part community meetings and small group activities could play in treatment; a more significant contribution from nurses to all these activities; and less reliance on physical methods of treatment. There was more contact between ward staff and general practitioners and social workers outside the hospital; the initial assessment of patients no longer assumed that the referred person would automatically be admitted to hospital; and the average patient population on the ward had been reduced. There was also a more defined structure for the management of the ward, and key staff members, including the consultants and ward sister, had clarified their new roles in this structure. In addition, some staff believed, in the words of the sister, that 'what we had gained most from our use of the social research adviser was the acquisition of a sophistication in the manner in which we tackled each new project, with foresight rather than hindsight, so that we undertook some form of examination before we embarked on any major organisational and treatment change'.

For my part, working with staff on this admission ward and the 'ups and downs' in the progress of this project had given me the opportunity to learn a great deal about how the elements of my new role could be productively mobilised in practice. In particular, I had seen how a continuing dialogue could be established with ward staff as a whole. Through this dialogue it was possible to help them analyse problems arising in their own work and provide a focus for the consideration of longer-term issues of ward organisation and treatment approach which were central to improving patient care. I had also experienced the considerable difficulties which staff faced in successfully establishing innovations in the complex and anxiety-prone setting of a busy admission ward; and learnt the need to be both patient and persistent in supporting staff in their efforts to overcome these difficulties. I had begun to recognise more clearly too, how wider organisational conditions in the hospital (notably in this case, continuity in staffing arrangements and support from more senior management) were important if significant innovations away from traditional medically-dominated approaches to care were to be sustained. The subsequent development of HIP provides, I hope, some demonstration of how I was able to apply and extend what was learnt from this first project in the many opportunities which followed.

Changing the Culture of Long Term Care

John Burgess, Lalchan Bhim and Clive Harries

The care of the long stay residents who form a susbtantial proportion of those in psychiatric hospitals has been under scrutiny in recent years. That the social organisation of an institution can have damaging effects on such residents is well known (Barton, 1959; Goffman, 1961). What perhaps is less well recognised is the scope that exists through changing the social organisation to achieve considerable benefits for these residents. Moreover it can be suggested that what has been learned from experiments in social care in psychiatric hospitals will be needed in whatever patterns of residential care evolve in the future (see Brown, 1973).

However, some policy makers in psychiatry assume that long stay residents will not exist in the future: that by devoting staff effort to the acute services, the long stay population in psychiatric hospitals will eventually disappear. This assumption needs to be thought about carefully. The problems of people by-passing general hospital or acute units and being admitted or transferred to the mental hospital has been described (Cmnd 4861, 1972), as has the subtle process by which individuals can become defined by staff as *chronic* and the decision then made to transfer them to long stay care (Suzuki, 1974). This suggests that in many places the long stay population of a hospital may be inadvertently 'topped-up'. Moreover recent enquiries have shown that problems can abound in this area of psychiatry (see SETRHA, 1976) and that these problems may attract very little medical attention.

The care of the long stay psychiatric patient is therefore an important issue. At hospital level the problem may be experienced and recognised mostly by the nursing staff, since they represent the major professional contact for long stay residents. The problem may be experienced as 'What to do next?' for the individual. After all, if an individual is transferred from a highly staffed 'acute admission' ward with its team's range of diagnostic and treatment skills, and these have not proved successful, what can a small group of nurses on a long stay ward do on their own?

The Setting

The work described here was undertaken by a group of staff in Ferndale — a long stay ward at Fulbourn Hospital. In 1975, when the project started, the ward accommodated 9 male and 20 female residents, including 3 from Broadmoor. The average length of stay of residents was 12 years, ranging from 2 to 37. Most usually the ward was staffed by two registered nurses, one state enrolled nurse, and a fluctuating number of nurses in training (four or five) one of whom was usually seconded from the local general hospital to the ward for six weeks. Consistent with the wider changes over some years in the hospital, the staff wore no uniforms and the ward was run on an 'open-door' policy. At the same time, the ward staff themselves felt 'forgotten' and made the observation that they were physically located at the 'back' of the hospital.

Unsuccessful attempts to improve care by the ward staff led the charge nurse to approach the social research adviser for help. As a result, the adviser joined the ward staff during their 'handover' meetings between shifts, to discuss some of the difficulties with them. One of the difficulties being encountered was that attempts to 'do something' to the residents using the traditional authority associated with the nurse's role had not proved successful. Equally, attempts to run the ward as a therapeutic community had not been productive and the residents seemed to remain as unresponsive as formerly. Also, the need to allocate a substantial number of learners to the ward for 'rehabilitation experience' during their nurse training was in conflict with the training value that the three senior staff felt the ward had to offer.

Exploration and discussion of these difficulties with the adviser led to agreement among the staff that they felt 'separated' from the residents, and in seeing little success in their efforts to improve care found it difficult to understand the reasons for the lack of response by the residents. This was perhaps reflected in the reliance on diagnostic phrases, such as 'chronic schizophrenic', when describing residents and their behaviour.

An Approach to Data Generation and Analysis

The adviser proposed that the staff might therefore consider trying to understand better how the residents experienced their life in hospital through the use of an interview method. Discussion of this idea showed that whilst aspects of some residents' lives were well understood by the staff (such as how they passed their time in the ward), much was not known (for example, how they spent their money, what exactly they did when they were out of the ward, and so on). This led to the staff identifying aspects of the residents' lives which they felt were important, and about which they thought they could valuably learn more.

With some help from the adviser a simple interview schedule was constructed which focussed on four basic areas. The first sought to piece together a picture of how the residents passed their time in hospital, day by day and at weekends. The second area concerned friendship patterns amongst the residents, and the third the residents' feelings about the staff and how they carried out their work. The fourth area explored how the residents learned about themselves, for example, how they knew they were dressed reasonably, or how they learned what others thought about them.

In preparation for carrying out the interviews, and realising that interviewing is not a topic normally included in nurse training, several staff meetings were devoted to this subject. Particular attention was given to the role the interviewer might adopt in approaching the resident. In deciding this the staff reviewed the experience of the transient general nurse students who, the staff observed, were frequently not identified by residents as 'real staff' and yet could sometimes obtain more response from residents. The staff decided therefore, that staff members would step out of their usual roles and would seek the residents' permission to be interviewed as well as arranging this at a mutually acceptable time and place.

As the initial interviews were undertaken, they were written up by the staff member, recalling where possible the words actually used during the interview. There was much discussion amongst staff at handover meetings, and considerable mutual support was given in the new venture as the interview material became available. At the same time early fears that the interviews might 'disturb' residents were shown to be quite unfounded.

The steady accumulation of interview material led staff to feel that they might be 'missing' the significance of much information, and that if all available interviews were reviewed together they might give a clearer picture of the ward as a whole. Since 'handover' meetings provided inadequate time to accomplish this, they held a special afternoon meeting. The adviser proposed that in preparation for this, staff members might independently read all available interviews and try to identify common themes which emerged. These views were collated for the meeting, and showed considerable agreement between the ward staff. In general, the staff felt that there was a high degree of insularity amongst residents most of whom showed little personal initiative, expressed little in the way of boredom, and seemed to see their lives more in terms of the past or the remote future than the present.

Themes were also identified regarding the process of rehabilitation, and staff roles. Some of the residents expressed concern about getting better. However, it appeared that 'getting better' was something which was just 'going to happen'. The idea of self-help was not widely recognised and often they seemed to see their disorder in physical terms. Ailments tended to be used as an excuse for remaining as they were and not making progress or participating in the ward programme as it stood at the time. Many residents seemed happy to be left to their own devices, although paradoxically, there was often a good response to ward outings and similar special events. Equally, many seemed to feel that nursing staff should control their physical environment by serving food, keeping the ward clean and so on. They seemed to see little other function for nurses, although there was an awareness of staff favouritism.

The staff also pin-pointed a number of characteristics regarding interaction in the ward. The interview data revealed a general lack of purposeful interaction between staff and residents who seemed to rely on staff approaching them rather than the other way round. There seemed to be a dislike of noisy and disturbed behaviour, and usually any cause of tension, anxiety and disturbance was seen to be located outside oneself. The expression of anger by an individual seemed to be the most important single factor determining whether residents disliked another resident. Otherwise there seemed to be a marked absence of feeling (particularly positive feeling) for others, and a tendency to await instructions; to be led, to be taken, or to be pushed into a situation. However, some residents seemed to respond positively to 'one to one' contact; apparently enjoying the interview situation and some suggesting that it might be continued.

The ward doctor, who had been visiting the ward regularly on a routine basis, became interested in the project. She read all the available interviews and independently recorded her views, which not only substantially confirmed the nursing and occupational therapist's ideas, but also helped the staff conceptualise and summarise the problems.

Changes in Staff Roles, Ward Organisation and Nurse Training

Consideration of the interviews and the factors identified as significant by the staff group did not lead to any immediate and dramatic changes in care. Rather, there was a slow development over eighteen months as one problem in day to day activities was worked on and led to others. Keeping this time scale in mind, it is possible to describe some of the ensuing changes and developments.

In the first instance the staff felt that the research tool (the interview) was sufficiently successful in its use and in its apparent effect on some individuals, to incorporate it into the routine nursing activities on the ward in the shape of follow-up interviews. This emerged in practice more as a *counselling* approach to care. The pattern that evolved was for a staff member to select a resident and to use the initial interview as a basis for developing further individual contact with the resident. The increase in interviewing and subsequent counselling led to staff identifying the need to review their experiences and make sense of the emerging material. At first the adviser took a supporting role here, helping staff to relate the experience reported by the resident to the social situation in which he or she found themselves, and to identify further areas that might be explored as the relationship flourished between the staff member and the resident. On occasions the ward doctor also took this supporting role, but as time went by the senior staff on the ward developed these skills and the adviser was able to withdraw.

One important aspect of this process entailed the use of the initial interview, once it was written up. At first its main use was by the staff member in reporting back to the other staff members; later however, the staff member returned to the residents and invited them to read it so using it as a stepping stone to further work, and removing any *mystique* from the situation. This also acted as a check on the validity of the written record, since the resident could (and on occasions did) challenge the record or change it.

This work gave the staff the confidence to structure their time with individual residents, and by using the framework of the initial interview, to change their perspective on the residents. In particular, instead of seeing residents as unresponsive, they came to see them as people with problems and difficulties, some of which were related to the social environment of care, and capable of solution. This added a purpose and goal to the new way of working, and in doing so, further encouraged staff to maintain and consolidate the changes in their new roles.

With this increasing emphasis on dyadic interaction, the function of the twice weekly meeting between staff and residents came into question. It was felt that this 'community meeting' had always been difficult to maintain, that interest in it was waning and in particular that it had many negative aspects (such as the reluctance of residents to attend it) which contrasted strongly with what were seen as the growing positive features of the counselling approach to care. Yet the staff felt strongly that some framework within which residents and staff could meet was highly desirable. As a result a series of small groups was organised, using information from a sociogram constructed by a student nurse during the first phase of interviews which enabled 'natural' groups to be identified. These groups differed from the usual small groups experienced by staff, for example in admission wards, in that instead of having what was seen as a psychodynamic orientation, they focussed more on practical issues of concern. These issues might range from the felt lack of privacy experienced by a group of lady residents to discussion of what residents did over the weekend, or the difficulties facing a member who was being divorced by her husband and needed to know where she could get practical legal advice. Thus such discussions could result in action plans evolving for individuals or groups.

Consistent with the decreasing feeling of staff/resident separation being experienced as time went by, the question of staff's fuller participation in the small groups was raised. In particular, residents became curious about how staff spent their off-duty time, and about aspects of their personal life. Attention to this question resulted in staff agreeing that it might be useful to share some of their life with residents, where it could be understood that a long stay resident might be deprived of normal experiences. Staff might do this, for example in describing a trip to the cinema and their feelings about the film they saw, or by satisfying residents' curiosity about who they were getting married to, and more importantly how they were going to find a place to live.

An important aspect of the small groups meeting regularly, was that residents were then provided with a choice of modes of interacting purposefully in the ward; either in a large community meeting, in a small group meeting or individually with a staff member.

The adoption of this counselling approach to care involved a change in the way nursing staff expected to approach residents. As has been described, the staff member sought the resident's permission to undertake the interview, and on the basis of what the resident said, tried to understand how the resident saw his or her life and problems. Most initial interviews took about an hour to complete, and within this framework helping relationships were encouraged to develop, first by the social research adviser and then by senior staff, as the patients' positive response to these relationships became evident. The staff conceived that they were able to develop a 'helping friend' or 'neighbour' type of role with residents, and as this aspect of work was discussed, its wider implications were realised which in turn led to further changes.

One example of changes in roles is afforded by the case of a nurse who had developed a warm relationship with an elderly man. In talking about weekends spent by the resident at home, the nurse learnt more about the relationship and attitudes of the wife to her husband. While the ward doctor herself was unable to set aside time to see the wife regularly, she recognised the new skills developed by the ward staff and was happy to encourage two of them to start discussions with the husband and wife, with support from herself and other ward staff. Through small innovations like this the traditional organisation of the ward changed considerably, as did the staff/resident relationships within this organisational framework.

Formerly, the staff group relied mainly on the charge nurse and the ward doctor to give direction to their activities with residents. This pattern, established for many years, meant that the role of the charge nurse was associated with meeting the dependency needs of both residents and other staff, and by responding to them, encouraging further dependency. This was reflected in the multitude of approaches to the charge nurse by individual residents seeking 'Permission to go to OT', or asking 'Will it be alright to do . . .'

As project work progressed, the organisation of the ward into three groups of staff and residents, together with a sense of purpose generated from individual work with residents, meant that there was less need to rely on the ward doctor and the charge nurse to give direction to activities, or, for particularly the charge nurse, to continue meeting the dependency needs of staff and patients alike, and the incidence of requests made to him was much reduced.

Later, it became apparent that the amount of ideas being generated by the staff group was increasing, and that some forum to contain and work on them was necessary. The afternoon research review meeting evolved as this regular forum. At the same time the increasing need to examine, implement and review ideas pointed up the need for a member of staff to occupy a work group leader role — this being taken in practice by the senior nurse on duty. The role was essentially to keep the staff group's attention focussed on work in hand against pressures to dwell on day to day events, and to form an agenda of items for discussion from topics raised by staff between the weekly review meetings.

With the new care pattern established, staff came to recognise that the approach was difficult to sustain, that 'the project was dropping to bits' at intervals. In particular, this was associated with the occasional absence of one of the three trained members of staff due to sickness, leave or courses, or with the problem of scheduled changes of nurses in training who outnumbered the senior staff and had most daily contact with residents. Nurses in training could change completely over-night because of the organisation of training allocation. Discussion of this problem with a group of trainees who were about to leave the ward resulted in a number of changes being made to the way in which new groups were received into the ward. First, new staff were sent a copy of a revised ward policy document which explained what would be expected of them, together with an invitation to visit the ward and talk with existing staff. Second, their duties were arranged so that they could be together with a senior member of staff during their first two days on the ward: several hours were set aside during this time to explain fully and discuss the ward programme, to meet patients, and to go with a senior staff member to their first small group meeting after which they could select a patient to interview.

Work on these problems raised wider issues in relation to helping nurses in training make the most use of a limited placement time. In particular, the difficulty of having to accommodate to a new style of working and developing new interactional skills raises the question of learners being allocated for longer periods in order to consolidate a new approach to care and newly learned skills. Equally the wholesale change of nurses in training on fixed dates clearly produces difficulties for staff and patients alike, suggesting that such mechanistic approaches to training programmes should be questioned.

Evaluation of Change

As this work progressed, staff became aware of various changes in individual residents and in the ward as a whole. It was residents them-selves who, in expressing enjoyment over being interviewed at the beginning of the project work, led staff to develop the subsequent counselling approach. Staff and patients alike also felt that the forma-tion of small groups would be a useful innovation. In many ways therefore, the residents have participated with staff in improving the care. At the same time individuals have themselves changed. Examples of this include a resident whose interest in cycling was re-awakened and another who, apparently as a result of an interview, improved her appearance and changed her job, later getting married. Another resident, again apparently as a direct result of reviewing her life in the ward with a staff member, became dissatisfied and found herself accommodation outside hospital, despite both psychiatric and physical handicaps.

The changing pattern of care attracted comment from both staff who retrospectively recorded their views having passed through the ward as part of their training, as well as from other staff who were associated with the ward over longer periods of time. One student nurse described her experience on the ward in the following way:

> This has been a most rewarding experience as I have tried to under-stand the feelings of my own group of residents and have come to see them so much more as individuals with so much in their personality make-up which is attractive . . . The interviews have served a double purpose in so far as the resident has come to see himself as having potential and several have expressed their desire to move on. It has also helped in a student role to have set ward work to do, and to have one's work discussed and evaluated, and to understand why people behave in the way they do, and then link it with classroom teaching.

From other comments like these, it was clear that these changes have potential for encouraging relationships to develop between staff and residents and for staff to feel that they both learn and achieve something of value. A student nurse described how he experienced the changed induction organisation of the ward:

> Small groups quickly provided opportunities to capitalise on relation-ships initiated from first interviews . . . improve contact between residents, residents and staff, and between staff. They also improve the ratio of staff to residents and the quality of contact involved. Before, a new staff member himself was faced with thirty strangers — now he quickly meets ten of them (his small group) and inter-views one or two. Within a fortnight he has a variety of strong contacts established which form his principal responsibilities whilst on the ward.

The views of a nursing officer associated with the ward were that the ward had improved the care it offered, and that this was reflected in the fact that the ward had resettled a growing number of residents, some of whom were originally thought to be poor resettlement candi-dates. Examination of records showed that for the three years 1974, 1975 and 1976 the number of residents resettled outside hospital were two, eight and eleven respectively. A social worker felt that the ward had developed 'a very warm client-centred approach to care' which contrasted very favourably with the former pattern of care, whilst the ward doctor described her experiences of the changing pattern of care as 'one of the most exciting and rewarding aspects of (her) work at the hospital'. This was echoed by one of the trained nurses who described it in the following way:

> This has been satisfying at two levels in a way that nothing else in psychiatric nursing has been. It is rewarding intellectually and also emotionally. To be able to examine one's own working critically and as a result of one's investigations help to bring about change is satisfying on an intellectual level. To help a person to think about what has happened, and is happening to them, and to help them change — this is emotionally satisfying. The nurse is learning both *from* the resident and later, as the relationship develops, *with* the resident.

During the two years that this work was being undertaken, one of the senior nurses involved was seconded to the Advanced Course in Psychiatric Nursing. His absence gave him the opportunity, as he described it, to stand back from working situations and to see what was happening in psychiatric hospitals — without being personally involved in decision making processes — and so reflect upon the project work being undertaken and consider wider questions relating to the way a hospital's organisation can support such initiatives, so harnessing the potential that exists amongst its staff more fully. As experienced at ward level, he suggests that a number of factors are important.

> Firstly, a degree of autonomy for the ward is necessary so that changes can be made without too much outside opposition; something that is difficult to achieve in some hospitals. Secondly, there needs to be a culture which encourages questioning by all staff, and for senior staff to listen to, and take notice of, junior nurses. Thirdly it is important that new expectations are agreed by all staff and not felt to be unachievable. In these circumstances such project work and resulting change can be achieved usually without extra cost, and without needing special, or extra staff, and without needing to select patients specially.

Work such as this described here needs always to be developing. There are continually further problems to be examined. In this case for example, attention was required to the half dozen residents apparently unaffected by the changes, to devise further strategies for helping them. There was also a need to explore how care in the ward related to that offered by other wards catering for long stay residents, so that existing alternatives and choices could be better related to future needs.

However, the basic lesson — that patients can be helped to change their roles of passivity and isolation, if staff can start to move out of their own complementary roles of authoritative control and superordinate distance — is not likely to be forgotten.

3 IMPROVING THE CARE OF THE ELDERLY
Bev Savage, Tony Widdowson and Tony Wright

The care of the elderly in psychiatric hospitals has proved to be an issue of continuing national concern in recent years. At Fulbourn, between 1973 and 1976, substantial changes have been seen in psycho-geriatric services with considerable impact on patterns of care. On Denbigh Ward in particular, a 33 bedded psycho-geriatric ward, staff have been engaged in a continuing series of projects. Here, staff involved report two key steps in their efforts to improve patient care. Bev Savage, the charge nurse on this ward, and Tony Widdowson, a student nurse who spent some months there during his training, begin by giving an account (based on Savage and Widdowson, 1974) of what was involved in revising the use of nursing resources so as to more effectively meet the varying needs of different patients. The developments in the nurse's role which this work encouraged were then a contribution to the next stage of achieving closer collaboration with social workers based outside the hospital, leading in turn to new arrangements for sharing in care. This is described by Bev Savage and Tony Wright, a senior social worker with Cambridgeshire Social Services (following Savage and Wright, 1976).

Important among the conditions for these developments was the role taken by the responsible consultant psychiatrist at the time, Oliver Hodgson. He supported both these and wider changes in psycho-geriatric services. He examines the need for such changes and the most appropriate role for the consultant to assume, in a contribution to Chapter 7.

Revising the Use of Nursing Resources
Bev Savage and Tony Widdowson

We first started discussing improving patient care in March 1973. Preliminary discussions as to how to divide the patient population into groups according to their needs led us to look at the degree of reality to which each patient responded.

At the top of our list were those patients who were fairly in touch with reality; they were aware of what was going on around them, had some concentration and were the easiest patients to get on with. Next came those who required support in concentration and encouragement to do tasks that were present in the ward. Finally came the patients who had poor concentration, who did not appear to know what was going on and were completely out of touch with reality. These were the most difficult to look after and, in some people's view, the most neglected.

Comments were made to the effect that the patients should be considered individually rather than as groups because of the considerable differences between them. Items such as intellectual performance, interests and physical disabilities needed to be examined. The needs of patients seemed an abstract conception as no one really knew what these needs were.

In view of these preliminary discussions, available staff time was thought to be an important factor if we were to consider trying to do anything new with patients. Staff felt that most of their work consisted of making sure that the patient was dry, and engaging in the tasks of undressing, toiletting, feeding and so on, and so little time was left in catering for the patient's less obvious needs. It was difficult for the staff to say exactly what they did for or with the patients during the times not occupied by routine work. It was thought best to do a detailed time study to see what work we were actually doing, and how much.

Various studies have been done on patient dependency, but most of these seem to have been physically rather than psycho-socially orientated, and seem to assume that once a patient became physically independent he needed no staff time. Thus most of these recorded studies were difficult to apply to Denbigh Ward and gave us all the more reason to carry out the study ourselves.

The questions that needed answering were as follows:

(i)   What do we spend our time doing? And how much time do we spend doing it?

(ii)   What difference does high and low staffing make?

(iii) What is the difference between weekends and weekdays?

To answer these questions the staff had first to look into the various activities they were engaged in during working hours. Although we were very unsure at the start, we managed in quite a short period to evolve 27 broad categories of activities which we felt covered most of our work (Table 3.1). The staff group then designed a time card for each nurse to complete during the working shift. The process of completion was attractively simple and required the nurses to enter on the card at 15 minute intervals the code number of the category of activity in which they had been predominantly engaged during the preceding 15 minutes.

Table 3.1: Categories of Activities on Which Staff Time is Spent

---

CODE CATEGORY

1. *Administrative* — telephone calls, report writing, requisitioning, other paper work. Normally in office.
2. *Dressing/undressing* and washing including toiletting, combing or brushing hair during the morning 'getting people up' process.
3. *Toiletting* — changing patients when incontinent, taking them to the toilet etc.
4. *Personal care* — combing hair (not when getting patients up), giving out dentures, brushing dentures pm, sewing on buttons etc.
5. *Preparing and serving meals* — including plates in oven, food in bain marie, etc. Including drinks and the odd sandwich.
6. *Laying tables.*
7. *Feeding patients* — collecting plates etc., wiping tables.
8. *Bed round.*
9. *Bedmaking* — including making up admission beds, turning down coverlets etc.
10. *Preparing for patient activities* — such as OT, getting the patients together, moving furniture before and after, etc.
11. *Joining patient activities* — OT, ward church services, etc.
12. *Bathing* — including hair washing, care of nails, etc.
13. *Time spent out of ward* — conveying or collecting items, pharmacy, medical records, etc. Not usually with patients — but may take a patient along.
14. *Time spent out of ward* — with patients. Canteen, walk, hairdresser.
15. *Washing patients' clothes.*
16. *Sorting clothes and laundry.*
17. *Domestic tasks* (usually done by the nurse) — cleaning cupboards, floors when patients incontinent, etc.
18. *Domestic tasks* (not usually done by nurses) — polishing floors, hoovering, washing up, etc.
19. *Staff time* — own time such as meals, etc.
20. *Staff time* — free time, waiting periods, discussions about patients, etc., handover meetings, etc.
21. *Talking with patients* — while not doing other things.
22. *Talking with visitors* — while not doing other things.
23. *Talking with other staff* — who come from outside ward, for example, unit officer, rounds, doctor, nurses, etc.
24. *Nursing procedures* — medication, suppositories; including drop everything, for example, patient choking.
25. *Admission procedure* — including paperwork, talking to patient and others, informing duty doctor, physical examination, patient's property, etc.
26. *Hospital time* — for example, playing cricket, asked to do medicines out of ward.
27. *Miscellaneous* — for example, tidying up clothing left about, tidying bathroom, putting laundry bags out, locking doors, etc.

At the end of the day the time cards were collected and the 15 minute periods for each category of nursing activity were totalled. Also calculated were the categories of nursing activities being undertaken during each quarter hour of the day. Thus it was possible to see:

(i)   How many quarter-hour periods of nursing time we spent on specific activities.

(ii)   Just what staff time was being used for at different times during the day.

The data were not quite complete because one afternoon shift time card (out of 103) went astray during the study. The results presented therefore are based on ten full days and one half day and not eleven full days. The time cards were completed over the eleven days from 23 May to 2 June 1973. This was a period during which there was a strong feeling of being short of staff, with some cover having to be provided from other wards in the area.

Table 3.2: Priority Uses of Staff Time, Predicted and Actual

Predictions — Before Study	Actual Time — After Study	Staff Time (hours/10.5 days)
1. Getting patient up or to bed: dressing, washing, toiletting etc. (category 2)	1. Staff time: handovers, discussion, waiting time, etc. (category 20)	55.6
2. Feeding patients (category 7)	2. Getting patients up: dressing, washing, toiletting, etc. (category 2)	41.6
3. Bathing (category 12)	3. Toiletting (category 3)	43.8
4. Toiletting (category 3)	4. Talking with patients (category 21)	43.1
5. Bedmaking (category 9)	5. Feeding patients (category 7)	42.7
6. Sorting clothes (category 16)	6. Bedmaking (category 9)	38.3

All results were collated by a member of the staff group and presented in such a way so that we could see the number of quarter-hour periods that we devoted to each nursing activity. These were then plotted diagrammatically to show the patterning of activities through the day. Before we engaged in the study we predicted how we thought we used our time (Table 3.2). The predictions were more or less correct but we were amazed that most quarter-hour periods of all were spent

Table 3.3: Total Number of Quarter-hour Periods for Each Category of Nursing Activity

Position	Code	Category of Nursing Activity	am*	pm*	Total
1	20	Staff time	119½	103½	223
2	2	Dressing/undressing	81½	107	188½
3	3	Toiletting	124½	51	175½
4	21	Talking with patients	79	93½	172½
5	7	Feeding patients	127½	43½	171
6	9	Bedmaking	143½	10	153½
7	19	Staff time	94	36	130
8	12	Bathing	76½	53	129½
9	5	Preparing and serving meals	88	39	127
10	1	Administrative	49½	23½	73
11	24	Nursing procedures	32½	31	63½
12	27	Miscellaneous	34½	20½	55
13	4	Personal care	29	20	49
14	15	Washing patients' clothes	20	28	48
15	16	Sorting clothes and laundry	16	24	40
15	13	Time spent out of ward	28	12	40
17	10	Preparing for patient activities	26½	3	29½
18	8	Bed round	0	28	28
19	14	Time spent out of ward (+ patients)	15	12	27
20	18	Domestic tasks (not usually done by nurse)	7	17½	24½
21	11	Joining patients' activities	17	0	17
22	22	Talking with visitors	1	10½	11½
23	6	Laying tables	5½	1	6½
24	26	Hospital time	2½	3	5½
25	17	Domestic tasks (usually done by nurse)	3	2	5
25	25	Admission procedure	3	2	5
27	23	Talking with other staff	1½	0	1½

* am includes data for 11 days: pm includes data for only 10 days

on the category 'staff time' (Table 3.3), which consisted of discussions about patients and handover meetings, etc. This was encouraging to us since, by reorganising some activities, it would enable the staff to engage in something new.

Nearly half the total working time was spent on activities directed primarily towards meeting the patient's physical needs (for example, dressing, toiletting and feeding). One-fifth of the total nursing time was directed more towards their mental needs (for example, talking with patients and discussions).

For at least two-thirds of the day one activity (or occasionally two) dominated any particular quarter-hour period. This suggested a fairly rigid routine in the ward. There seemed to be many activities in which all available staff on duty engaged, all getting people dressed, all feeding patients or all bedmaking. The onset of a particular activity tended not to be gradual but started at fairly rigid times (particularly meals). This we termed the stop-go effect.

Before doing the time study, staff thought that there was a marked difference in the service to patients on low-staff days compared with high-staff days. The study showed us how the extra time is spent when more staff are on duty. A clear effect of more staff is that more time is spent feeding patients. In general, all available staff help with meals. Another clear effect was that less time was spent on bedmaking, but paradoxically, it was noted that sometimes two people make beds quicker than four people. There was also evidence that scheduled bathing was attempted only when there were more staff on duty.

It followed, then, that only slightly more talking with patients occurred on high staff days, so that the extra time was spent mainly elsewhere, in carrying out physical care. So, we were broadly doing the same thing but more of it. Comparing weekends with weekdays, the study showed that more time was spent talking with patients and in free-time discussions during weekends. This may account for the more relaxed atmosphere reported at weekends. Once we had appraised the amount of time spent on various activities, and could see that the time available could be used differently, we continued with our original idea of looking at individual patients and their needs in order to improve standards of care.

Patient Assessment

It was decided to formulate a programme of 'tests' by which we could assess the patients on their physical, mental and social abilities in relation to the life they led on Denbigh Ward. This was also done to find out what each individual patient's capabilities were, and to see if there was any way of grouping the patients.

The staff drew up 24 tests to use in the assessment. We evolved these tests by looking at many aspects of individual patients — for example, Mrs Smith held onto chairs and tables when she walked around the ward so the physical ability to walk became a test.

These 24 tests were carried out by observing the patient, as in the physical ability to walk; by questioning the patient, as in the mental ability to remember recent events in the ward; and by both observation and questioning as in the social ability to carry out a conversation. The

Table 3.4: Showing Tests Devised to Assess Patients' Capacities

---

		Score
1.	**How well does she walk?**	
	(a) Requires maximum assistance: wheelchair or walking aid.	1
	(b) Walks with difficulty, but can manage without assistance.	2
	(c) Experiences minimal or no difficulty in walking.	3
2.	**How well can she hear?**	
	(a) Considerable deafness present.	1
	(b) Hard of hearing, have to raise voice to be heard.	2
	(c) No difficulty in hearing.	3
3.	**How well can she talk?**	
	(a) Incapable of forming intelligible words.	1
	(b) Experiences difficulty with speech, but can generally make herself understood.	2
	(c) No difficulty in talking.	3
4.	**How well can she manage to feed herself?**	
	(a) Cannot feed herself, needs spoon feeding.	1
	(b) Can manage with assistance, experiences difficulty managing cutlery, messy eater.	2
	(c) Manages well, good eater.	3
5.	**Can she manage to dress?**	
	(a) Requires to be dressed.	1
	(b) Needs some assistance for example with zips, tights etc. but can manage up to a point.	2
	(c) Can dress without assistance.	3
6.	**Can she manage to wash herself?**	
	(a) Needs someone to wash her.	1
	(b) Needs some assistance or prompting, for example in putting plug in hand basin, finding towel, etc., but can manage some of the process.	2
	(c) Needs little or no assistance.	3
7.	**Can she manage to bath herself?**	
	(a) Needs to be assisted completely.	1
	(b) Needs some help or prompting.	2
	(c) Needs little or no assistance.	3
8.	**Is she continent during the day?**	
	(a) She is often incontinent and/or needs taking to toilet.	1
	(b) Only occasionally incontinent and/or needs reminding to go to toilet.	2
	(c) Rarely incontinent, toilets self.	3
9.	**Is she continent at night?**	
	See 8 above.	

Table 3.4 *(cont.)*

_____

		Score
10. How aware is she of the names of others with whom she is in contact?
    (a)   Knows no names.   1
    (b)   Knows one or two names.   2
    (c)   Knows three or more names.   3

11. How aware is she of changes in events in the ward? (ward activity)
    (a)   No correct answers.   1
    (b)   One correct answer.   2
    (c)   More than one (2+) correct answers.   3
    (Questions asked were: 'Who is the newest patient here?' 'Who is the newest nurse here?' 'How many tablets do you have?'. Names were not required.)

12. How aware is the patient of another's distress and does she bring it to the attention of a nurse if she sees it? e.g. a patient falling.
    (a)   No recognition of another's need for help.   1
    (b)   Recognises the need for help but does nothing.   2
    (c)   Recognises need for help, and brings it to attention of a nurse.   3

13. How aware is she of time?
    (a)   No appreciation of time.   1
    (b)   Cannot read the clock or give meal times but shows an appreciation of the passing of time.   2
    (c)   Has a good appreciation of time; many correct answers.   3
    (What is the time? Meal times? Time usually go to bed?)

14. Does she know generally where she is? (general place)
    (a)   Very little or false knowledge of where she is.   1
    (b)   Knows she is in hospital — but not which ward.   2
    (c)   Knows name of hospital and ward.   3

15. Does patient know where her bed is? (local place)
    (a)   Does not know.   1
    (b)   Usually reliable, but sometimes makes mistakes.   2
    (c)   Knows reliably.   3

16. How well does she remember things in her past life? (memory past)
    (a)   No correct answers.   1
    (b)   One or two correct answers.   2
    (c)   More than two (3+) correct answers.   3
    (When were you born? Are/were you married? How many children? Remember World War I? What dates?)

17. How well does she remember recent events? (memory present)
    (a)   Remembered nothing.   1
    (b)   Remembered event recently — but no details.   2
    (c)   Remembered event reasonably accurately.   3
    (An extraordinary event was devised to assess this: a mock fire drill. Two days later the patient was asked to remember the event. Do you remember? How long ago was it? What happened?)

_____

Table 3.4 *(cont.)*

		Score
18.	What sort of temperament does the patient have? Is she generally hostile/ friendly towards other patients?	
	(a) Usually hostile to other patients.	1
	(b) Has variable hostility/friendliness, or displays no emotion to other patients.	2
	(c) Generally amiable or friendly to other patients.	3

19. Does she respond to patients/staff when they talk to her?
    (a)   Makes no response or shows no understanding.   1
    (b)   Appreciates she is being spoken to, but shows little understanding.   2
    (c)   Shows good understanding and makes appropriate responses.   3

20. Can she carry on a conversation?
    (a)   Makes no verbal response, or an inappropriate one.   1
    (b)   One party (usually staff member) stimulates other who does not contribute other than answering the dialogue.   2
    (c)   Both parties contribute to a continuing appropriate dialogue.   3

21. What sort of relationship does she have with nurses?
    (a)   No apparent relationship.   1
    (b)   Relationship only seems to exist at an authority level e.g. with a nurse.   2
    (c)   Relationship with nurses at a social level (as well as authority level).   3

22. Does she have a relationship with another (other) patients?
    (a)   No apparent relationship.   1
    (b)   A variable relationship e.g. existing only temporarily in moments of crisis.   2
    (c)   Has a strong relationship (either positive or antagonistic) with at least one other patient.   3

23. Does the patient help in ward? (e.g. laying tables etc.)
    (a)   Never.   1
    (b)   Occasionally.   2
    (c)   Regularly.   3

24. Does the patient help other patients? (e.g. to a chair for lunch or undressing)
    (a)   Never.   1
    (b)   Occasionally.   2
    (c)   Regularly.   3

    It was felt that the assessment dimensions above, although sometimes overlapping and interdependent, could be seen as falling into three main areas:
1. Tests of physical capacity.   (1 to 9)
2. Tests of psychological capacity.   (10 to 17)
3. Tests of social capacity.   (18 to 24)

Table 3.5: Assessment Ratings of Patients' Capacities

PATIENT	1	2	3	4	5	6	7	8	9	10	11	12	13	14	15	16	17	18	19	20	21	22	23	24	25	26	27	28	29	30	31	32	33	Total
TEST																																		
Feeding	3	3	3	3	3	3	3	3	3	3	3	3	3	3	3	3	3	3	3	3	3	3	3	3	3	3	3	2	2	3	1	2	2	94
Hearing	3	3	2	3	3	3	3	3	2	3	3	3	3	3	1	2	3	3	3	3	3	2	1	1	3	2	2	3	3	2	3	3	2	84
Walking	3	3	3	3	3	3	3	3	2	3	3	3	3	3	3	2	2	3	3	3	3	3	2	3	3	1	2	3	2	2	2	2	1	83
Talking	3	3	3	3	3	3	3	1	3	3	3	3	3	3	3	2	2	2	2	2	2	2	3	3	3	3	3	2	1	1	1	1	1	82
Responsiveness	3	3	3	3	3	3	3	2	3	3	3	3	2	3	3	3	3	2	3	3	3	2	3	3	2	2	1	2	2	1	1	1	1	80
Relationship – staff	3	3	3	3	3	3	3	3	3	3	3	3	3	1	2	3	2	3	3	3	2	3	3	3	2	2	1	1	2	2	1	1	1	78
Washing	3	3	3	3	3	3	3	2	3	3	3	2	3	3	3	3	3	3	3	3	1	3	2	2	1	3	1	1	1	1	1	1	1	77
Dressing	3	3	3	3	3	3	3	3	3	3	3	3	3	3	3	3	2	3	1	1	3	2	2	1	1	1	1	1	2	1	1	1	1	75
Place – local	3	3	2	3	3	3	3	3	3	3	3	3	2	1	3	2	3	3	3	3	3	2	2	1	1	1	2	2	2	1	1	1	1	75
Incontinence – day	3	3	3	3	3	2	3	3	3	3	3	3	2	3	3	3	3	1	3	3	3	3	3	2	2	1	1	1	2	2	1	1	1	73
Conversation	3	3	3	3	3	3	3	1	3	2	2	3	2	2	3	1	3	2	3	2	1	2	2	2	2	2	2	2	1	1	1	1	1	70
Incontinence – night	2	3	3	3	3	1	1	3	3	3	3	2	2	2	3	1	3	1	3	3	3	2	1	3	3	1	1	1	1	1	1	1	1	68
Temperament	3	3	3	3	3	3	3	2	2	3	2	2	2	2	3	3	2	1	3	2	3	2	3	2	2	2	2	1	1	1	1	1	1	68
Ward activity	3	3	3	3	3	3	3	3	2	2	3	3	1	1	2	2	2	3	2	1	1	3	3	2	2	1	1	2	1	1	1	1	1	66
Place – general	3	3	3	2	3	3	3	3	2	2	2	2	2	1	1	2	2	3	3	3	1	2	1	1	1	1	1	1	1	1	1	1	1	64
Time	3	3	3	1	3	3	1	3	3	1	1	2	2	1	3	1	1	2	1	2	2	1	1	1	1	1	1	2	2	1	1	1	1	60
Help situation	3	3	3	3	3	1	3	3	1	1	1	2	2	3	3	3	2	2	1	1	1	1	1	1	1	1	1	1	1	1	1	1	1	58
Relationship – patients	3	3	3	2	3	2	2	2	3	1	1	1	2	2	3	1	1	2	2	2	2	2	1	1	2	2	1	1	1	1	1	1	1	58
Memory – past	3	3	3	2	3	2	3	2	1	2	1	1	2	2	3	3	3	2	2	2	2	2	2	2	1	1	1	1	1	1	1	1	1	58
Memory – recent	3	3	3	1	3	3	2	3	2	1	1	3	1	1	2	2	3	2	1	1	1	1	2	1	1	1	1	1	1	1	1	1	1	56
Helping patients	3	3	3	3	3	1	1	1	3	2	2	2	3	3	3	1	1	3	1	1	2	2	1	2	1	1	1	1	1	1	1	1	1	55
Bathing	3	3	2	1	3	2	2	2	1	2	2	1	1	1	2	2	2	1	1	1	2	2	1	1	1	1	1	1	1	1	1	1	1	53
Helping staff	3	1	1	1	3	3	1	2	2	3	3	1	3	1	1	2	2	1	1	3	1	3	2	1	1	1	1	1	1	1	1	1	1	50
Names	3	1	1	1	3	3	1	2	2	1	1	3	1	1	1	1	1	1	1	1	1	1	1	1	1	1	1	1	1	1	1	1	1	45
Totals	71	70	65	64	64	62	60	59	59	58	57	55	54	54	54	53	52	52	50	47	48	47	46	40	39	36	34	32	31	30	30	27	26	

Rating: 1 – poor   2 – moderate   3 – good

gradings for each test were by number, 1 being poor, 2 moderate and
3 good (Table 3.4).

There was a great deal of discussion between staff during the assessment. We had first to clarify each grading, and a consensus had to be
reached before testing began. For example, in grading the patient's
ability to talk the staff recognised that talking was important in the
patient being able to function autonomously both in and out of
hospital. We graded the physical ability to talk as:
1. Poor – the patient was incapable of forming intelligible words or of
   communicating.
2. Moderate – the patient experienced difficulty with speech but could
   generally make herself understood.
3. Good – the patient had no difficulty in talking.

This example illustrates how we went about forming a consensus of
all the 24 categories. It took about two-and-a-half months to complete
the assessment programme, the results of which were recorded. The
patients' names were arranged along the top from number 1, on the
left, who scored the highest, to number 33, on the right, who scored
the lowest. The tests themselves are similarly arranged on the list from
category number 1, at the top, which gained the highest total of points
scored by the patients, to category number 24, at the bottom, which
gained the lowest total (Table 3.5).

This chart showed, as we had thought, that the patients fell into
three main groups. It also appeared that it was the middle group, not
the last, which gained the least amount of attention from the staff. We
could see the reason for this. Because the top group were fairly well
socially adjusted, we could sit and talk with them, and because the
bottom group were so incapable, they gained a lot of physical care and
attention from the staff. The middle group really had neither.

Our discussions during the assessment gave us many clues to our
actions afterwards and the chart enabled us to pick out various groups
of patients. For example, one category on the chart was 'Awareness:
place – general'. This test was devised to see whether the patients knew
that they were in Denbigh Ward at Fulbourn Hospital. There were quite
a few patients who did not know this and scored 1.

Groups of six were then invited to a quiet place in the ward, where
we asked them questions like 'Where are you?' and 'Do you know
where you are?' continually letting them know where they were. This
process was repeated until, when a patient was asked where she was, she
would be able to recall that she was in Denbigh Ward at Fulbourn
Hospital. This form of re-educating the patients was used to combat

other incapacities — knowing the time for example.

Subsequent Changes

These results, together with those from the first part of our project, showed that compared with time spent on physical tasks, a relatively small amount of time was spent on the patients' psychological and social needs. It was, therefore, decided to change the ward routine to give the staff more time with the patients. This in turn led to other changes.

There is now a clear tendency on behalf of the staff to break up the rigid routine we have been used to. Particular activities tend to be gradual and with a purpose behind them. A noticeable feature is that staff are engaged in different tasks at different times rather than everyone doing the same thing at the same time. The pressure to keep to a rigid, fixed routine has now altered.

An example of this is the period between seven and eight in the morning. Then everyone used to be engaged in getting patients dressed, toiletted and washed, and when there was a staff crisis patients were not, we felt, adequately cared for because all of them had to be having breakfast at 8 a.m. We were, in fact, fighting time and everyone became anxious if the patients were not ready by 8 a.m. A later breakfast now gives us ample time to care for the patients adequately, and the anxiety of staff in respect of time has tended to disappear.

Discussions with the night staff, which have arisen from the confidence about changing the morning pressure, have now led to the patients being left in bed until the day staff come on duty. Reports from the night staff have stated that patients sleep much better and there is less wandering at night. Perhaps the greatest benefit is the loss of the old institutional habit of getting patients up early.

Since the alteration of meal milestones in the routine, the patients have breakfast at different times during the first part of the morning according to how much they can do for themselves and how long it takes them to get dressed and washed. We cannot get all the patients up at the same time and in the past some patients had been sitting at the table for an hour before breakfast. The last meal of the day, a sort of high tea, was found to be too early at 4.0 p.m. This period has now moved to 6.0 p.m. We were fortunate in acquiring an evening domestic to wash up after this period following discussion with the domestic superintendent.

Greater autonomy for patients is something that we have examined closely and we are getting surprising results. Patients are engaged in tasks, for example clearing away tables and other household activities, which they would have been carrying out in their own homes. It was apparent right from the start that it was quicker for the staff to do everything for the patients such as bed-making, washing and so on, but this was a far cry from retaining or developing skills which patients had had outside the hospital. Over the years patients have been placed in the position where everything is done for them and although the new method requires a great deal of added effort on behalf of the staff, we realise it is for the better.

Time which we have free to talk to the patients is more concentrated on an attempt to work to a plan. We endeavour to achieve a purpose, however long it may take, in patients who are to some extent disabled. We can now say that an amount of time is directed purely towards the patients' minds. When extra staff are in the ward, they too, can be directed towards a purposeful end.

Morale within the ward team has certainly been raised during the course of the project and we can at least say that the work we are doing is conducive to treatment. Seeing the patient as an object rather than a human being is, we hope, something of the past. It is also true that everyone has enjoyed looking at the patients in a different light from that of purely physical care. Crises do still exist in the ward in relation to staff but not to the same extent. We feel that we are better adapted and, when we are short of staff, we can cope comfortably with ward situations.

The project has evidently changed the attitudes of staff who have been in the ward for quite some time. In discussing the results they tended to agree that patients were less incontinent and appeared much more responsive to their environment. All agreed that work was more satisfying and interesting than the former pattern of care, and that they knew much more about the patients and what was going on in the ward. One said that she found herself thinking about the ward when she was at home and trying to formulate further improvements.

There was a general feeling that routinised tasks were less important and that staff were encouraged, and felt free, to use their own initiative and discretion much more over what they did with patients. In turn this posed further problems. For example, if a patient was now expected to continue to exercise, say, domestic skills, the problem arose of 'How can I help Mrs A to do X, when I know she is capable of doing it?' Two nurses recognised that they did not quite feel fully at home with the new pattern of patient care, but felt this was hardly surprising in view of the rigid routine that they had been trained in. But all wished to stay involved with the developments.

The work described so far led to considerable changes in the way staff saw the care of patients in their charge. However, the changes also acted as a catalyst to further changes in the wider psycho-geriatric service, which will now be described.

Collaboration with Social Services in Shared Care
Bev Savage and Tony Wright

At a time when the resources available to the elderly are increasingly burdened, the need for comprehensive client assessment and the co-ordination of hitherto independently functioning organisations is paramount. There is a need for closer co-operation between caring professionals. One way of achieving this is to blur the boundaries between hospital and community care.

It was within this climate and building on the work already described in this chapter which was leading to substantial innovation in nursing care, that Fulbourn Hospital and Cambridgeshire Social Services embarked on a joint project. It proved to be an exercise not only in practical co-operation between two traditionally separated professional disciplines, but also an opportunity for each to develop understanding of the work of the other. It resulted in improved working relationships between the two disciplines and enabled the management of the problems of the so called confused elderly to be shared and improved. We describe here the background of some of the changes, and make some interim observations on the new system of care.

Formerly the psycho-geriatric wards in the hospital were organised so that one ward served as an admission ward. The demand for elderly patients to be admitted was such that empty beds on other wards were used to take an overflow of patients from the one admission ward. Some psycho-geriatric wards catered more particularly for severely disabled patients — whilst others cared for the more ambulant patient. Some ten wards, therefore, backed up the one admission ward. Altogether, there was a general feeling that the demand for beds was too great; that the services were about to break down.

With a lengthy waiting list of up to 30 patients on occasions, the feeling was prevalent amongst staff that the psychiatric hospital was seen by others as merely a dumping ground for the elderly. Ward staff having little contact with the external agencies, had some feelings of impotence, as they were unable to influence — or to participate in — the decisions of those outside the hospital who determined who would receive care in it.

Outside the hospital, Cambridgeshire Social Services came into being with the implementation of the Seebohm Report. It was organised into five geographical divisions. Each division comprised a number of geographically organised generic social work teams led by a senior social worker. The social services were also responsible for a number of residential homes for the elderly, including one for the elderly mentally infirm. As places became available in such homes, prospective cases were reviewed by representatives from each division at a regular joint meeting. There was difficulty because demand for residential places frequently exceeded the supply.

Clients identified as psycho-geriatric in the primary care setting were usually referred for a domiciliary visit by a consultant psychiatrist. Most frequently, if accepted for psychiatric care, the client was then placed on the hospital's waiting list to await an available bed. There was little local authority social work contact with psycho-geriatric wards, and the organisation of hospital care was such that a client could be admitted one day, and the following week might have been transferred to another ward. From the community services viewpoint, this effectively lost the person within a large institutional setting.

In the report on the studies undertaken by the ward's nurses, it was noted that staff had constructed an assessment schedule by which to quantify and on which to record the capacities and social functioning of each patient in the ward. This had resulted in their discovering features of the way care was organised which they felt might serve to influence a patient being seen as deteriorating. This enabled them to make changes in the way care was managed which sought either to delay, or partially reverse some of these processes. A more rehabilitative approach to care began to emerge.

It was during this period, and as part of an attempt by the hospital and the social services to achieve closer collaboration – that a member of the local authority social services became interested in the activities of the ward staff, and the changes they were making. As a result he recognised that the assessment schedule devised by the nurses might be a valuable tool for use in the client's home setting. With some modifications this proved possible and ward nursing staff were invited to assess prospective clients in their homes. This complemented the usual social work assessment, which focussed more on the circumstances of the whole family.

During the early stages of planning how ward nurses could most effectively assess patients in this way, the consultant psychiatrist and the unit nursing officer made the suggestion that two beds might be

given to the particular division of the social services with whom the
ward nurses were starting to collaborate in making assessments of
prospective clients. (This number was subsequently increased by stages
to seven.) Orginally the intention had been to simplify the management
of potential crisis situations occurring in the community population
served jointly by the ward and this social services division. After discussion the suggestion was accepted on a trial basis to be reviewed as it
developed. The actual use of these beds required some thought.
However, agreement was quite rapidly reached between the ward staff
and the social services divisional staff.

How the New Care System Works

When a social worker feels that a client would benefit by psychiatric
hospital admission, they make a written assessment of need. This is
done in liaison with the general practitioner. The ward is informed, and
a nurse from the ward visits the patient and completes an assessment
schedule derived from the one evolved in the ward setting. Each week
the social work and nursing assessments are then discussed fully at a
meeting between the ward staff and the referring social worker. It is at
this point that joint decisions are made as to how clients and their
families can best be helped. It may be by further social work and/or
nursing help in the home setting, or it may involve admitting the
patient for varying periods. The final decision is then communicated to
the general practitioner. Where a client is admitted, the social worker
organises the client's admission and keeps in touch with the patient
on the ward, either in person, or through the regular liaison social
worker. This has been found to be a vital part of the service. Frequently
the social worker can keep contact with the patient whilst working with
the family by arranging for supportive services and preparing them for
the client's return to the home setting.

If there are more clients than available beds then the priority
decision rests finally with the social services, an infrequent occurrence
in practice. When the patient is discharged, a further assessment is made
by the nurses, comparable with the first and this is passed to the social
worker involved.

The new system is not without its difficulties. The problems of
clients and of their families still have to be worked on, priority
decisions have to be made and so on. However, one problem that seems
to have become smaller over the two years that the experiment has
been in progress is that of relatives' reactions to a client's discharge.
At the start of the experiment it was recognised that relatives

resisted the client's discharge. It is a firm impression that such resistance is now less frequently encountered; that temporary admission to the ward often relieves family stress by the sharing of care with them; and that it enables families to cope more easily when the client returns home.

In essence, therefore, the ward staff limited their psycho-geriatric work to coincide with the work of a particular social service division and so to provide a service to a population of 108,450 of whom about 16,944 (15.62 per cent) were over the age of 65.

The same method of referral (direct to the ward staff) was open to general practitioners who have clients within the population served by the ward. Whilst traditional referral channels to a hospital psychiatrist were still open to general practitioners, and were preferentially used by many, the action which follows is often the same in that the nursing staff are commonly requested to make an assessment by the psychiatrist receiving the referral.

During these developments, a number of meetings with relatives have been held on the ward, for the purpose of explaining more fully the aims of care on the ward. Additionally a number of divisional social work meetings have been held in the hospital, enabling ward staff to attend and to meet the full social work team.

Reviewing Experience to Date

As the service developed, the staff involved became aware that more questions were being asked than could be answered; in particular, 'Is the service an improvement?' There is no doubt that this question is extraordinarily difficult to answer. For example, an elderly lady who is just coping with her life may have her wishes not to be admitted respected. This is likely to be seen as an improvement by the client, although not necessarily by the individual referring the lady. Such dilemmas abound for those involved in work with the elderly and their relatives.

In attempting to review the effectiveness of the new service, it was also recognised that comparable data before and after the changes were not available. The data presented in what follows, therefore, summarise the experiences during a twelve month period, and provide data with which future experiences can be compared.

Before the experiment started there was a waiting list of psycho-geriatric patients for admission to the psycho-geriatric service. Being placed on that waiting list might involve a wait of up to three months before help (which was then seen as being provided only by admission)

Table 3.6: Source of Referrals and Outcome of Assessment, 12 Months, 1974-5

Referral Agent	Admitted N =	%	Not Admitted N =	%	Totals N =	%
G.P.	19	51	18	72	37	60
Social Workers	14	38	3	12	17	27
Internal Hospital	1	3	4	16	5	8
General Hospital	3	8	–	–	3	5
Totals	37	100%	25	100%	62	100%

could be given. During the course of the experiment the waiting list has disappeared. There follows an assessment of the process by which assessment and admission services are now provided.

Table 3.6 shows the number of assessments made during a recent twelve month period, the source of referral, and the number of referrals who subsequently were or were not admitted to the ward. It can be seen that the largest number originated from general practitioners. A small number originated from other (mainly admission) wards in the hospital and from the local district general hospital. Examination of the records of patients admitted during this period shows that the average length of time elapsing between referral and admission was 12.51 days. It can be seen that 37 out of 62 clients referred (that is 60 per cent) during this period were admitted to the ward.

The speed with which the service can be provided is important. Since the experiment involved (in the main) decisions being taken at a weekly joint meeting, two measurements are significant, namely the time elapsing between referral and assessment of the client, and secondly the time between assessment and admission.

Of the 37 patients admitted to the ward following assessment, the number of days that elapsed between the receipt of the referral by the ward staff and their completion of the assessment ranged from 1 to 25 days. However, 51 per cent of assessments were completed in 48 hours and 83 per cent within 7 days. The average time that elapsed between receiving the referral and completing the assessment was 3.75 days.

Of the clients admitted, four patients (11 per cent) were not assessed at the time. They were clients known to the ward team and for whom assessments had previously been completed before the 12 month period commenced. Two clients (6 per cent) for whom assessment took longer than seven days to complete (19 and 25 days respectively) were referred as non-urgent.

Turning attention to the second measure of the service provided, the time that elapsed between a client being assessed and subsequently being admitted, examination of data showed that over half (53 per cent) of clients were admitted within a week of the assessment being made, the average length of time being 8.81 days (this excludes the 4 patients discussed previously who were not assessed at the time).

Discussion of these data led to a detailed examination of the features of all cases in which admitted clients had not gained access to the ward within twelve days. (Twelve days may be regarded as a reasonable time, given that joint decision making meetings were held weekly and a referral might be received immediately following the weekly meeting, so that a client who did not need emergency action might be admitted in the week following the next joint meeting.) A separate review of these clients was undertaken to see if delay could be related to a shortage of available beds or to blocked beds, common explanations for the resurrection of a waiting list. The review was also important since, in a number of cases, admission had been arranged on the spot when the assessment had been made. This indicated a capability for immediate action when judged necessary, and also confirmed the validity of the original idea of the nursing officer and the consultant, that the new service might help to meet crises. It made the question 'Why did it take so long to admit some clients?' assume some importance.

Examination of the ten individual cases revealed that three of the clients were accepted for admission, but other ways of managing the case were being tried out first. In each case it was the social worker involved who decided the time at which admission was eventually needed. A further three clients were accepted for admission, but were in local authority residential accommodation and ward staff were advising on alternative ways of managing difficulties before admitting them. An additional two clients were in the local general hospital and required to complete treatment before admission, and a further client was being looked after by two retired nurses who welcomed advice on her management by the ward staff; eventually she fell by the fire and burned her hair and was admitted within 24 hours. The final client was referred as non-urgent, requiring assessment as an in-patient, but was the only case for whom a bed was not immediately available.

Examination of the outcome for admitted patients shows that of those 37 patients admitted for care, 27 (73 per cent) were discharged, four (10.8 per cent) died and six (16.2 per cent) remained as in-patients.

Benefits of the Changes

In reviewing the data above, it seemed to us that the picture that emerged was better than we had expected. In particular, it had been anticipated that the time elapsing between referral and assessment, and between assessment and admission, would have been longer; and that the number remaining in care would have been higher than in fact proved to be so. We ourselves, therefore, learned from the exercise of reviewing the data.

Certain benefits clearly emerge from the experience of providing the service. Ward staff visiting and assessing clients in their homes, on occasions jointly with the social worker, enables the problems encountered in the home situation to be recognised and discussed in the ward prior to admission, and the nursing approach to individuals tailored accordingly.

Equally, social workers now knowing more about the care given to patients in the ward, are able to give a first hand account of that care to clients and their families in preparing them for an admission to the ward. Similarly ward nursing staff, now knowing more about the work of social workers, are able to advise on the desirability of having a social work assessment as well (for example, when assessing cases referred by general practitioners). Thus a degree of role sharing has been achieved by developing closer professional working relationships between nurses and social workers, whilst each retains their distinct, though complementary, professional skills.

During the two years of the experiment, an awareness has developed of the complex referral procedures that preceded the referral of a client for psycho-geriatric care. Frequently, it appeared that a client had had multiple referrals to different services before finally being referred for psycho-geriatric care. It was almost as though the client was the ball in a pin-ball machine, with each service deflecting the client on to the next. From our review, particularly of the more recent cases – it appeared that the former complex pin-ball model of referral to psycho-geriatric care had been simplified.

Wider Implications

The experiment described above was confined to one ward and a single social service division. Over a period, the model it provided enabled other wards in the psycho-geriatric service at the hospital to become similarly linked with other social service divisions. They have developed their own styles of joint working relationships. It is not possible to make meaningful comparisons between these different services and working relationships because generally accepted methods of systematically recording data have not yet been worked out. It is possible, however, to comment on the effect of the zoned services as they relate to the overall services provided for psycho-geriatric clients by the hospital. It is reflected in the total admission and discharge figures for the years ending March 1973 (before the zoning was effective) and March 1975 (after zoning had become better developed). These are shown in Table 3.7.

Table 3.7: Showing Admissions, Discharges and Deaths of the Elderly 1973 and 1975

	Admissions	Discharges	Deaths
1973	187	162	77
1975	282	244	67

It can be seen that there was a considerable (about 50 per cent) increase in workload for the psycho-geriatric service as a whole. The large increase in admissions was managed without any increase in the number of long-stay beds (indeed, a few beds were taken down during this period, and so reduced former over-crowding) and without resort to a traditional waiting list, which disappeared. This increase in workload was achieved by reorganising and utilising the existing but formerly underused resources of nursing skills, and did not involve the new establishment and appointment of separately designated psychiatric community nurses. In essence, zoned wards as described increasingly developed as community wards. It is clear that some of the benefits discussed above in terms of improvement in ward care could not have been achieved without the ward staff's involvement in developing care outside the hospital.

The work described in this chapter was undertaken over a period of four years and has opened up further questions about the organisation of services for the elderly and how they can be helped. Psycho-geriatric care would seem to be a relatively fruitful, if neglected, field for study.

4 RE-EXAMINING NURSING MANAGEMENT AND TRAINING

Maurice Fenn, Ruby Mungovan, David Towell, Jim Aitken, Clive Harries, Aggie Lloyd, Ian McRae and Joan Murrell

Efforts to improve patient care have often been seen to require at ward level some re-examination of the existing forms of management and procedures for training key staff. However, these factors at ward level are typically part of wider patterns and arrangements which equally require attention if the optimum conditions for innovation are to be established. This proposition has particular force in the case of nursing: nurses provide a large proportion of the care available to clients of the psychiatric services; nursing management and training have both been the subject of substantial criticism and detailed investigation at national level. More locally, the two projects reported here illustrate how at Fulbourn, staff themselves were able to tackle problems in nursing management and training, including problems which followed from attempts to implement the recommendations of such national investigations.

In the first account, attention is drawn to the Report of the Committee on Senior Nursing Staff Structure ('Salmon', 1966) which led to substantial changes in the formal organisation of nursing administration in hospitals. Despite these changes, considerable difficulty was experienced by nursing managers in developing the new roles and approaches upon which the success of this reorganisation depended. Particular difficulties were encountered in relation to the new role of unit nursing officer, which is crucial to providing the supportive leadership necessary to facilitate ward-based improvements in nursing practice. At Fulbourn, these difficulties became the focus for study by a project group made up of all ten members of the nursing administration. On behalf of this study group, Maurice Fenn, the principal nursing officer, Ruby Mungovan, one of the seven nursing officers, and David Towell describe (following Fenn et al, 1975) the efforts made to identify and examine these difficulties and the changes it was possible to introduce in the process of gradually developing the nursing officer role between May 1972 and a review of progress in mid 1974. (Maurice Fenn describes more fully the closely related philosophy of management he was evolving during this period, in Chapter 7.)

In the second account, attention turns to arrangements for nurse training. The focus is on the secondment of general nurses to Fulbourn, but the approach demonstrated has wider relevance to improving the value of training activities, and is especially pertinent to the proposed implementation of the Committee on Nursing's recommendations for future nurse training, in which such secondments will assume increasing importance ('Briggs', 1972). Following concern about the benefits derived from this particular secondment scheme, a working party made up of staff from Fulbourn and its neighbouring general hospital set out to examine this scheme in more detail. The core members of this working party: Ian McRae, Aggie Lloyd and Clive Harries, respectively tutor, ward sister, and senior nursing officer at Fulbourn; Joan Murrell and Jim Aitken, tutor and nursing officer at the general hospital; and David Towell, describe the several components of this project undertaken between May 1972 and June 1974 (based on Aitken et al, 1974).

In both these accounts, those involved draw out some implications of their work for the reorganised NHS, for example in showing what needs to be done if national 'blueprints' are to be effectively realised, and in demonstrating possible benefits from closer collaboration between staff in different parts of the district service. At the same time, ways in which innovation at hospital level may be facilitated or constrained by still wider patterns and arrangements are also suggested.

Developing the Role of Unit Nursing Officer

Maurice Fenn, Ruby Mungovan and David Towell

The gradual implementation of the recommendations of the Salmon Committee has brought substantial changes in the pattern of nursing administration in British hospitals. The attempts to fully implement these changes however posed widespread difficulties, as the Department of Health and Social Security's pamphlet 'Progress on Salmon' (1972) indicates. According to this pamphlet, particular difficulties have been found in successfully establishing the new 'clinical/ managerial' role of the 'unit nursing officer' in the face of pressure to continue in the traditional role of 'assistant matron', a problem accentuated where nursing officers share a central nursing office.

At Fulbourn Hospital, efforts had begun in 1965 to create 'functional' nursing units and in 1971 other efforts were made to strengthen the role of nursing officers. At the time the work to be described began however, the six day-time officers continued to share a central nursing office and were experiencing some difficulty in meeting the various demands upon them to their own satisfaction. These difficulties probably generated the original motivation for undertaking an examination of the role of unit nursing officers and the functions of the central nursing office. We set out here to describe our approach to tackling these problems and review the developments which took place in the unit nursing officer's role at Fulbourn from the beginning of this work in the summer of 1972 up until mid-1974.

The Clarification of Problems

This project began with the nursing administration inviting the social research adviser to help in their review of the problems of nursing officers. After discussion it was agreed that the adviser would assist in identifying and clarifying these problems through individual and group discussion with members of the nursing administration, and through regular attendance at their weekly administrative meetings. At these meetings the adviser also sought to promote discussion of the implications for nursing organisation of the specific issues arising for administrative action.

It emerged from these initial discussions that the changes consequent upon the implementation of 'Salmon' at Fulbourn had brought a number of inter-related problems for the nursing officers. They were finding themselves increasingly stretched between the demands of their units (particularly as the nursing officer's role expanded to include new areas of activity like liaison with the community services) and the traditional requirements for central administration associated with their position. A concrete manifestation of the difficulties here was the need to carry.out what was regarded as less important clerical and administrative work in the central office, when they would have preferred to be fulfilling professional responsibilities in their units. More generally nursing officers found other people's expectations to be out of alignment with what they themselves now saw as their proper roles.

These problems were discussed at length at a special evening meeting of the nursing administration, with particular attention being given to possible changes in the work of nursing officers and the ramifications these changes might have for other hospital staff. Among the issues considered here were the appropriate style of management in a decentralised organisation; the current content of the nursing officer's work and which aspects of this might be reallocated to other roles; the consequences of occupying a central nursing office; and ways in which communications to this office might be dealt with.

The social research adviser was able to help the meeting in the examination of possible forms of systematic investigation into these issues which might provide a basis for planning changes in the existing situation. Out of this emerged the decision to undertake as a first step, a study of communications to nursing officers.

A Study of Communications

Working together with the adviser and assisted by a charge nurse attached to the nursing officers for in-service training, the nursing officers collectively planned a study which aimed to examine the current functions of nursing officers and the central nursing office in the communication system of the hospital. This study was intended to show in some detail which other staff were initiating communications with nursing officers, on what subjects, and requiring what sorts of action, so as to provide a basis for nursing officers to review their current role at Fulbourn with their various role partners.

More specifically the study was designed to contribute information on a number of pertinent questions including:

(1) How much of their time were nursing officers spending dealing with communications which might be regarded as not part of their job?

(2) What kinds of communications might more appropriately be dealt with by other staff?

(3) What administrative assistance might be of value in the central nursing office?

(4) What need was there for continuous manning of the central nursing office by nursing officers?

(5) What factors determined the extent to which unit staff directed communications to their own unit nursing officer?

The method of study devised involved nursing officers themselves recording on pre-coded forms (Table 4.1) some limited information on every alternate communication received by them (which were, or would otherwise have been, received in the central nursing office) over a period of one week. The pre-coded form was itself constructed through a set of trials and discussion among the nursing officers. During the week of the study the nursing officers also kept a record of how they spent their time when not in the central nursing office.

The work involved in devising this study, and the experience of systematically observing their own activities in itself seemed to increase the nursing officers' awareness of their current role. To obtain a

Table 4.1: Pre-coded Form for Nursing Office Communication Study

1.   Initials   Date   Episode No.

2.   Time

3.   Communication type
           Letter   Person   Int.   Tel.   Ext.
                                Int.   Bleep   Ext.

4.   Rec'd direct   ☐   Passed on by   ☐
                                   other N.O.

5.   Rec'd in   ☐   Elsewhere   ☐
      office

6.   Communication   other ☐   self ☐
      initiated by

7.   From whom   ward ☐
      C.N. ☐   Drs (Cons) ☐   Other Depts ☐
      Other N. ☐   Drs (Duty) ☐   Hspl Sec ☐
      Patient ☐   Drs (Other) ☐   Wages ☐
                                         MRO ☐
                                         Lodge ☐
                                         Warden ☐

      Nursing Admin.   C.H. ☐
                       E.R. ☐

      Other (specify) ☐

8.   Who did they want?   Self ☐   Any N.O. ☐
      Other (specify) ☐

9.   (If relevant)
      was other on duty?   Yes ☐   No ☐

Table 4.1 *(cont.)*

---

10. In your opinion who ideally should have dealt with this, if not you? ☐

11. Subject of communication concerned with your unit?
    Yes ☐   No ☐

    Category   Prof ☐   Gen. Adm. ☐
                Nursing Adm. ☐ Other ☐
                Personnel ☐
    Brief comments on subject, or don't know ☐
    ☐

12. Your function   Info./advice   Instr./decision
              Given   ☐   ☐
              Rec'd   ☐   ☐

13. Required action   14. Was further action
                                        required on your part?
    Emergency ☐   Yes ☐
    Quick ☐
    Today ☐   No ☐
    Longer ☐
    None ☐

15. Brief comment on actions taken if required
    ☐

16. If relevant, which other N.O. informed?
    N 1 2 3 4 5 6 TL ER CH MF
    ☐

17. Duration of episode (in minutes)
    0-2   2-5   5-15   Specify
    ☐

Table 4.2: Analysis of Time[a] Spent out of the Nursing Office

Unit Officer	WORK IN UNIT[b]			OTHER					TOTAL
	Unit Meetings	Unit Other	Total	Other Meetings[c]	Hospital Rounds[d] Routine	/Special	Other[e]	Meals	
1	3.15	2.00	5.15	1.40	0.50	–	3.55	2.10	13.50
2	4.05	4.05	8.10	3.25	2.25	–	–	3.00	17.00
3	1.30	2.30	4.00	2.40	2.00	3.15	4.15	2.35	18.45
4	4.55	0.35	5.30	1.40	5.10	4.30	2.25	0.40	19.55
5	9.05	2.15	11.20	4.40	1.00	–	–	3.20	20.20
6	4.10	11.10	15.20	3.45	2.20	–	–	4.45	26.10
Total	27.00	22.35	49.35	17.50	13.45	7.45	10.35	16.30	116.00

Notes:

a Time is expressed in hours and minutes
b Work in Unit. Some of the time included under 'Unit Meetings' may in fact refer to 'Unit Other'. 'Unit Other' includes informal discussions with Unit staff, and visits concerned with the day-to-day running of the wards.
c 'Other Meetings', includes the nursing administration meeting, hospital staff meeting, and various committees and working parties.
d Hospital rounds 'Special' refers to escorting visitors and explaining to them the functions of individual units, etc.
e 'Other' relates to visits to other departments concerned with nursing and general administration, including records, pharmacy, reception, hospital secretary's department and senior nursing administration.

more comprehensive analysis of the information collected in the communication survey however, the hospital sought the help of the regional hospital board computer services department. Staff of the latter provided very valuable assistance in solving the problems of coding and analysis of data, and in undertaking the computer analysis. While this was being done, the in-service trainee prepared a preliminary analysis of the data in order to provide the nursing officers with material for immediate discussion, and to enable them to decide which of the more complex analytic operations should be asked of the data processing.

Beginning with the simpler data from the records of time spent, Table 4.2 shows the way in which the nursing officers used their time when not in the central nursing office over the week of the study. Examination of this table drew attention particularly to the wide variations in the time spent by nursing officers on the wards of their units.

Subsequently the computer analysis of the coded communication episodes produced a number of significant further findings. Over the week as a whole the total number of in-coming communications to the central nursing office was 762. The proportion of communications each nursing officer received which were concerned with their own unit varied from 36 per cent to 55 per cent and on average some 60 per cent of the communications dealt with by nursing officers in this context were not concerned with their unit. Detailed information was also obtained on the types of communications received, their distribution through the day, the urgency of action required, the other staff who might have dealt with particular issues, etc.

From discussion of these findings a number of implications were drawn both for changes nursing officers had already made in their work, and for further possible innovations. For example, the study suggested that renewed attention might be given to the elimination or transfer of some of the general administrative work then being under-taken by nursing officers and gave impetus to the effort to acquire some secretarial cover for the central nursing office. It also provided support for changes both in the duty times of nursing officers and in the pattern of office manning.

In short, undertaking this study provided nursing officers with both a new perspective on the relevant issues, and an informed basis for the consideration of further changes designed to facilitate the more effective performance of their role.

Reviewing Progress

Looking back in 1974 over a period of two years, a number of changes could be identified, introduced in collaboration with other concerned staff, which have arisen from discussion within the nursing administration of the results of the study of communications and the nursing officers' experiences in performing their roles. While all these changes are related, it is useful to distinguish those concerned with policy formation and co-ordination in the nursing administration as a whole; those focussed on the unit nursing officer's role and the processes of unit management; and those affecting the work carried out in the central nursing office.

Beginning with developments in policy formation and co-ordination in the nursing administration, previously, priority had been given to co-ordination of unit activities within the hospital. This has given way to a new emphasis on the co-ordination of each unit's activities with the relevant extra-hospital services, as attention has been directed towards developing treatment policies and facilities to best meet the needs of different types of client. Following on from this and consistent with the trend towards decentralisation, nursing officers have been encouraged to take responsibility for developments in their units within the context of general understandings established in the nursing administration about the kinds of policy which would be supported. This has been aided by the principal nursing officer's efforts to delegate more effectively and to make freely available to nursing officers relevant information about both wider developments in treatment services (e.g. the longer-term plans of the regional hospital board and social services departments) and interesting work in the psychiatric specialities being done elsewhere. As part of other changes in management systems at hospital level, joint monthly meetings of the nursing and professional administrators have been instigated, and representatives of the professional administration have begun to attend unit meetings, with concomitant improvements in understanding and in the way problems are dealt with in some areas. And through an extra daily meeting with each other, nursing officers have sought to facilitate better co-ordination of policies between units and to provide a forum for working through the conflicts which necessarily arise in the management of a decentralised hospital.

These changes in the pattern of nursing administration together with the rationalisation of work carried out in the central nursing office have both permitted and encouraged a number of developments in the roles of nursing officers and in the way units are managed. Nursing officers

have been able to give more time to work in their units and thus to
develop new components to their roles in relation to unit staff:
examples include increased involvement in work with the community;
extensions to the nursing officers' supportive clinical role; and greater
participation in the training of more junior staff. These changes in the
content of roles have been associated with a longer term evolution in
nursing officers' philoposphy of management and attitudes to subordinates: more open styles of leadership have developed in which emphasis
is placed on acting as a supportive consultant to unit staff who have
discretion to try out their own ideas, rather than maintaining close
supervisory control on their activities. This has in turn implied a concern to establish relationships in which people on the wards could
draw on the nursing officers' experience, skills and expertise to develop
their own. In addition, steps have been made towards the introduction
of an effective system of 'acting-up' so that rather than nursing officers
'covering' for each other, responsibility for unit management is
retained within the unit in the absence of the unit nursing officer. The
opportunities for charge nurses and sisters to 'act-up', together with the
pattern of in-service training, also seem to have increased understanding
of the nursing officer's role and fostered staff identification with units.
And within units, new forums of various kinds have been established
for communication, collective discussion and development of policy
among nursing and other professional staff.

Parallel with these developments in the unit nursing officers' role,
considerable effort has been devoted to reviewing the traditional
functions served by the central nursing office and rationalising the work
carried out there. Thus there has been increasing acceptance of the
capacity of ward staff to take responsibility for administrative tasks
traditionally controlled by nursing officers, and correspondingly a
number of these tasks (e.g. planning and making alterations to staff
duty times; ordering transport) have been decentralised to ward level.
Some tasks carried out by nursing officers have been abolished, reduced
or eliminated through transfer to other relevant staff and this process
has been particularly facilitated by the introduction of a secretary/
assistant into the central nursing office, who has also been able to deal
effectively with many general enquiries. Encouragement of other staff
to make use of the 'bleep' in contacting particular nursing officers, in
conjunction with the circulation of nursing officers' duty times to the
wards and the switchboard, have also reduced the frequency of redundant telephone calls. And together these changes have permitted
substantial revisions to the duty times worked by nursing officers, with

a reduction in the time worked out of office hours, less time devoted to routine 'rounds', and less requirement for 'central office' duties now covered by the 'duty nursing officer'. In turn these changes in hours of work and central office responsibilities have made nursing officers more available for unit work, and more able to commit themselves ahead to future engagements.

While the substantial changes which have been achieved have led to considerable benefits, particularly in improving staff relationships and policy development within each unit and facilitating better patient care, there is a sense in which these benefits have now become taken for granted and nursing officers are more aware of the problems which remain or indeed which have been increased by the trend towards decentralisation. Foremost among these problems is the feeling among nursing officers that their efforts at communication and co-ordination among themselves have lagged behind the development of more autonomous unit activities and that therefore they are not working together effectively as a group. The symptoms of this problem are recognised in the competitiveness between nursing officers and the not infrequent conflict between units, sometimes displaced into trivial difficulties between nursing officers or expressed in negotiation over more realistic issues like the transfer of patients. In turn this problem may well be related to continuing ambivalence over the question of whether to maintain a central nursing office: on the one hand nursing officers see the desirable aspects of establishing separate unit offices; on the other hand they still have to face the sometimes contrary expectations of other staff and perhaps feel reluctant to lose the group solidarity traditonally represented by the existence of a common office. (It also seems likely, however, that the retention of a central nursing office has been influenced by the adoption of a relatively 'flat' administrative hierarchy in which the nursing officers are in a 'line' relationship with the principal nursing officer, and senior nursing officers have 'staff' functions.)

More generally it seems that these problems may be related to wider organisational issues facing the hospital. Recognising that not only the nursing administration but also the division of psychiatry and the professional administration are involved in policy making which ultimately affects patient care, the question being raised in the context of NHS reorganisation is that of whether adequate machinery exists at hospital level for consultation and joint planning between the professional groups. The analogy of six 'little hospitals' sometimes used to refer to the nursing units and the difficulties of the nursing officers, suggests the hypothesis that the nursing administration is having to carry the main weight of holding the hospital as a whole together. All this has indicated the need for further work to develop a hospital level management system appropriate to the requirements of the services based on Fulbourn, while at nursing officer level seeking to find new ways of working together which match this form of organisation.

Dilemmas of Innovation

This account has attempted to summarise the main steps from the initial clarification of problems, through the more systematic investigation of some aspects of these problems, to the work done in gradually bringing about organisational changes, which have together led to developments in the roles of nursing officers at Fulbourn. As well as being a valuable learning experience, participants in this project have derived satisfaction from overcoming difficulties and recognising the benefits of these changes for their work. At the same time this experience has suggested the importance of not underestimating the problems to be faced in changing roles and organisation. Over a period of two years, members of the nursing administration have had to invest time and energy in discussing new ideas among themselves and working through desired changes with other staff who would be affected. Within the group of nursing officers, this has sometimes meant meeting the anxiety of putting aside the security of established aspects of the role in exchange for the uncertainty of new activities in which individuals may initially feel less confident. Particularly for long serving staff, such changes may also be taken as an unfavourable reflection on the value of their past activities. And other staff may be affronted by not being able to rely on nursing officers for what has traditionally been expected. Moreover, given the continuing problem for unit officers of balancing the 'here and now's' with the 'tomorrow's', encountering these difficulties may discourage the longer term examination of their work which projects like this imply.

Faced with all these dilemmas, the process of change in this project has been facilitated by the wider culture of the hospital in which attempts at innovation are positively valued; the facilitating role taken by senior staff notably in this case the principal nursing officer; and the availability of the social research adviser to assist in work of this kind. The latter has been useful not only for his technical contribution to the design of research, but also because his presence has helped to make the study group a protected forum in which the focus on longer term issues could be sustained and some of the emotional issues associated with change coped with more readily. This in itself has brought some further dilemmas however, seen for example in the tendency at some stages of the work for the study group to act as if this project belonged to the adviser rather than to the group, and occasionally perhaps to entertain the notion that if only the adviser would go away then so would the problems. For this work to continue therefore, it has been important that the staff involved are prepared to accept responsibility both individually and collectively for trying to bring about change.

In sum, the substantial developments in the 'clinical/managerial' role of unit nursing officers emerging from this project have furthered the hospital's move from a centralised pattern of organisation to a more open structure with peripheral foci of activity (see Hunter, 1973) increasingly sensitive to patient need. These inter-related developments have brought with them personal, professional and organisational dilemmas and the added dimensions have required a continual updating of communicating and co-ordinating machinery. The considerable efforts required to bring about these changes even where a blueprint (in the form of the Salmon report) was already available are perhaps also suggestive of what needs to be done on a much wider scale if the maximum benefit is to be derived from the reorganisation of the NHS as a whole. What seems certain is that this changing organisation and the evolving needs of clients will make role review of this kind a continuing concern of nursing administrators.

Enhancing the Value of General Nurse Training by Psychiatric Secondment
Jim Aitken, Clive Harries, Aggie Lloyd, Ian McRae, Joan Murrell and David Towell

Since the introduction of the 1969 Nurse Training Syllabus, students undertaking general training have had more opportunity to spend three months nursing in a psychiatric hospital. This secondment has existed in the past in some hospitals on a limited scale, but its objectives and benefits were often obscure. Conscious of this, Fulbourn and its neighbouring general hospital set up a working party in 1972 to formulate objectives, and later, to monitor the progress of nurses both during their secondment and after their return to this general hospital. The working party has included representatives of ward, tutorial, and nursing administrative staff from both hospitals. We describe here the progress in this work as seen from the summer of 1974.

Shortly prior to this project beginning, the general hospital had introduced a 'two plus one' system of training which essentially condenses the experience required under the 1971 General Nursing Council syllabus into a two year training programme after which state examinations are taken. The third year is spent as a 'junior staff nurse' although registration is not achieved until the end of the third year. While some secondment to Fulbourn had existed for a number of years and indeed had settled into an almost taken for granted pattern, by early 1971 the increasing number of nurses being seconded, their new syllabus and the more enquiring students this syllabus attracted, together began to generate a felt need for review of the secondment arrangements.

The very fact that there were more seconded nurses made Fulbourn staff think more carefully about what these students should be doing during their three months in the psychiatric hospital. Such reconsideration was further stimulated where seconded nurses themselves raised difficult questions about the aims of secondment, particularly relating to the value of this part of their training and the ways in which it should be relevant to their general nursing. Initial attempts by concerned staff to answer these questions suggested that more fundamental attention to the purpose of these secondments was required, and it was at this stage that the assistance of the social research adviser was first invited.

The Exploratory Research Phase

In this invitation, the principal tutor at Fulbourn asked the social research adviser's help in designing an evaluation questionnaire for seconded nurses to get more scientific feedback from them about their views on the secondment experience. It might be noted here that distributing questionnaires is initially what many hospital staff think research is; certainly in the early stages of this work there were times when the adviser felt that the main task had been displaced from improving the secondments to collecting more data from the nurses, the usefulness of which was uncertain. The adviser's response to this first request was twofold: first to propose that clarifying the aims of this secondment should logically precede designing an evaluation; and second, to suggest that if there were going to be changes made in the secondment arrangements, it would be useful from the beginning to get together a working party representing staff who would be involved in these changes and which could give sanction for any work that was done. In this way a group was created which had authority to take action on the issues of concern. This group began in fact by commissioning from the adviser a small exploratory study of one set of seconded nurses, designed to find out more about their experiences in the psychiatric hospital and what they seeemed to gain from these experiences. This study also sought to discover the main problems these nurses were encountering and their own views on how this part of their training might be improved.

The method the adviser adopted was to undertake group discussions with the whole set of eighteen nurses, at the beginning, middle and end of their secondment, and five weeks after their return to the general hospital; supplementing this by more frequent discussions with two pairs of nurses throughout their period in the psychiatric hospital.

Without attempting to go into the detailed results of this study, it will be useful to summarise the main points reported back, both verbally and in writing to the working party, because it was these points which provided a basis for much of the work which followed.

To begin with, the report indicated a number of problems identified by the nurses themselves, which had implicit in them the need for some changes. For example, the nurses were clearly dissatisfied with having to choose whether to take this or some other secondment option during their introductory course before having any experience even of general nursing, and not therefore being able to make an informed choice between the alternatives. In addition, these nurses were critical of some of the arrangements for the course and its contents, including the lack of preparation before the secondment and the ineffective use made of some of the time spent in the training school.

From the comments and experiences reported by these nurses in the discussions, it was also possible to infer some things about what they seemed to gain from the secondment and to identify some more fundamental problems. At the end of the secondment the overall response of the majority of these nurses seemed to be a quite positive feeling about the time spent in the psychiatric hospital. It appeared likely that they had acquired a more accurate view of what a modern psychiatric hospital is like, and lost some of their fantasies about psychiatric patients. Because of this, they anticipated being less apprehensive about the patients said to be suffering from mental illness they met in the general hospital. Moreover, in their own assessment of the benefits of secondment, these nurses emphasised the effects of this experience on themselves, particularly in increasing their self-awareness and self-confidence.

This seemed linked to what these nurses were learning about the appropriate approach to relationships with patients in the psychiatric hospital, and perhaps to new conceptions about what understanding and helping patients involves. This led the adviser to raise as one key question, whether there were any ways in which these nurses could be helped more effectively to learn about this aspect of nursing.

Following from this was another important question, that of how far what was learned by these nurses during the secondment was transferable to their general nursing. On this point the adviser reported that during the secondment, these nurses felt that what they were learning would help them understand the behaviour of patients in the general hospital and encourage them to give more attention to the psychological aspects of patient care. On the little evidence available from the later interviews however, it appeared that the gains in this direction were fairly limited: these nurses experienced strong pressures to readjust back to what were normal general nursing practices on their return to the general hospital. This in turn raised the question of whether there might be some way of reinforcing and extending their learning about relationships with patients once these nurses had returned to the general hospital ward situation, and providing more support for them in this aspect of their work.

Finally, the adviser reported to the working party that a number of these points strongly suggested the need to clarify both within the working party and for the nurses, what the aims of secondment were and particularly the extent to which this training experience was intended to be a contribution to the nurses' skills at general nursing.

Working on Improvements

This report served a catalytic function for the working party in providing a focus for activity through which the group took up the task of devising improvements to this training course. During the first few meetings, some improvements to the secondment were readily agreed in response to the problems identified.

These improvements were: first, that the general students would be allowed to make the choice over which secondment to do later in their training; second, that as a contribution to their preparation, nurses coming to Fulbourn on secondment would have the opportunity to discuss what they might experience there with a nurse who had already completed her secondment; and third, that in order to increase the link between the seconded nurses and their general hospital, a member of the general hospital tutorial staff would have a standing invitation to the weekly discussion periods arranged for the seconded nurses in the training school at Fulbourn.

Table 4.3: Statement of Objectives for the Three-month Secondment
of Trainee General Nurses to the Psychiatric Hospital

A. Increasing the nurse's skill in psycho-social aspects of nursing.
    (i) The nurse should increase her recognition and understanding
         of the problems experienced by people in hospital, and learn
         to relate to people in ways which are helpful to them in coping
         with these problems.

B. Increasing the nurse's knowledge about modern psychiatry and
    providing an insight into psychiatric nursing.
    (i)   The nurse should increase her knowledge of the nature and
          origin of what may be described as common psychiatric dis-
          orders, the kinds of treatment which may be offered to psychi-
          atric patients, and the nurse's contribution to this treatment.
    (ii) The nurse should become aware of the hospital and com-
          munity services — both available and developing — which may
          contribute to the treatment and care of people requiring
          psychiatric help, and their families.
    (iii) The nurse should increase her understanding of the develop-
          ment of psychiatric care and its relationship to change in
          public attitudes towards 'mental illness'. The nurse should
          become familiar with the main provisions of the 1959 Mental
          Health Act.

C. Contributing to the nurse's understanding of the effects of ward
    organisation and staff relationships on patient care.
    (i)   The nurse should become aware of the importance of team
          work, collective decision taking, effective communication and
          supportive staff relationships, in the psychiatric hospital.
    (ii) The nurse should increase her awareness of the relevance of
          these points to the general hospital.

D. Contributing to the nurse's self-development.
    (i)   The nurse should increase her self-understanding and self-
          awareness through experiences in the psychiatric setting and
          learning from these experiences in discussion with others.
    (ii) The nurse should become more self-confident through taking
          the opportunities available to explore ways of approaching
          people and learning from these explorations.

The working party during further meetings devoted much time and thought in attempting to formulate more precise objectives for the secondment scheme. Not without some difficulty, tentative agreement was finally reached that the objectives of this secondment, that is what nurses can be expected to gain from their three months in a psychiatric hospital and the contribution this should make to their training, can be summarised in four main areas. (See Table 4.3).

Much debating took place, especially around what came to be seen as the main objective, that of 'increasing the nurse's skill in psychosocial aspects of nursing'. This area presented difficulties until it was recognised that any patient in any hospital has problems. Thus the psychiatric secondment should assist general nurses to recognise and understand these problems, and to contribute to their resolution through relating to people in a helpful manner. The seconded nurses themselves brought out this theme in the initial study; it was their own views on what was gained from the secondment which provided a useful guide to the working party in formulating realistic and attainable objectives.

This statement of objectives provided a new basis to reformulate the programme and improve the induction, thereby dealing with some further problems revealed in the exploratory research. Regarding inadequate preparation for example, the working party attempted to reduce this problem by sending prospective seconded nurses a copy of the objectives, together with an introductory letter. This letter was designed by the working party in consultation with a newly arrived group of seconded nurses and contained a brief outline of the placements each would undertake, together with arrangements for duty times and transport, as well as some details about the induction phase and the training school programme. On arrival at Fulbourn, this introduction was supplemented by a two-day induction period which included contributions from ward staff designed to help clarify for the nurses what would be expected of them.

Similarly, in relation to the problems in learning about relating to patients, more time was introduced into the training school programme for the nurses to spend discussing their experiences and anxieties. In addition, the working party encouraged the development of experiential learning groups (regular meetings of a small group of nurses with a staff member more experienced in understanding relationships) on the wards to which these nurses were allocated.

Further Developments

Meetings were then arranged with charge nurses from all the wards to which the general nurses were allocated. The task of these meetings was to identify what features of each ward could contribute to attaining the objectives set out for the secondment. The charge nurses themselves gradually undertook responsibility for arranging these meetings of what came to be known as the 'ward resources' group.

Although participation in this group has been variable, a substantial amount of work has been done in discussing and clarifying the objectives described. Out of this work there has been considerable learning, and with the help of members of the working party, ward staff have been increasingly able to identify those aspects of the trainees' experiences in each of their wards which might contribute to achieving these objectives.

Efforts have also been made to establish feedback mechanisms to assist in further review of the secondment experience. One contribution to this review comes from informal discussion with the seconded nurses during and at the end of the course. This is being supplemented and made more systematic through the regular administration of a semi-structured evaluation questionnaire designed for the purpose. It is envisaged that the response to these questionnaires will provide one basis for assessing what benefits student nurses derive from the secondment, devising improvements to the course, and monitoring changes introduced by comparison of answers from successive sets of students about their experiences. A sub-group of the original working party was set up to analyse the responses to this 'monitoring' questionnaire. The sub-group meets quarterly to examine the completed questionnaires in detail and to prepare a summary of the results. This summary is then circulated to people concerned with the secondment, including those ward sisters and charge nurses who provide placements on their wards for seconded nurses, those organising the secondment, and educationalists from both hospitals. In this way it is possible to make further changes in the secondment arrangements in the light of new information.

The monitoring questionnaire may prove particularly useful in relation to one of the unresolved dilemmas of the secondment: the issue of the appropriate number of ward placements to include in a three-month period. Some evidence from the exploratory study suggests that if the total length of the secondment itself cannot be extended, then it might be preferable for nurses to spend most of their secondment on a single ward, rather than the two placements currently favoured by the General Nursing Council. The questionnaire provides one tool for assessing an experiment in which different patterns of allocations are compared.

Transferability of Learning

Other problems remain, the most fundamental of which seem to be concerned with the extent to which learning gained through the secondment experience in the psychiatric hospital is applicable in the very different environment of the general hospital. With this problem in mind, during the process of formulating the objectives, representatives of the working party arranged to meet with ward sisters and nursing officers in the general hospital to report on their work and raise for discussion some of the issues which were then emerging.

These meetings began with the working party representatives describing some of the positive things general nurses gained from the secondment, but going on to report the difficulties these nurses themselves anticipated in giving any greater attention to the psychological care of patients in the general nursing situation. Not surprisingly, this message received a somewhat mixed response. However some interest was identified, and later one sister volunteered her ward for an experiment designed to develop group discussion methods of relevance to tackling these difficulties. Modelled on the experiential learning groups already established at Fulbourn, the intention in these groups was to provide new opportunities for general nurses to learn from their experiences of working with patients and to support them in coping with the problems which can arise in this work. An experienced psychiatric nurse, herself a member of the secondment working party, agreed to make her time and skills available to help with this initiative.

This experiment in a medical ward has confronted a number of problems in developing this approach to nurse training in a general hospital context. First, given the high pressures deriving from the focus on physical nursing care, staff experienced some guilt in engaging in a ward based activity which is not directly patient centred; in fact where the acknowledged main beneficiaries are the nurses themselves. Second, there seemed to be anxiety among some staff that allowing people to express their views might only encourage them to be critical of the established order of things. And third, there has been some discomfort within the group when people expressed their feelings about sensitive issues, even while it was generally accepted that nurses of necessity face traumatic experiences in their work and that new staff in particular may benefit from support in coping with these difficulties. Nevertheless these groups have developed as a regular activity on the ward and the sister has assumed the main leadership role, with the gradual withdrawal of the experienced psychiatric nurse as confidence in this approach has grown.

From the experience so far, it is possible to identify a number of benefits derived from these meetings: junior nurses are using the group to orientate themselves to distinctive clinical features of the ward and its related practical nursing procedures; to discuss problems encountered in conversation with patients often relating to queries patients raise about the nature of their illnesses; and to share feelings about traumatic events in their work as nurses like those associated with unexpected death. At the same time more senior nurses have been able to use the groups to help clarify what is expected of the ward's nurses and provide increased support for their junior colleagues. If this experiment proves to have any wider validity, then one valuable means of reinforcing what nurses learn about relating to patients during secondment, might begin to be established.

The Process of Innovation

The main steps over the first two years in this attempt to improve the value of training by secondment are summarised in the model of the change process represented in the diagram (See Figure 4.1). In passing, this account has sought to imply that although perhaps logical, this process of innovation has by no means been straightforward. The experience of participants in this work has illuminated not only the difficulties of working effectively together over a sustained period but also the recalcitrance of wider aspects of hospital organisation to even modest changes.

Although clearly a basic necessity in the reorganised health service, collaborative work between nurses in general and psychiatric hospitals is probably still the exception rather than the rule. Among the problems in such collaboration experienced in this project were the difficulties of finding a shared language with which to discuss issues, and the tendency of traditional stereotypes about different types of hospital to influence behaviour in the present. In the early stages of this work progress was slow; first, because of the ambivalence of the Fulbourn participants, who recalled periodically how badly the general hospital was said to treat psychiatric nurses on secondment there, and so wondered whether it was worth making much effort on something where general nurses would be the main beneficiaries; second, because of the inclination of sub-sections of the working party to fly off onto consideration of new problems usually relating to the 'other side's'

Figure 4.1: Model of the Change Process in Improving the Value of Training by Secondment

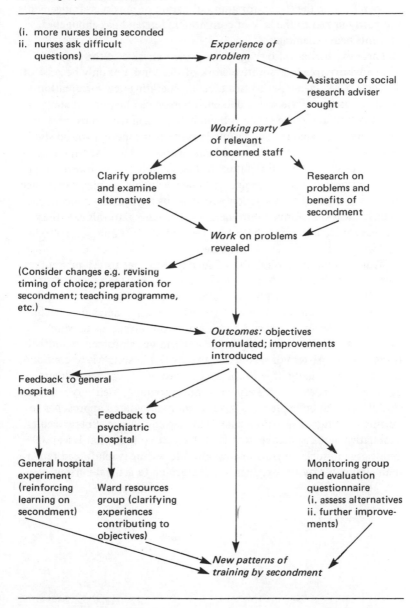

(i. more nurses being seconded
ii. nurses ask difficult questions) ⟶ *Experience of problem*

Assistance of social research adviser sought

Working party of relevant concerned staff

Clarify problems and examine alternatives

Research on problems and benefits of secondment

Work on problems revealed

(Consider changes e.g. revising timing of choice; preparation for secondment; teaching programme, etc.)

Outcomes: objectives formulated; improvements introduced

Feedback to general hospital

Feedback to psychiatric hospital

General hospital experiment (reinforcing learning on secondment)

Ward resources group (clarifying experiences contributing to objectives)

Monitoring group and evaluation questionnaire (i. assess alternatives ii. further improvements)

New patterns of training by secondment

hospital before any issue was resolved. Similarly later in the formulation of objectives, there was considerable conflict within the working party, partly reflecting the 'taken for granted' nature of previous arrangements and partly linked to the lack of common understandings about the concepts being examined.

These experiences also suggest the potential value of the presence of an advisory role in innovative work of this kind, not only because of the social research adviser's assistance in generating new information, but also because of the way a detached person can help to encourage a group to hold on to the total problem being examined against pressures to fragment or avoid this, and provide support for more involved staff in working through the emotional issues associated with social change.

In recognising these difficulties, it needs emphasising however, that participation in innovative projects can be a valuable learning experience for staff and give the satisfaction which stems from seeing concern and creative ideas transformed into meaningful changes. In this case these changes should contribute both to improved nurse training and also in the longer term to better patient care.

While arguing the desirability of such innovations to secondment training, it is important to note in conclusion a substantial reservation which arises from this work. The value of secondments between such diverse nursing cultures as currently exist in many general and psychiatric hospitals seems to depend considerably on the extent to which learning in one situation is applicable and can be reinforced in another. If the existing pattern of secondments between hospitals is to continue, and more particularly, if with the acceptance of 'Briggs' secondment becomes a more substantial aspect of nurse training, then very considerable efforts will be required to develop more integrated approaches to nursing in different situations such that learning can be experienced as cumulative, not disjunctive; that is in this case so that what is learnt about psycho-social nursing in a psychiatric setting is reinforced rather than eliminated by the experience of returning to general nursing.

5 SUCCESS AND FAILURE: LESSONS FROM THE ANALYSIS OF PROJECT EXPERIENCE

David Towell and Clive Harries

The main contribution of the Hospital Innovation Project at Fulbourn has been through the wide variety of projects like those reported in Chapters 2, 3 and 4, which have been initiated since 1972. Support to these project activities has also been the main demand on the social research adviser's time. In taking stock of this work, Table 5.1 provides a complete list of major projects undertaken between 1972 and 1977, together with a measure of the duration of each project. Table 5.2 lists the shorter projects undertaken in this period.

These projects have focussed on various issues of policy, organisation, training and patient care, arising at different levels in the management and provision of services. Work has been undertaken in many areas of the hospital and involved different professions. The resources invested in this project work and the nature and extent of innovation have also varied considerably. Some of the projects have been judged productive by those mainly involved; others have seemed disappointing; and sometimes these judgements have differed according to the perspective from which they have been made.

As active participants in this work, we have shared these feelings of success and failure. Reflecting on our experiences, we have increasingly recognised that in struggling to achieve innovation, realistic hope needs to be combined with some preparation for disappointment: success can only be sought at the risk of failure. In exploring the contribution of project work therefore, we have equally been concerned to examine where innovation was not achieved or not sustained and to identify problems arising in the hospital which were not tackled at all. We have also been interested in weighing the benefits derived from project work against the costs involved in bringing about change and establishing new practices.

Our aim here is to develop a fuller understanding of the processes through which project work was carried out and change occurred. From the analysis of Project experience, we seek to identify how projects were initiated and the steps which then followed. We examine the relationships among the various characteristics of different projects. We explore particularly the ways in which innovation in aspects of hospital

Table 5.1: List of Major Projects, 1972-1977

		Duration
1.	Series of projects on the development of new approaches to treatment in an admission ward including exploratory survey of problems (arising out of disagreements re nursing uniform); introduction of counselling groups for staff in the ward; review of ward organisation and management; exploration of ways of improving links with extra hospital services; and study of patients' experiences in hospital.	March 1972 – Sept. 1973
2.	Evaluation and improvement to the training of student general nurses seconded to Fulbourn for three months.	May 1972 – Dec. 1973
3.	Survey on the use made of volunteers within the hospital.	May 1972 – Sept. 1972
4.	Examination of the work of unit nursing officers, the functions of the Central Nursing Office and efforts to develop new role for nursing officers.	May 1972 – Dec. 1973
5.	Study of the problems experienced by wards and departments in relation to the services provided by the Area Supplies Department, and introduction of improved procedures.	Sept. 1972 – May 1973
6.	Study group to examine the training arrangements through which nurses acquire professional attitudes.	Sept. 1972 – Nov. 1972
7.	Review of treatment needs and improvement of rehabilitative facilities for long-stay patients.	Nov. 1972 – Sept. 1973
8.	Series of projects on the use of nursing resources in psycho-geriatric care, including time study of nursing activity; assessment of patient needs; and development of new patterns of liaison with community services.	Feb. 1973 – June 1977
9.	Organisation and assessment of a working conference on the management of disturbed behaviour.	Aug. 1973 – Nov. 1973
10.	Experiment in helping to provide experiential learning groups for nurses in a nearby general hospital.	Oct. 1973 – June 1974
11.	Working groups to review inter-professional co-ordination arrangements at hospital level.	June 1974 – Aug. 1974
12.	Improving the nursing care of patients in a long-stay ward through staff examination of patients' own views about life on the ward.	April 1975 – Sept. 1976

Table 5.1 *(cont.)*

		Duration
13.	Assessment of patients' performance at work as an indicator of successful occupational resettlement, leading to further reappraisal of industrial rehabilitation services.	April 1975 – October 1975 and Sept. 1976 ongoing
14.	Second series of projects in the area of psycho-geriatric care which incorporated: re-zoning the work of psycho-geriatric wards to correspond with the work of Social Service teams; improving the assessment of prospective psycho-geriatric patients; and preparing a national conference to review changes in roles and services required to provide better psycho-geriatric care.	Sept. 1975 – June 1977
15.	Improving the statistical information system relating to the patient workload of the hospital.	Sept. 1975 – June 1977
16.	Preparation of ward policy on a long-stay ward and training a ward team to present this process to a national conference.	Oct. 1975 – Dec. 1975
17.	Describing and measuring aspects of the psychiatric service to the community undertaken by the hospital's nursing staff.	May 1976 – Oct. 1977
18.	Appraising the work of a psychiatric hospital chaplain.	June 1977 ongoing
19.	Assessing the amount of nursing time required to meet the needs of psycho-geriatric patients.	Sept. 1977 ongoing
20.	Retrospective review of a cohort of patients referred for long-stay care, and subsequent consideration of topics raised by the review, including improving the assessment process, and the management of the long-stay service.	Sept. 1977 ongoing

performance was or was not brought about.

All this is not an easy task. The nature of HIP – as a multi-faceted approach to service development – is such that even where changes can be identified, the causal linkages and critical conditions involved are often hard to isolate. Assessment of these changes requires attention both to intervening variables (for example, relating to ward organisation or staff morale) and more directly to consequences for patient care and welfare. Appropriate indices on which to base this assessment can be difficult to establish, particularly where innovation implies a re-examination of ends as well as means.

Faced with these difficulties, one response adopted in other work

Table 5.2: List of Minor Projects, 1972-1977

		Raised
1.	Review of arrangements relating to staff induction	Feb. 1972
2.	Assessment of staff requirements for child care facilities	March 1972
3.	Review of arrangements for student nurse progress assessment	May 1972
4.	Survey on the use of nursing uniform in long-stay wards	June 1972
5.	Review of the functions and developing the role of group leader in a day centre	Sept. 1972
6.	Survey to generate proposals for the provision of new social facilities for patients	Feb. 1973
7.	Preparation of comparative statistics on sickness and absenteeism among nursing staff	Feb. 1973
8.	Examination of the use of nursing resources outside the hospital	April 1974
9.	Developing new functions for staff attached to an ECT Department	April 1974
10.	Review of unit administration	May 1974
11.	Assistance to staff in coping with change in an admission ward	Feb. 1976
12.	Exploration of alternative models for a geographically zoned psychiatric service	April 1976
13.	Production for teaching purposes of role play videotape showing multi-disciplinary team reviewing crisis in patient care	July 1976
14.	Review of retrospective and prospective developments in a long-stay ward	Sept. 1976
15.	Review of staff and patient roles in industrial therapy and the closer integration of its work with the staff of the long-stay area of care	Oct. 1976
16.	Video training tape 'Looking at the Elderly'	Feb. 1977
17.	Preparation of a day conference to enable the staff of the long-stay area of the hospital to present their work to other hospital staff	June 1977
18.	Re-organisation of staff roles in a geriatric ward to give a better serivce to the community	Sept. 1977

of this genre (see for example Wieland and Leigh, 1971) has been to commission a separate evaluation exercise. While this response has some advantages, an independent evaluation might easily have required more resources than the Project itself and seriously affected a central feature of our approach – that analysis and evaluation should be an intrinsic aspect of the development of HIP. Rather then, the staff involved in particular projects and the Steering Committee for the Project as a whole have continuously been engaged in examining the process of change and assessing the benefits of innovation. Similarly, we have encouraged these efforts and particularly sought to understand more fully our own contribution to project activities.

Accordingly, we recorded extensive notes as each project proceeded as well as on events of wider significance affecting the hospital. Discussions with the external consultant to the Project provided one important forum for reviewing these developments. Interviews between the adviser and an uninvolved colleague (see Klein, 1974) covering the first eighteen months of the pilot stage were also recorded. Accounts of some projects have been prepared by the staff mainly involved. Of necessity, the focus of much of this information has been on projects in which the adviser participated. Through our presence in the hospital however, we have also gained less systematic knowledge of issues being examined and changes occurring in other ways, and of persistent problems which did not seem to be tackled. All this information has been subsequently utilised in this fuller examination of Project experience.

We have identified significant aspects of innovation in organisations and developed a conceptual framework to guide the comparative analysis of project activity, drawing on relevant social science perspectives summarised in the Introduction. Applying this framework to HIP, a schema has been constructed for ordering the data generated in each project. (The schema is attached at Appendix B.) Comparison across projects along the dimensions specified in this schema has provided the means for developing inferences about the relationship between the conditions, strategies and outcomes to project work. These inferences have then been tested against all the data available.

We begin with this comparative analysis of project activity, examining particularly the main projects initiated between 1972 and the end of 1975, where it is now possible to review the outcomes to this work. Building on this analysis, we then explore further the nature of the social research adviser role and its development over the first five years of this Project, with successive role occupants. At the same time, in

describing a set of strategies for innovation and identifying the conditions where these might be productive, we are also seeking to provide
some practical lessons of wider relevance, both for related social action
programmes and other service development advisory roles.

Comparative Analysis of Projects Undertaken Between 1972 and 1975

As our schema for the analysis of project work implies, the approach to
innovation developed in HIP projects can be examined in terms of a
simple general model of the change process. This model is represented
diagrammatically in Figure 5.1. The schema distinguishes a number of
stages from the experience of a problem by staff, through the initiation
of project activity, undertaking investigations and considering their
implications, to the introduction and establishment of particular
innovations. However, as will already be clear, this change process can
be complex and lengthy, with many of these stages of project work
overlapping and being repeated. This schema offers then a framework
for analysis, not a mechanistic description of project development.

Origins of Project Work

A variety of influences and rationales contributed initially to making
particular issues a focus for staff attention. External changes could
generate problems inside the hospital. A major example here was NHS
reorganisation, the effects of which (with the disappearance of the
Hospital Management Committee) highlighted deficiencies in the
management structure of the hospital and led to a project to examine
the need for new co-ordination arrangements among the professions at
hospital level. A more local example was the need for re-zoning of
geriatric services following the geographical reorganisation of the
county social services department.

Wider ideological changes in psychiatry had their impact too, as
was reflected in the admission ward project where there was evidence
of conflict between the traditional medical and emergent social psychiatric approaches to treatment. The combination of such external trends
with developments internal to the hospital could also generate problems
which became the focus for projects. One example was provided by the
decreasing use of electro-convulsive therapy which raised concern about
the future function of staff attached to the hospital's ECT department.
Another example came from efforts to develop extra-hospital facilities
and services, which raised new questions about the appropriate roles for
the nurses involved. More generally, progressive expectations about the
quality of care, particularly when combined with the arrival of new

Figure 5.1: A General Model of the Change Process in Project Work

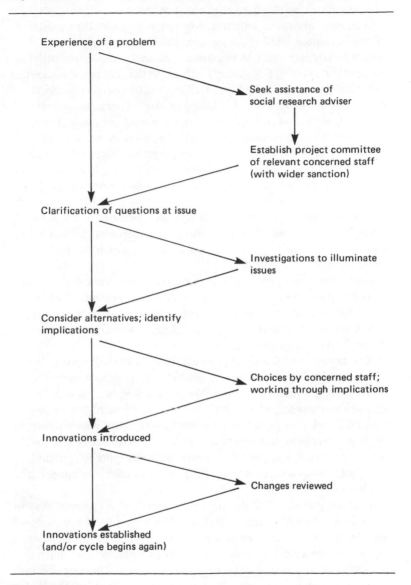

staff in key positions, could lead to the desire to innovate – the psycho-geriatric ward work being one such instance.

A number of project initiatives were encouraged by the experience of conflict among staff which led either to the desire to provide 'objective evidence' for one's position or to seek outside resolution of the problem at issue. For example, debate within a hospital committee about the provision of child care facilities led to a project to assess staff needs in this area. The working party on information systems arose initially from divergent views among consultant medical staff about how equitable was the distribution of work between them.

The rationale for a number of other projects arose from a desire to review the value of earlier innovations – for example a new method of student nurse progress assessment; or to collect information of relevance to pending policy decisions – for example what might be the most appropriate new social facilities to provide for patients. More generally, projects were initiated either from a sense of dissatisfaction where staff were not sure what to do, or from a growing belief that 'research might be a good thing'.

Quite commonly, the origin of projects could be regarded as multi-determined in the sense that a range of different influences had led to a problem being crystallised as requiring attention. In such cases therefore, the various interested parties might have different reasons for inviting attention to these problems.

The experience by staff of problems in their work did not in itself of course lead to the social research adviser being approached or projects being initiated. Some problems were perceived to require immediate responses, while with others, the staff mainly concerned might feel well able to tackle the issues involved without assistance, or might not recognise any potential value in the existence of HIP. In some cases too, it was possible – sometimes over quite long periods – that problems would persist with little evidence of staff attempts at resolution.

In three quarters of all the projects undertaken, it appeared that an initial link between concerned staff and the adviser had been encouraged by an intermediary, most often a Steering Committee member, but sometimes a staff member involved in an earlier project. Indeed in nearly half of the first stage projects, the principal nursing officer played some sponsoring role. The latter's active support for the Project as a whole then was one important influence on the fact that more than half these projects primarily affected nursing staff. It seems likely that the relatively autonomous peer group organisation of senior medical staff on the one hand, and the separate functional organisation of service departments on the other, made it more difficult for the chairman of the division of psychiatry and hospital secretary respectively to play similar sponsoring roles, except in areas for which they were directly responsible. This partly contributed to the fact that only a few projects primarily affected medical staff or the service departments.

There was also some evidence in relation to a number of key problems facing the hospital that no one felt confident of their authority to instigate a project. This seemed particularly likely where agreement among the consultants would have been a pre-condition for successful project work (for example, on the sectorisation of admission services or the creation of a hospital management team).

As the Project developed, the possibility increased that rather than direct sponsorship, project initiatives could arise out of lateral contacts between staff in different areas and through growing awareness of HIP in the hospital. One example was the work on changing the culture of long term care which arose indirectly from a hospital workshop on HIP. Another example was the project on experiential learning groups for nurses in the nearby general hospital which emerged from the intersection of two earlier projects, that on seconded nurses and the admission ward experiment in counselling groups. This process of project diffusion could still leave the overall distribution of projects patchy however, reflecting the segmented structure of the hospital (particularly the separation between caring and support services staff) and the tendency of successful project work to lead to further work in the same areas.

Tables 5.3 and 5.4 show the distribution of the first sixteen major projects and constituent part-projects according to the nature of the issues examined, the areas of the hospital, and the professions mainly involved.

Investigation of Problems

In the next stage of project development the adviser's stratgey was typically to seek to involve relevant staff in examination of the problems at issue and to ensure that adequate sanction was obtained for any work undertaken. From the beginning the adviser emphasised the issue of the use to which any investigations would be put and sought to see that those who were likely to be affected by innovations participated in their creation. Indeed in retrospect, the importance of this condition has been reaffirmed by evidence that failure in this respect was possibly the most significant factor in those projects where

Table 5.3: Distribution of Projects According to Issues Examined and Areas of the Hospital, 1972-1975

ISSUE EXAMINED	AREA OF HOSPITAL				
	Acute	Long Stay	Geriatric	Other	Total
Policy and Administration	1	1	1	4	7
Organisation	2	1	2	2	7
Training	2	2	2	2	8
Practices of Care	1	5	2	—	8
Total	6	9	7	8	30

Notes: Frequencies refer to number of projects or significant part-projects relevant to the categories shown.
'Other', includes projects affecting several areas, senior management or support services.

Table 5.4: Distribution of Projects According to Professions Mainly Involved, 1972-1975

Professions involved	Nurses	Doctors	Paramedicals	Administration and Support services
Number of projects/ part-projects	16	5	6	3

little was achieved by way of innovation.

Another possibility at this stage of project definition was that the problem raised would be identified as of substantial concern only to the individual raising it. Some small projects took the form therefore of a series of consultations with the adviser, as for example in work on developing the role of group leader in a day centre. In some other cases, initial discussion suggested that the issues being raised would best be pursued without further involvement of the adviser.

Where however it was possible to identify an appropriate set of staff in relation to a proposed project, the adviser stressed the idea that staff groups were themselves responsible for tackling problems, rather than himself accepting either the role of problem-solver or research assistant. This strategy sometimes required hard negotiation in the face of contrary expectations from some of the staff involved. For example in the seconded nurses project the adviser resisted the initial request for him to prepare an 'assessment questionnaire' until collaborative work had begun on the objectives of the training course which was to be assessed.

Commonly the adviser used the work done with staff in clarifying the problems of concern to help widen and reconceptualise the questions at issue. Sometimes this involved diagnostic studies in which the adviser made a research contribution – the beginning of the admission ward project described in Chapter 2 provides a detailed example. In this as in other cases it was important that the collaborative nature of project work was such that both staff and the adviser had some influence in shaping project activities. Here the authority the adviser derived from the 'official' definition of his role and the initial 'contract' he established with the staff group concerned, usually meant that he was able to encourage attention to the issues which seemed most salient to the tasks of that group.

One possible outcome from the work on problem definition was the decision that participants already had in their own experience all that was required to evolve desirable changes. In these cases (and also where time constraints prevented any further investigative activity) the work consisted mainly of reviewing these experiences in the light of relevant conceptualisations and thus planning requisite innovations. Even this could be a lengthy process in which staff involved needed to examine more systematically their own experiences and explore with each other the appropriateness of past practices. An example here was the project involving the hospital secretary, principal nursing officer and chairman of the division of psychiatry, which led to establishing a tri-partite co-ordination committee for the psychiatric services based on the hospital.

More frequently, however, indeed in nearly all sustained projects (as distinct from short-term consultations with the adviser) a next stage was to carry out some more or less systematic investigation designed to further illuminate the problems identified. The accounts provided in the preceding chapters well represent the types of investigation undertaken, and the staff contributions to these research activities. Generally it was the case that the research design and methods employed were shaped flexibly by the issues being investigated and the staff resources that could be made available. Common were open-ended and exploratory techniques (most often interviews) or the design of tools specifically for the purpose in hand.

These investigations had a variety of functions and the degree of emphasis on technical research issues varied accordingly. In a number of projects the primary requirement was for factual information (for example, on the amount and nature of the work of nurses outside the hospital; on the potential demand for child care facilities, etc.). In some, while information was required, the research activity also had the function of raising fresh issues for the respondents (as for example a request to long-stay ward treatment teams to complete questionnaires on the rehabilitation needs of patients) or of giving the investigators a new perspective on particular problems. In others, the investigations provided an initially safe focus from which to begin tackling difficult questions (as in the nursing administration 'communication study'), a way of breaking through traditional defensive views of a problem (as in the study of the way time was used by nurses in the psycho-geriatric ward), or a further opportunity for reconceptualising significant issues.

Table 5.5: Distribution of Projects According to the Method of Research Employed and the Personnel Mainly Involved in the Research Activity

| | PERSONNEL INVOLVED | | | |
METHOD OF RESEARCH	Concerned staff	Attached trainees	Social research adviser	Total
Participant observation	—	1	1	2
Interviews/ group discussions	3	3	2	8
Questionnaire	5	—	—	5
Special instrument	6	—	—	6
Statistics	3	3	—	6
Review of experience	7	—	—	7
Total	24	7	3	34

Note: Frequencies based on 34 research exercises carried out as part of major and minor projects 1972-1975.

Table 5.5 shows the distribution of projects according to the method of research employed, and the personnel mainly involved in the research activity.

A number of dilemmas were involved in the choice of research methods. An appropriate balance had to be sought between the use of methods technically most suited to the problems being examined, the staff skills and time that could realistically be made available for research activity, and the degree of validity required for the different functions these investigations served.

One bias to be countered here was the tendency of staff to regard research and questionnaires as synonymous, when other methods might well have been more useful. In some projects for example, an open-ended approach to seeking the patients' perspectives on particular aspects of hospital life proved to be a valuable impetus to fresh thinking by the staff concerned with those patients, even though other more structured methods might have given the appearance of collecting more systematic data.

Another dilemma concerned the sophistication of research activities and their relationship to a sense of staff 'ownership' of the project. For example, at one stage of the work with unit nursing officers, a computer was used for analysis of data from the 'communication study': the apparent complexity of the print-out encouraged staff dependence on the social research adviser's interpretive skills in this area and staff increasingly perceived this as 'his' project, with a consequent falling off in project work in the adviser's absence. The significance of the choice of methods is further illustrated by comparison of two different projects on long term care. In the project to change the culture on one long-stay ward, the use by staff of a simple interviewing technique provided the basis for radical changes in the nursing role and approach to relationships with patients on the ward. By contract, an earlier project on a ward for severely damaged patients, in which the Gunsberg progress assessment charts were introduced to measure change in patients, proved to have little application: the results of this work seemed too abstract and long-term for a ward in which there were a plethora of more immediate concerns and a rapid turnover (supposedly for 'training' reasons) of junior nurses.

Problems of relevance and 'ownership' also entered into the question of who should undertake investigative activities. In some projects, research exercises were carried out by trainees (for example, cadet nurses, administrative trainees) attached to the staff group concerned. Experience suggests this research was only likely to be utilised where three conditions were satisfied. The problem investigated had to be of real salience to the staff group. A project committee was required to support and give wider sanction to the trainee's work. The trainee needed to be involved for a period long enough to contribute to all the main stages of the project. In short, the project was fully integrated with the work of the hospital. For example, all these requirements were met in a study by an administrative trainee of the problems experienced by wards in using the services of the area supplies department. Other exercises where trainees were given 'projects' to do without establishing these conditions typically proved less productive. The same was usually true of 'projects' undertaken by staff attending off-the-job management courses, unless these focussed on issues currently emerging in the manager's own job, and the arbitrary time scale of the course happened to coincide with the appropriate evolution of the project in question.

It should finally be noted here that while a number of projects sought to learn more about patient views and experiences, and the outcomes of some projects included greater participation by patients in treatment and assessment processes, only rarely were patients represented on project committees. We remain uncertain about whether the greater involvement of patients in these stages of project work would have been desirable.

Examining the Implications

As many of these observations suggest, the next stage, that of working through the implications of findings, developing new conceptions of problems with the staff concerned and planning desirable changes, may in fact have started almost from the beginning of many projects. Again as the accounts in Chapters 2, 3 and 4 indicate however, this working through process, particularly if it was to lead to substantial changes, might be a lengthy and difficult undertaking, with many ups and downs, considerable work for the participants, and sometimes the need for continued support from the adviser.

A fuller analysis of what is involved in these processes can be attempted. The commitment to undertaking a project could from the beginning reflect some confidence among staff in their own potential capacity to bring about change. Starting from how these staff defined their own situation, the investigative work and examination of findings provided opportunities for fresh thinking in which new options might be identified. Thus the reconceptualisation of problems could increase the awareness and widen the choices of those involved. Through the mobilisation of staff skills, it was possible to fashion alternative practices out of these ideas, having regard to relevant constraints like the resources available. Innovations were then introduced when the decision was taken to adopt a particular option. These innovations could be regarded as established when authoritative sanction had been generated for this change.

As the preceding accounts have also illustrated, working towards the implementation of new practices commonly met ambivalence or opposition from at least some staff, especially where changes in professional roles and attitudes were required. Difficulties could arise from the disruption of established ways of working and social relationships often entailed. Guilt might be generated by the unfavourable reflection on past activities which innovation sometimes implied. More generally, change was likely to challenge the existing systems of defence against anxiety embodied in traditional arrangements. In overcoming such problems therefore, it was important that the staff involved be provided with support and the opportunities to review their own activities, experiment with new practices, and carefully work through emotional issues in a protected forum.

Attempts to fulfil these conditions were made in a number of ways in various projects. In many, project committees performed an important function in providing one forum in which a relatively long-term focus on the problems being considered could be maintained against the demands from more immediate matters. At the same time these committees gave participants the opportunity to explore the difficulties involved in the process of change. An example comes from a project on the rehabilitation of long-stay patients, where part of the problem was the tendency of both nurses and occupational therapy staff to see each other as the source of difficulties affecting the rehabilitation of patients, but where the project committee entailed working together on inter-related tasks in a way which might have been a model for collaboration in the treatment enterprise. In such cases as this, there was usually a strong belief among staff in the social research adviser's supposed ability to maintain a non-partisan role.

An important dilemma in this work of project committees however was their relationship to the wider groups of staff who might be affected by the changes being considered. In the cases where these were coterminous, it has been argued that difficulties might well arise in finding time for the project under pressure from day-to-day affairs. More often, the wider group would delegate the main work to a representative project committee: but then there might be considerable difficulty in maintaining the wider group's commitment to the project and any changes proposed. It was in some of these cases that reports on investigations tended to become ends in themselves rather than contributions to innovation.

The notion of research itself also could provide a 'protective envelope' within which staff could examine ideas and make preparations for their later application in a way which, at least to begin with, could be detached from everyday activities in the hospital. The idea that commissioning research might be used as a delaying tactic needs to be balanced by recognition that in some cases delay may have the positive function of contributing ultimately to productive change. Similarly, the maintenance of an attitude of experimentation could help to provide the space necessary to introduce and test particular innovations, as was illustrated by the admission ward experiment in 'counselling groups'.

Support for staff in these processes could be derived from three main sources. Staff involved in projects were often a significant source of mutual support, particularly where the concepts of teamwork and participative modes of working were already developing. In another sense, the social research adviser's contribution to projects often seemed to provide for staff some confirmation of their value and some assistance in facing the difficulties to be overcome. Important also, was the leadership of more senior staff, particularly perhaps in providing the conditions in which staff groups in project work could assume the authority necessary to accomplish innovations. One example was the principal nursing officer's willingness to encourage the project on the role of unit nursing officers, despite opposition to this work from other senior staff. In addition, the interest of external agencies, either laterally connected to the changes being considered (as with the social services department in the case of the later stages of the psychogeriatric project) or more generally interested in innovation (as with the other health service staff who participated in the national conferences on aspects of work at Fulbourn), could provide further encouragement to internal action.

Outcomes to Project Work

Overall much of this project work was associated with a considerable range of substantive innovations in hospital organisation and practice. As the preceding analysis has indicated, the ways in which change occurred were often both subtle and complex, but it can be confidently inferred that the Project as a whole substantially contributed to these innovations.

From a review in 1977 of the first sixteen major projects undertaken,

Table 5.6: Twenty Significant Outcomes from first Sixteen Major
Projects and Persistence of Innovations Two Years after their
Introduction

INNOVATION IN POLICY AND ADMINISTRATION

- Developments in policy formation and co-ordination in the nursing administration (4)*
- Introduction of secretary to the central nursing office and revision to central administrative arrangements (4)*
- New procedures for requisitioning and condemning supplies, and increased feedback to wards about progress of requests (5)*
- Extensions in the uses of volunteers within the hospital (3)
- Clarification and development of policies for the treatment provided by a specialised long-stay ward (16)

INNOVATION IN ORGANISATION

- Establishment of tripartite interprofessional coordination arrangements for hospital management (11)
- Development of a more 'clinical/managerial' role for nursing officers and associated changes in unit management (4)*
- Creation of organisational conditions more supportive of a social psychiatric approach to treatment in an admission ward (1)*
- Developments in collaboration and team work among professions involved in the rehabilitation of long-stay patients (7) (13)**
- Developments in liaison between ward staff and social services teams managing and providing hospital and community care for the confused elderly (8) (14)**

INNOVATION IN TRAINING

- Introduction of 'counselling groups' into ward-based training for nurses and other staff (1)*
- Clarification of objectives, revised arrangements for, and continuous monitoring of secondment training of general nurses (2)*
- Experiment in experiential learning groups for nurses on a general hospital ward (2) (10)
- New training methods for staff involved in the assessment of psycho-geriatric referrals (14)
- Development of working conference methods for exchanging and disseminating experience of new approaches to care (9) (14) (16)**

INNOVATION IN PRACTICES OF CARE

- Increased emphasis on the patient's experiences in hospital as an aspect of treatment, and new opportunities for 'social learning' in an admission ward (1)*
- Patient participation in assessments, linked to provision of wider range of facilities for occupational and domestic rehabilitation for longer stay patients (7) (13)**
- New approach to social therapy on a long-stay ward and development of a culture supporting greater patient autonomy (12)*
- Revised use of nursing resources to facilitate patient-centred care and attention to psychological needs on a psycho-geriatric ward (8)**
- Development in assessment processes linked to new patterns of intervention and treatment for the confused elderly inside and outside hospital (8) (14)**

Notes: Numbers in brackets refer to projects as listed in Appendix A.
* Evidence of persistence of innovation two years after introduction.
** Evidence of persistence of innovation and further development through project work in two years after introduction.

it was possible to identify more than fifty specific innovations which had arisen from this work. (Appendix A describes each of these projects more fully.) Table 5.6 summarises twenty of the more significant outcomes according to their relevance for policy and administration, organisation, training, and practices of care. Table 5.6 also indicates the extent to which there was evidence two years after the introduction of each innovation that these changes had become firmly established or indeed further developed in subsequent work.

Other less concrete but nevertheless important outputs from these projects could be identified. In some cases there were improvements in staff morale, perhaps best illustrated by the psycho-geriatric ward project which made hitherto unpopular work both stimulating and rewarding to a number of junior staff. More generally, participation in project work seemed to be a potent form of staff development through 'action learning': providing opportunities for staff to combine analysis of their own work situation with the experience of acting positively to influence that situation. And wider changes could be seen in the organisation and culture of the hospital as a whole (to be examined further in Chapter 6).

Most significant however was the impact of HIP both directly and indirectly on patient care. Changing practices in order to improve care could entail or be assisted by changes in a number of contributory factors, including the ways in which staff and physical resources were used; the patterns of management and collaboration between the professions and others involved; the training and ongoing support available to staff; and the professional attitudes and roles adopted. In this light then, not only work primarily concerned with the interface between staff and patients but also many other projects, could be seen as ultimately having implications for the services provided by the hospital.

While of course HIP was not the only source of change at Fulbourn during this period, it can be concluded that the Project did achieve much which was very positively valued by those involved.

These successes need to be assessed against some appreciation of the costs this work incurred. One cost was the resources invested in the post of social research adviser and other consultancy to the Project: in the pilot stages these activities were externally funded but now the hospital is financing a full-time adviser from its own budget. A second cost was the staff effort and time devoted to project work: in a few projects this amounted for all the staff involved to a total of some hundreds of hours spread out over one or two years, but in no case was this more than a very small percentage of the working time these staff had available.

There were also costs in providing the resources necessary to implement some innovations. For example, new facilities for rehabilitation included the use of a house in the hospital grounds (previously a staff residence) for the preparation of patients for resettlement in 'group homes'; the administrative changes in the central nursing office required the appointment of an additional secretary. In this respect, increases in the resources for psychiatric services were a valuable support, and in some cases a requirement, for particular developments. It is noteworthy however that more than four fifths of the innovations which have been identified were achieved essentially through the alternative use of existing resources.

Any assessment of the output from projects should also take account of what was not achieved. We have argued that in work of this kind, it is realistic to be prepared for some disappointment. Mention has already been made of significant problems facing the hospital, particularly in the second stage of the Project, where the resources represented by HIP have not been used at all. In addition, there were some projects in which either no innovations were achieved, or any changes seeemed hardly commensurate with the staff effort invested – although there may have been some learning for those most involved. One example here was the study group on how nurses acquire professional attitudes. In some other projects, innovations were introduced but these were not sustained long enough to become effectively established. Two years after their initiation, this already seemed to be the case for one quarter of the changes identified in Table 5.6, and subsequent experience has suggested that others are also at risk.

These disappointments can partly be understood as arising from a failure to establish the conditions or utilise the strategies which have been seen to influence the productivity of project work during earlier phases of the change process. Two further conditions can be suggested as of particular importance in the extent to which innovations became institutionalised.

First, some innovatory processes were clearly endangered by staff movement, particularly where one or more key staff (like a senior doctor or ward sister) changed during a project. The course of successful project work usually entailed the gradual development of shared commitment among staff involved throughout; not only might this commitment not be shared by newcomers, but also new senior staff might feel the need to demonstrate their own capacity for innovation by introducing further changes. Frequent/and substantial changes among junior staff within project areas could also be disruptive, often requiring that major efforts be invested in maintaining (rather than further developing) an innovation, in the face of successive waves of staff requiring training in the new methods. In these circumstances, the process of innovation could adopt more of an oscillatory pattern. For example, efforts to develop more effective socio-therapeutic approaches to treatment in admission wards were typically subject to periodic 'swings back' to more traditional medically-oriented practices. These observations suggest the need for attention to the wider factors shaping hospital staffing practices (particularly in the arrangements for staff training) if these are to be more conducive to sustained innovation.

Second, the institutionalisation of innovations was influenced by the degree to which change in particular areas was reinforced by supporting conditions in the wider systems of which these areas were part. Important to such support was the establishment of organisational and management arrangements which provided for staff involved in innovation something of a protective boundary, within which they could manage the development of new practices affecting their own work. Also significant here was the extent to which innovation in one area was strengthened by complementary changes in related areas, such that a jigsaw of wider interlocking patterns was created.

In another sense however, it was in the nature of HIP that the institutionalisation of innovation was always likely to be temporary in a longer-term perspective. The process of innovation is in principle a continuous one, in which while there could be identifiable achievements, this work is never fully completed, and subsequently new ideas and changing demands can be expected to pose fresh problems for attention. In this context, it is possible to think of the HIP approach to innovation itself being institutionalised, so that in particular areas, staff would continue to engage in systematic examination of problems arising in their work and to make sustained efforts to bring about informed change. In 1977, this seemed to have occurred in some areas of the hospital: most clearly evident where early project initiatives have led on to extensive series of projects, as for example on problems of long-stay and psycho-geriatric care. Further factors which appear relevant to this persistence of the HIP approach include the increased confidence in this approach which staff groups might acquire through the experience of some success in earlier projects; the mediating influence of key sponsors of the Project (notably Steering Committee members) in sustaining interest in areas where they were themselves involved; and continuing informal links between some staff members and the social research adviser, whose availability served to symbolise the potential relevance of HIP to new problems which arose.

Finally, some observations can be made on the diffusion of innovations between parts of the hospital. It was noteworthy that in those few projects in which the substantive innovations introduced might have been directly relevant to other situations, the diffusion process was very slow. For example it was a year or more before the developments in experiential learning for staff on the admission ward or the new relationship with social services achieved on the psycho-geriatric ward proved to be of interest elsewhere. By contrast, it seemed that the more general concern with bringing about change was much more readily spread into new areas and the wider influence of the HIP approach on the efforts of many staff to contribute to informed innovation could be identified even where projects were not explicitly undertaken. Here it might be hypothesised that while the increasing autonomy of staff groups and the rather segmented structure of the hospital were conditions quite favourable to innovation, these same conditions made the ready diffusion of particular innovations unlikely. It was also probable of course that the staff first to initiate projects were likely to be those most motivated to make changes within their areas of responsibility. More generally, the experience of this work suggests that attempts to 'short-cut' the working through of change by directly transferring new practices from elsewhere, may inadequately recognise the significance of each staff group having to 'make' their own innovation.

The Role of Social Research Adviser

Much of this analysis of project activity has implicitly shown what the work of the social research adviser involved and how this role contributed to change within the hospital. On the basis of this analysis and further reflection on our own experiences, we draw together here a more general summary of the main lessons we have learnt about the nature and requirements of this new role. We also examine how the role developed and was established as a central feature of HIP.

Nature and Requirements of the Advisory Role

It will be recalled that in our original plans for this Project, we formulated a distinctive definition of the social research adviser role: this role was to provide a service to staff members through which they could seek help:

(i)   in identifying and clarifying problems arising in their day-to-day work;
(ii) designing and carrying out investigations relevant to these problems; and
(iii) working through the implications of such investigations with a view to bringing about improvements in hospital organisation and practice.

What this entailed can be inferred from the detailed review of Project experience. Clearly the adviser worked with staff to establish and maintain appropriate sanction for project activities; collaborated with staff in conceptualising, widening and defining the questions at issue; and assisted in finding ways of enriching the information needed to examine these issues, planning more systematic studies, and developing tools for self-evaluation. The adviser contributed to the further efforts involved in making use of such investigations; working through the difficulties staff were confronted with in achieving change; and providing support during the introduction of innovations.

At the overt level these contributions have required some technical skills in research design and methods, linked to an appreciation of what kinds of investigative work might be feasible in the light of the resources available to this Project. Necessary too, has been some conceptual framework for understanding and analysing the substantive problems of the hospital, such as that provided by our *social science perspectives.*

It also became increasingly apparent from the experience of project work that the advisory role has a number of latent components, the most important of which seem to include:

(iv) encouraging staff groups to hold on to the total problems being examined in the face of pressures to fragment or avoid this;
(v) helping staff work through emotional aspects of problems and redefine existing expectations of themselves and others, in preparation for changing roles and relationships; and
(vi) providing support for staff in the process of innovation by carrying for them some of the uncertainty about change, while underlining their capacity and authority for taking creative action.

As has been seen, the adviser could use his presence during projects and the belief in his neutrality to help create a protected forum in which problems could be fully examined. He could then support staff in making more explicit, and questioning taken for granted assumptions; reviewing ends as well as means; and thereby releasing staff to explore new possibilities. The confidence, both realistically and unrealistically located in him, meant that the adviser could serve as a temporary 'container' for some of the anxiety necessarily generated during change. And his availability seemed to symbolise the authority staff groups could assume in the effort to achieve innovation in their own situation.

Again these latent components of the advisory role required some conceptual framework for interpreting the processes of social change, both so that staff could be helped to see the ways in which problems they experienced were related to wider organisation dynamics, and also to guide the adviser's own strategies of intervention.

In addition, these aspects of the role demanded a considerable emotional contribution from the adviser: most readily identified in our experience of the substantial investment by staff in our supposed objectivity; our skills as mediators between conflicting parties; our capacity to resolve problems; and less commonly, the opposite of all these traits. A further requirement therefore was some skill on the adviser's part in resisting pressures to himself 'take over' the problems of staff, while at the same time continuing to provide appropriate support for their work in tackling these problems. In turn this entailed the adviser's sensitivity and willingness to reflect on his own input to project activities.

Developing and Establishing the Advisory Role

This understanding of the social research adviser's role emerged gradually from our experiences during the Project. At the beginning of the pilot stage, David Towell's previous work at Fulbourn had already provided some opportunities for mutual exploration with staff of the likely benefits from further collaboration, and given him a stock of goodwill on which to draw in susbsequent work. At the same time, his transition into this new role was both marked and supported by three main steps: the creation of the Project Steering Committee; the dissemination of information about the Project in the hospital; and his appointment to the staff of the Tavistock Institute.

These arrangements provided a strong base from which the first adviser was able to develop a consistent definition of this role: emphasising the collaborative nature of project work and the importance of its relevance to significant problems; resisting alternative expectations about the nature of his services; and negotiating with each group of staff an appropriate contract for any assistance he gave.

It was essentially through this process of multiple negotiations that the many different projects were instigated and the Project as a whole was realised.

At each stage of project work however, the attempt to fulfil this new role raised testing dilemmas. An early and continuing dilemma related to the degree of initiative to be taken in project work. Should the adviser seek out project ideas or only respond to requests? When ideas were raised, should he actively encourage their translation into projects? Later in projects, should he take initiatives, for example by writing reports, to keep work moving forward? An associated dilemma concerned the amount of influence that the adviser exerted on the scope of projects. How far should he accept problems as first presented, or seek to question the issues being raised? How could a balance be struck between undertaking work on perhaps less significant problems, and importing too many of his own ideas about what was significant into project work?

Other dilemmas arose in relation to research activities. Sometimes the adviser suggested that the most productive strategy would be for staff to undertake some investigative work, while they sought a research contribution from him; at other times the adviser himself volunteered an exploratory piece of research. How was the choice between these alternatives to be judged? Sometimes staff saw research reports as ends in themselves, while the adviser was encouraging the use of these reports in the examination of change. How could these conflicting expectations be bridged?

Underlying all these dilemmas was the more general problem of how the adviser could ensure that his contributions were such as to maintain the autonomy of staff groups and develop their own capacity to continue the process of innovation. As the preceding analysis has suggested, through struggling to resolve these dilemmas, successful strategies relevant to different phases of project work were identified. Through learning from the experience of particular projects and the opportunities to review this experience with an external colleague, the initial definition of the advisory role was filled out and its nature further illuminated. Thus over the pilot stage the adviser became more confident in his practice of this role and shared expectations with hospital staff were increasingly in evidence.

On this basis, consideration began of how the Project itself could be established as a more enduring contribution to the hospital's work. As the overview of Project development in Chapter 1 has described, the contingencies involved in funding HIP after the pilot stage played an important part in subsequent events. It was not until eighteen months later that Clive Harries was able to take on the full-time social research adviser role.

Of particular significance in maintaining HIP over the intervening period between April 1974 and October 1975 was the emergence of the Innovation Forum (IF). Some staff had already taken an interest in projects elsewhere in the hospital and Clive Harries had acted as adviser to one substantial study. IF was an attempt to widen these processes through establishing a regular meeting for staff to draw on each other's skill and experience in developing new project activity.

With support from the Steering Committee, Clive Harries became IF convener and David Towell initially provided one model to participants of how staff could act as consultants to each other in assisting project work. At its most active, IF met weekly with three or four projects for discussion; an attendance of six to twelve staff; and a wider circulation list of some 40 people. As well as support for projects and continued representation of the HIP approach, the forum provided a new means of sharing project experiences and disseminating information across different parts of the hospital: in pursuing these aims, IF participants also arranged an internal conference and exhibition to publicise HIP.

More subtly, IF was an important transitional mechanism in the further development of the Project. On the one hand, it permitted the first adviser to gradually withdraw from his role in the hospital in a way which underlined the capacity of staff themselves to continue the HIP approach: insofar as the advisory role was a significant source of support in the process of change, IF provided a means whereby this support role could be transferred back into the hospital. On the other hand, IF gave Clive Harries the opportunity to build on his earlier experience of taking the advisory role and to demonstrate more widely in the hospital his value as a resource to HIP, in preparation for what was to be his succession to the full-time social research adviser role in the second stage of the Project.

These experiences also gave further support to the view that the advisory role could become part of the hospital's establishment and therefore an internal staff role, provided certain conditions were met. The importance of consistency in the practice of this role and comple-mentary expectations among other staff have already been emphasised. In addition, it was anticipated first, that this should be a full-time post so the occupant would not be subject to conflicting pressures arising from other internal duties. Second, the role would need to be outside any particular professional domain and responsible to a multi-professional steering committee: thus providing sanction for a service to the whole hospital and reducing the likelihood of problems being compartmentalised according to professional divisions. Third, continuing benefit was expected from some external consultancy to the Project and outside interest in subsequent developments.

When funds became available through foundation support for the second stage of HIP, these conditions were established; the new post advertised; and Clive Harries appointed as social research adviser. Given these arrangements, the second adviser was able to complete the transition from an administrative role in one profession (he had been senior nursing officer) to an advisory role for all the hospital.

In subsequent work, Clive Harries has been developing his own definition of this role, building on what was learnt from earlier stages of the Project and also drawing on his distinctive experiences, for example of nursing research and the Hospital Advisory Service. It has thus proved possible for a second incumbent of the social research adviser role to play a full part in sustaining HIP in the changed organisational environment at Fulbourn which has followed NHS reorganisation: but not without confronting significant new difficulties (as Clive Harries describes in Chapter 6).

Lessons from these further developments have been of particular importance in our efforts to utilise aspects of the HIP approach in related projects elsewhere. Analysis has suggested that given the conditions which have been identified, the value of the advisory role to the hospital depends not so much on the specific background and skills of the role occupant as on the wider functions served by the availability of this role: crucially in representing to groups of staff the authority they have to seek and implement informed change. Moreover as the innovation forum began to demonstrate, there may be a number of alternative means which in appropriate circumstances can stimulate staff to examine critically their own work and provide some of the support necessary in working through the problems involved in achieving innovation. We have inferred that any future action programmes of this kind, while building on previous experiences, should aim to create new development strategies best fitting the particular circumstances and resources available. We explore the implications of these points in more detail in the Conclusion.

6 ORGANISATION FOR INNOVATION: SUPPORTING CONDITIONS AND THE IMPACT OF NHS REORGANISATION

David Towell and Clive Harries

The instigation of the Hospital Innovation Project at Fulbourn was encouraged by the view that in some ways the hospital might prove to be a fertile site for such an experiment. Subsequent experience suggested that this approach to innovation in particular projects both drew on and contributed to a number of more general developments in the organisation and culture of the hospital, increasingly in evidence over the first stage of the work. Building on the analysis in Chapter 5, David Towell sets out here to identify more fully the organisational conditions required to facilitate informed innovation in psychiatric care. He also explores what part HIP as a whole played in creating and strengthening these conditions at Fulbourn between 1972 and 1974. Clive Harries then shows how NHS reorganisation affected these achievements of the pilot stage: providing an unusual insight into the impact at hospital level of major administrative change and perhaps wider illumination of what further developments will be required if the intended benefits of this reorganisation are to be more fully realised.

A Model of Innovatory Organisation
David Towell

A starting point for the development of HIP was a concern with how psychiatric services should be organised and managed so as to ensure the effective use of resources in responding to changing demands for care. As Clive Harries argues in Chapter 1, the inability of psychiatric institutions to change themselves has come to be seen as a major problem, notwithstanding the substantial improvements in provision which have occurred in many places over the past 20 years. Much of the sociological work in this area has also been devoted to highlighting the factors hindering change in custodial institutions or, in the case of literature on therapeutic communities, often stressing the complementary theme of the significance of highly charismatic leadership in overcoming such hindrance. My own recent experience has itself served to underline how, particularly in large hospitals, dominant features may

131

still include a sense of isolation from the community being served, a traditional rigidity and pattern of hierarchical dependence, a confusion in management and lack of collaboration between the professions, and a pessimistic climate in which awareness of resource constraints and memories of past failures drown individual initiatives.

However much of the discussion in the preceding chapter has shown how a wide range of internal and external pressures ideally requires that psychiatric hospitals should be continuously involved in innovation, if high standards of care are to be developed and maintained. On this view then, informed change is central to the ordinary business of management and professional practice.

In considering how such change can be encouraged, the *social systems approach* provides a useful theoretical framework for analysing the task and organisation of psychiatric care. Such analysis suggests in the light of observations made at Fulbourn that three main factors need to be taken into account in the design and development of more responsive forms of organisation.

First, there is the nature of therapy itself. There are wide variations in treatment and care according to the group of patients concerned, the therapeutic approach favoured by relevant staff, and the resources available. In each case however, the quality of therapy is crucially dependent on the interaction between patients and the 'front line' staff actually delivering care, whose commitment and contribution is therefore of fundamental importance. Moreover, to the extent that treatment involves providing support for patients in their personal growth and exercise of autonomy, it is essential that staff themselves should be able to demonstrate confidence in self-development and learn in an open, questioning way from their own experience.

Second, the division of labour in psychiatric hospitals is such that patient treatment entails drawing on the skills and integrating the activities of a range of different practitioners. Each is organised into professional specialisms claiming, to varying degrees, the right to control their own work. Further complexities arise from the existence of multiple power structures and the differences there can be in the principles informing the organisation of each discipline. At both ward and higher management levels therefore, there is likely to be a need to superimpose some unifying boundary on the total service to patients in the face of cross-cutting professional and administrative distinctions.

Third, since the hospital is only one part of the total system of patient care, it follows that what is done there will affect and be affected by what is done in other parts of this system. Attention is also required therefore to the integration of hospital provision with the contribution of community resources (including the patient's family) and other agencies (general practitioners, social services, housing authorities, etc.).

Developing this analysis and drawing further on the experience of HIP, it is possible to make more explicit inferences about the organisational conditions required to facilitate innovation in psychiatric care and encourage fuller utilisation of the potential contribution of staff. These conditions can be specified by a sequence of working hypotheses outlining a model of innovatory organisation.

A Sequence of Hypotheses

It has been suggested that hospital organisation must necessarily be built on a matrix arising from the interaction of different disciplines and client groups:

Working Hypothesis One A focus on the services to be provided requires that the basic units of therapeutic organisation should typically be multi-disciplinary treatment teams in which different professions co-operate in the care of particular sets of patients and recognise the interdependence of their contributions.

Differences in the organisation of professional specialisms and in the level of expertise and experience of individuals will imply variations in the degree of discretion expected of particular team members:

Working Hypothesis Two These teams will need to develop a participative mode of working to ensure that different skills and experiences are appropriately mobilised in the task of treatment and to encourage positive staff involvement in the work which constitutes psychiatric care.

In addition, these teams will want sufficient autonomy for staff to use their knowledge and initiative in responding to particular problems which arise, and to establish collaborative working relationships with staff in a range of external agencies also contributing to the total pattern of care:

Working Hypothesis Three The flexible and responsive provision of treatment services entails a considerable measure of decentralisation in the management of the hospital and the hierarchical professions, such that treatment teams can become largely self-managing groups within broader policy frameworks.

It follows that a form of leadership and authority structure for the hospital as a whole will be required which sustains these conditions and provides support for staff initiative, while also actively monitoring and co-ordinating related activities and representing the common interests of the institution. Implicit here is a view (developed more fully in Chapter 8) which identifies the main function of the management of any system as being to define, jointly with participants, the task of this system and then to provide the boundary conditions within which relevant staff can manage their own work so as to perform this task most effectively:

Working Hypothesis Four To meet these requirements an effective management structure for the hospital is likely to entail the existence of an authoritative multi-disciplinary management group for the institution, in a negotiating relationship with the management of constituent parts of the hospital: seeking to provide the optimum conditions for each part to carry out its work, while representing the wider opportunities and constraints that derive from consideration of the service as a whole.

Such an approach to multi-disciplinary management has further implications for management within particular disciplines:

Working Hypothesis Five If multi-disciplinary collaboration is to be sustained, the dual accountability of staff to management teams and to their own disciplines requires recognition by the relevant managements and clarity about the extent of the individual's authority to represent his discipline within the team context.

Some degree of conflict is inevitable in the various relationships between teams, disciplines, and levels of management:

Working Hypothesis Six In order to encourage the constructive mediation of conflict, leadership is required to foster mutual understanding and provide flexible mechanisms for the resolution or arbitration of disagreements.

Permeating all these aspects of organisation is the institutional climate of shared attitudes and beliefs which enter into the motivation for change:

> *Working Hypothesis Seven* Informed innovation is more likely to the extent that the hospital culture encourages staff to question traditional arrangements; exercise detachment in the examination of their work; accept uncertainty in the course of seeking new practices; and recognise their own authority to initiate action.

The analysis of Project experience has pointed to a variety of ways in which these processes of change can be stimulated and assistance provided in working through the problems which necessarily arise:

> *Working Hypothesis Eight* Innovation is further encouraged to the extent that opportunities exist for staff to exchange experiences with others engaged in seeking improvements; managers at all levels demonstrate through their own exercise of authority that openness and experiment are highly valued; staff in key roles provide appropriate leadership; and through these or other means transitional support is available in coping with the anxieties generated by change.

Finally, the factors affecting the persistence of innovation identified in the preceding analysis of individual projects, can be generalised to suggest what is required to sustain these conditions in the hospital as a whole:

> *Working Hypothesis Nine* Where the innovatory organisation is part of a larger health service in which different conditions prevail, firm management arrangements through which the institution as a whole is represented to the wider service, decentralisation to facilitate such institutional management, some stability in staffing, and appropriate training arrangements for newcomers, are each likely to help protect these elements of organisation and culture from external disruptions.

The precise ways and the extent to which these conditions are realised in different situations will of course be variable. The meaning of these hypotheses can be further illuminated by considering organisational change at Fulbourn during successive stages in the development of HIP.

The Contribution of HIP

It is clear that the Hospital Innovation Project could not have been successfully launched without some active sponsorship from key power holders in the hospital and an authority structure which already permitted staff some freedom to explore problems and the time to participate in such activities. Equally, advantage was only likely to be taken of such opportunities, where some staff members were positively committed to their work and saw some need for (and possibility of) change. Indeed as has been implied, the differential development of project activities in different parts of the hospital can be related to the extent to which these requirements were satisfied. Moreover as noted in Chapter 1, many of the conditions identified above had antecedents in the history of Fulbourn prior to 1972. At the same time however it is also evident from the analysis of Project experience that HIP as a whole substantially contributed to the further development of these aspects of hospital organisation and culture. Again here there is a problem of attributing causality to elements of a complex, interactive process, but it is possible to identify some of the more important influences deriving from the Project.

The formation within the hospital of the Steering Committee to guide the Project was itself a crucial step in providing appropriate leadership and hospital-wide sanction for innovation, underlining also the need for multi-disciplinary collaboration in this activity. The Steering Committee met about eight times each year, with the social research adviser taking the secretary role. Typically meetings were devoted to reviewing the current state of project work, examining wider developments in the hospital and the value of the Project as a whole, and (by the second year) considering ways in which HIP could be sustained at Fulbourn after the pilot stage.

Initially members came to meetings with different ideas about the Project, but there was evidence in discussions over the first year of increasing convergence towards a shared view and through this, a clarification of the functions to be fulfilled by the Steering Committee. In particular this committee assumed responsibility for relating the Project to the overall management of the hospital. It also played a leadership role in encouraging the involvement of staff in project activities and providing support for staff in their efforts to translate the results of project work into productive innovations.

As Clive Harries describes further later in this chapter, for most of the period since 1972, the Steering Committee has been the only forum in which senior representatives of medicine, nursing and administration have met regularly together in a management role at hospital level. An important latent function of these meetings (and HIP more generally) seems therefore to have been that of helping to preserve the identity of Fulbourn as an institution, in the face of other factors tending to reduce the hospital to a place in which different groups of professionals – each with broader disciplinary identifications – practised their own specialisations. The committee not infrequently then was used by its members to exchange information and ideas about wider issues confronting the development of services based on the hospital. In the second stage of the Project, this became an explicit item in which the current state of the hospital was reviewed as part of examining how the conditions necessary to support project work could be sustained. These regular meetings were significant too in maintaining continuity in the leadership of the Project over a number of key staff changes at senior level.

In addition to the development of the Steering Committee, project work contributed directly to strengthening these organisational conditions in several ways. One project examined directly the need for new hospital management arrangements in 1974. Other projects on the management structure of the hospital aided the process of decentraltion and the emphasis given to the multi-disciplinary management of particular sets of services in relation to external agencies and the client groups or geographical areas being served. Most important here was the extended project on developing a new role for unit nursing officers, but this was paralleled by other work, including an experiment in attaching 'link-administrators' to these service management groups.

In other projects too, a significant influence arose from the definition of the social research advisory role and the adviser's approach to ensuring adequate sanction for project activities. As seen earlier, the first steps in project work typically involved identifying a group of staff (often multi-disciplinary) who could be regarded as responsible for taking action on the problems of concern and who would collectively decide on the next steps to be taken. The adviser's availability to such groups then further represented the authority they had to engage in innovation, and supported the process of decentralisation. At the same time, through a focus on defining groups of staff in relation to the task under review, a number of projects (for example, those on rehabilitative processes, psycho-geriatric care, and training by secondment) led to different relationships being established across pre-existing organisational boundaries such that innovation within the hospital was facilitated.

Several projects also had a primary focus on the organisational requirements for improved patient care, permitting exploration of how each profession's distinctive contribution could be integrated in the task of treatment. Moreover projects like those on the admission, long-stay and psycho-geriatric wards all demonstrated the significance of staff developing their own roles in the direction of greater autonomy, flexibility and openness, in order to improve care for these different sets of clients.

More generally, the project activities as a whole, both through their impact on staff development and their encouragement of certain ideas about the desirability and means of achieving informed change, contributed to the growth of what can be described as a culture of self innovation in the hospital. Among the aspects of this culture which Steering Committee members were able to identify from a review of their own experiences, were a sense of reduced dependency of staff on the hierarchy, a more widespread capacity to cope constructively with anxiety, and a trend for initiatives to be taken for their intrinsic value rather than to gain the approval of more senior staff.

All this was particularly evident in the nursing discipline where more direct evidence of this new culture could be found in the changing functions of the central nursing office, which no longer needed to serve as a control point from which authority for a wide range of ward level decisions had traditionally been sought. The many project initiatives taken by nurses also underlined the movement away from a situation in which nursing dependence on medical leadership made doctors the main source of innovation.

Two further aspects of this culture — observable in the working of the innovation forum — were an increased ability among staff to exercise some detachment in looking at their own work and a related increase in acceptance that open disagreement need not be experienced as destructive of inter-personal relationships. These trends seemed to be reflected too in increasing trust between staff at different levels of the professional hierarchies. (Further evidence for these observations is reported in Chapter 7.)

Some of these developments, both in the identity of the whole hospital as an innovating institution and in the self-confidence of individual staff members, were further reinforced by the external recognition given to HIP by a succession of interested visitors, by the working conferences on particular issues which Fulbourn staff organised, and especially by the King's Fund Conference in November 1973.

In sum, by 1974 there was significant evidence that many of the conditions intrinsic to the model of innovatory organisation which has been proposed were being practically realised at Fulbourn; and that HIP increasingly symbolised for staff the capacity they had to become their own agents of informed change. By this time however, the hospital was immersed in a much wider process of administrative restructuring in the NHS as a whole. This subsequent experience was to provide a not necessarily welcome opportunity to test further some of the working hypotheses which this analysis has suggested.

The Impact of Reorganisation

Clive Harries

The basic objective of Government in reorganising the NHS in 1974 was to encourage the more rational and effective use of resources in providing improved health care for the people (Cmnd 5055, 1972). More specific objectives included the promotion of greater integration of services, new thinking about health care, more forward thinking about the pattern of services in relation to the needs of particular client groups, and greater encouragement to innovation more generally. It seemed clear from the achievements of the Hospital Innovation Project in the pilot stage from 1972 until 1974, that to the extent these objectives were really pursued, the approach developed at Fulbourn should make a major contribution to the success of reorganisation locally.

However, the experience of reorganisation in the first three years after April 1974, both at Fulbourn and also nationally, has been associated more with disruption and disappointment than with much progress on these objectives. It can of course be argued that even without the further constraints imposed by the economic crisis, some years will be required before the intended benefits of reorganisation can realistically be expected to materialise.

Following reorganisation, officers all over the country at regional, area and district levels were confronted with the problems of introducing the new management structure and trying to make it work. In the case of those districts or areas where there existed a large psychiatric hospital, and where few, if any, of the newly appointed officers had sound management experience in psychiatric care, they were also confronted with understanding an organisation where patient needs, policies and practices differed, often radically, from their own previous experience. Questions regarding 'What is best for psychiatric patients?' 'How far is it possible, or even desirable, to exercise direct management control?' 'Who is, or really can be, responsible?' had to be considered by these officers. At the outset, establishing contact with senior hospital officers was a priority together with appointing people to posts which emerged in the new structure. Together with ironing out financial policies and other priorities within the district or area, these issues were topics of dominant concern.

Clearly, these difficulties encountered by new officers at district level and above cannot be isolated from the experience of senior officers at hospital level following reorganisation: issues of responsibility, multi-disciplinary collaboration and delegation now pose widespread problems throughout the psychiatric service. This has been well illustrated in the Report of the Committee of Enquiry at St. Augustine's Hospital (SETRHA 1976), and the ensuing discussions in many journals, although the resolution of these issues may typically be less clear.

Study of the development of HIP since 1974 has provided an unusual opportunity to understand further the impact of reorganisation at hospital level, and begin to identify what staff will need to do to overcome the damage and realise the benefits from this major organisational change.

It will be recalled that although hospital staff were committed to continuing HIP after the pilot phase, efforts to raise funds to sustain the social research adviser role in 1974 were unsuccessful. The innovation forum had, however, provided some support to staff trying to undertake project work in this period, and it is significant in relation to what followed, that the one new project to which David Towell contributed, was concerned with interprofessional co-ordination arrangements at hospital level. This project could be seen in retrospect as a first effort to plug the dyke in hospital management which reorganisation had created.

In September 1975 the hospital was awarded a grant from the King's Fund and I took up post. As former senior nursing officer, I was known in the hospital and had been closely associated with HIP during the first phase, both as a Steering Committee member, and in taking an advisory role in a few projects. This analysis of subsequent developments is based on my experiences in the social research adviser role and observations on what was happening at Fulbourn between 1974 and 1977.

Changes in Organisation and Management

The changes occasioned by the new management arrangements following reorganisation gradually began to alter the stable, supportive management structure which had existed prior to reorganisation, in which HIP project activity had flourished. Initially this was expressed by some senior and middle managers as 'we are going to miss the HMC', together with some uncertainty and apprehension over what would be expected of them by newly appointed district managers and the new Area Health Authority. Following the disappearance of the Hospital Management Committee, the next visible changes occurred when the new structure made the incumbents of the posts of hospital secretary and principal nursing officer redundant, and David Storr and Maurice Fenn were required to seek posts elsewhere.

Slowly the significance of these events became evident, clarifying some of the important functions of the HMC, and shedding some light on the loss of the roles of principal nursing officer and hospital secretary. In an important way the meetings of the HMC had acted as a regular forum for lateral contact between the senior managers in the hospital. Frequently, prior to an HMC meeting, officers would meet to discuss items on the agenda. Over the years, this process provided a management forum where the implications of decisions could be examined, talked through and agreements made; in particular, where the implications of decisions by one professional group could be examined against the needs of patients and other professional groups. Thus the HMC meetings, and the processes surrounding them, acted as an informal 'check and balance' in the management processes of policy formation and decision taking in relation to psychiatric care. Additionally the principal nursing officer and hospital secretary, who shared the same boundaries to their responsibilities, had developed aspects of their roles to provide a similar function at hospital level, collaborating laterally to facilitate day to day work, both informally and at regular meetings. The loss of both the HMC and these two significant role occupants therefore left a vacuum which was partially filled by the increasing preoccupation on the part of senior officers with the necessity of establishing relationships and working arrangements with their superiors in the new manangement structure outside the hospital. This effectively diminished the possibility of lateral collaboration in decision taking and, apparently by default, encouraged the processes by which professional groups operated more in isolation.

These changes, of course, had their impact on the Steering Committee, which became something of a thermometer for assessing the climate at senior management level. The redundancy of the principal nursing officer and hospital secretary, and my assumption of the social research adviser role necessitated a restructuring of the Steering Committee. As an interim measure the chief nursing officer and the (former) group secretary were invited to join the committee. Later, with their leaving, the newly appointed senior nursing officer, divisional nursing officer and sector administrator became members, together with a consultant nominated by his colleagues to represent them on a proposed hospital management team. These substantial changes over a period entailed some hard work on the part of the convenor (David Clark) as new members learned afresh about HIP and the functions of the Steering Committee.

During this period the Steering Committee was the only multi-disciplinary forum at senior level where events preoccupying one professional group, which might have implications for another, could be examined systematically. An example of this was provided by members discovering that they had been contacted independently regarding the provision of a regional security unit. This independent contact had not encouraged the professions in the mutual consultations necessary to work out a shared response to issues which should have required joint consideration.

A further significant change with which the organisation had to contend during this period took place in medical staffing. In the period prior to reorganisation two new consultant psychiatrists were appointed, and later a professor of psychiatry. Many staff perceived their approach to care as more 'medical' than that of the existing clinical teams and as such considerable periods of time had to be spent on the part of staff, both in clinical areas and at higher levels, in re-negotiating roles, and accommodating to new expectations.

Gradually the problems being experienced at a senior level in the hospital were transmitted through to the level of patient care. One senior administrative nurse felt that lines of communication 'had been elongated to the point where nothing happened', and that the new management 'could not understand the flexible approach which is necessary to running a psychiatric service . . . they think that everything is of a physical nature, one bed, one patient — therefore everything, staff ratios, revenue for services . . . are all geared to this theme'. This feeling of impotence was also observable at middle management level: particularly amongst the nursing officers, one of whom thought that 'there's no doubt the place is going to the dogs — we are becoming much more bureaucratic, and less professional in all that we are having to do . . . procedures for this and that, more and more memos are flying about and much less time for patient care than we used to have'. Tracing this down to the ward level a charge nurse reported, 'The whole place is dropping to bits — you can't get an answer to anything' and illustrated his feeling with a series of unresolved queries, the resolution of which would have entailed an element of lateral communication between professions, and would have been solved easily at hospital level before reorganisation.

The disintegrating effect of all this was reflected by a student nurse who remarked, 'There's really not much point in doing anything new now because someone "up there" will decide in the end, anyway.'

A striking example of the way policy changes and reduced flexibility emanating from above the level of the hospital had consequences on work at ward level was afforded by a new approach to managing the nursing staff establishment. Formerly the hospital nursing policy had been to make preparatory adjustments to staff numbers so that as student nurses qualified they were absorbed into the trained staff establishment, and the financial budget was not exceeded. Following reorganisation this was replaced by a more rigid policy which meant in practice that a stated number of nursing staff in each category was not to be exceeded. It became necessary for one group of student nurses to be told shortly before their examination that there would not be jobs for all of them if they qualified. This decision generated considerable hostility towards senior nursing staff at the hospital with obvious implications for efforts to undertake longer term projects to develop services. In one project in which two of these student nurses were involved, the attention of the whole staff group turned for a period from project activities to the more immediate task of providing support to the students concerned.

During this period of change the project sponsoring role played by Steering Committee members was also diminished so that many of the projects current during the second experimental phase of HIP resulted from contacts established by me in my former post as senior nursing officer whilst sitting in on, and contributing to projects, or on occasions taking the advisory role myself.

As might be imagined all this was a distinct change in the climate of innovation which had previously existed and been fostered by HIP. It was reflected in the projects which were current at the time: in a review of project work during 1976 the Steering Committee noted existing projects were spread wide and somewhat encapsulated in their occurrence and that the resources represented by HIP were not being well used in relation to tackling the major problems facing the hospital.

Through its developing awareness of the implications of issues such as these, the Steering Committee increasingly identified the need for some form of 'Hospital Management Team'.

The Implications of Changes for Innovatory Activity

In the preceding section, David Towell identified on the basis of his experience at Fulbourn between 1972 and 1974 the elements of an organisational model for encouraging staff to engage in adaptive and innovatory activities to meet the changing demands on psychiatric services and care. Within the changed circumstances occasioned by the reorganisation of the NHS an opportunity was afforded to examine further the relevance of these organisational conditions in supporting the programme of informed change represented in the HIP approach.

If we examine the working hypotheses suggested by David Towell and summarised in Table 6.1 against the experience of the hospital following reorganisation and the problems perceived by staff, it can be seen that the main conditions were differentially affected — but that none were strengthened or enhanced in the direction of helping further innovatory activity develop.

With regard to multi-disciplinary teamwork — it is evident from the feelings of staff that this was not only seriously curtailed at senior management level following reorganisation — but that it was sadly missed as well. As a result difficulties were posed, for example, in mediating between the demands and requirements of different clinical teams. Although multi-disciplinary collaboration continued at the patient care level, it was weakened to an extent by an increasing concern with vertical relationships within disciplines at the expense of lateral relationships between team members.

The participatory way of working, in evidence during the first experimental phase of HIP work and a key factor in much of the project work, was also affected. This was reflected in the feelings expressed earlier by staff at different levels in the organisation. These feelings indicated that there was a general agreement that the tradition of having a say in decision making was seriously undermined. A consequence of this was that people at clinical level felt that the discretion and autonomy that had been previously increasingly encouraged, and which were consistent with developed decentralised management, were being curtailed.

Existing working links with external agencies concerned with particular client groups were not so seriously affected at least at the patient care level in that most such links had been developed out of clinical teams' day to day work, and were sustained by daily demand.

The nature of leadership in the hospital was also subject to change. It has been argued that senior officers in the hospital, when the HMC was in being, exercised an implicit collective leadership. This was particularly evident in many issues which necessitated collaboration

Table 6.1: Organisational Conditions Facilitating Innovation: The Impact of Reorganisation

Organisational conditions facilitating innovation – developing during pilot stage of HIP	Impact of NHS reorganisation and related changes on these conditions at Fulbourn
Hypothesis One – on the requirement for professional collaboration in multi-disciplinary treatment teams	Teamwork put under stress by increasing emphasis on disciplinary allegiance, 'vertical' rather than 'lateral' relationships, and reduced decentralisation
Hypothesis Two – on the requirement for a partici-pative mode of working	Effective participation similarly undermined, including by more decisions being 'sent down from above' and less support for the use of discretion
Hypothesis Three – on the requirement for decentralisa-tion in management and greater autonomy	Trend towards decentralisation reversed by creation of the district management tier, imposition of more rigid controls, and pre-occupation with 'accountability upwards'
Hypothesis Four – on the requirement for multi-disciplinary management for the institution in support of management for its parts	Institutional management structure similarly weakened by the stronger orientation to disciplinary and functional management, the creation of non-matching administrative arrangements for different disciplines, and the loss of the Hospital Management Committee
Hypothesis Five – on the requirement for recognition of the dual accountability and clarity as to the authority of team members	All these changes contribute to a reduction in shared understanding of the requirements for appropriately articulating service management with disciplinary and functional management
Hypothesis Six – on the requirement for means of constructively mediating conflict	In addition, more compartmentalised leader-ship and the loss of management forums reduce the organisations' capacity for conflict resolution
Hypothesis Seven – on the requirement for a culture encouraging questioning and the use of initiative	Uncertainty among senior managers and changed authority relationships associated with incorporation into the district structure begin to undermine the 'culture of self-innovation'
Hypothesis Eight – on the requirement for oppor-tunities to exchange experiences and receive support during processes of change	Similarly the weakening of institutional manage-ment, increased segmentation in the hospital, and less effective leadership reduce the support available and staff groups become more isolated
Hypothesis Nine – on the requirement for protecting the innovatory institution from wider disruption	In sum, multiple changes including increasing direction from above, weakening of institu-tional identity, and rapid turnover in senior staff, all prove disruptive of established conditions

between the professions — such as the setting up of a multi-disciplinary Housing Council to aid the resettlement of long-stay patients, or displaying encouragement for the actions of another professional group in their success in tackling a difficulty.

The maintenance of a culture of innovation was also affected by these organisational changes. In the face of more centralised management, less collaboration between professions at a senior level, and the erosion of opportunities where inter-unit dialogue could be fostered, innovative activity tended to be more confined or to remain encapsulated, as was noted earlier.

An example of this was evident when staff from the 'disturbed' ward prepared to present their ward policy at a national conference. They rehearsed the presentation using the staff from other long-stay wards as an audience. Although one or two other wards felt that they too might revise their ward policies, issues such as the redundancy of newly qualified staff, the distribution of staff and the appointment of senior staff, intervened. These issues — spaced over a period of time — conspired to distract attention from innovatory activity and to leave such innovations as there were, relatively isolated.

However, one area of the hospital was able to sustain a series of projects for a time. The staff in the psycho-geriatric area had been the largest users of the social research adviser's services during the first two years following reorganisation. The question of interest is 'why should the psycho-geriatric area — of all the care areas in the hospital — find itself able to sustain an extensive series of projects?' One reason could be the association of the current social research adviser with projects which arose in that area during the first experimental phase of HIP work. But this does not wholly explain the innovatory success of the area, given that (as part of the hospital as a whole) they too faced the changes described earlier which confronted all psychiatric hospitals in the Health Service.

In looking at this question, it seems possible to identify some distinctive aspects of organisation in this area which seem to have helped in this work. Three factors discussed earlier as important in sustaining HIP activity seemed to remain intact.

First, the external cross boundary work with other agencies sharing a concern over a common client group was generalised and reinforced by day-to-day work. In other words the work of staff continued to be in demand by others outside the hospital, giving perhaps a sense of purpose and of value to their activities, particularly through the collaboration being established with social services. Second,

there was a sense of having the opportunity to influence the development of care plans for the elderly at a higher level, by psychiatric
nursing and consultant participation in the Health Care Planning Team
for the Elderly. This had the effect of maintaining the feeling not only
that they could be part masters of their own destiny, but there was
something of value that they could offer to wider planning processes.

Third, the style of supportive leadership developed by the consultant
at that time was added to by an active outgoing leadership style at
nursing officer level. This leadership, exercised by individuals who were
also members of the Health Care Planning Team for the Elderly, meant
that the staff of the psycho-geriatric area were kept fully informed of
proposed developments. Discussion over issues arising from proposals
was encouraged and the wider staff's views were carried forward into
the Health Care Planning Team.

However, even here these achievements have been made precarious
by changes in medical leadership for these services which has led to
divided responsibilities between consultants and a series of interim
measures which have increased the uncertainty of the staff involved.

The Future

Viewed against both the achievements of the pilot stage of the Hospital
Innovation Project and also the intended objectives of NHS reorganisation, this case study of the impact at Fulbourn of the disruption
occasioned since 1974 perhaps conveys a gloomy picture of the current
state of the NHS at local level. Indeed to the extent that the earlier
work at Fulbourn succeeded in creating staff morale and ways of
working which provided some resilience against this disruption, it can
be expected that in many other situations, there have been considerably
greater problems.

Although the description of changes has focussed so far on the more
negative effects in the hospital of reorganisation between 1974 and
1977, there was a strong feeling that the very presence of HIP activity
had itself made some contribution to ameliorating the more negative
consequences of NHS reorganisation as experienced locally. First,
Steering Committee members have been able to share some of the
problems experienced individually by members and give a degree of
mutual support in adversity. Second, the continuance of some project
work at patient care levels was seen as useful in maintaining some focus
of attention on the resolution of difficulties being experienced in day
to day work against the pressure to become preoccupied with the more
intangible problems of the hospital. The project enabling the geriatric

area to re-zone its services with reorganised social service teams was an illustration of this.

There have also been some important new projects initiated in the first two years since I took up my post as social research adviser. The project concerning the psychiatric nursing service to the community has raised fresh issues concerning future developments. Equally a review of patients moved into the long-stay area of care has drawn attention to the disabled psychiatric patient in the community, and to the relationship of the hospital with community services. Both of these projects raise potentially important issues for future examination.

Against this background, at the time of writing at the end of 1977 there are encouraging signs that Fulbourn had made the first steps to repair some of the damage of reorganisation. Out of a series of discussions, firm proposals have been generated by the new sector administrator for forming a 'Hospital Management Team', and this was established in November 1977. Within three months it had represented some of the hospital's needs to the District Management Team. There is a growing sense that a multi-disciplinary representation of the hospital's needs might now become a reality, reflecting a movement to re-establish effective collaboration at a senior level, and an attempt to retrieve some collective identity for the family of psychiatric services based on the hospital. The Hospital Management Team has also managed to secure NHS funds for the post of social research adviser, thus making HIP a more permanent experiment.

As these efforts are made to re-establish organisational conditions favourable to innovation and service development, it appears reasonable to hope that with the benefits of nearly six years experience, the Hospital Innovation Project will have a significant role to play in helping staff to develop further the effective therapeutic organisation and culture which was emerging prior to 1974.

Finally, this account of the impact of reorganisation serves to underline the important conclusions about the organisational conditions required for innovation derived from the first stage of HIP. Just as in individual projects, the hospital conditions of multi-disciplinary collaboration, decentralisation and staff stability were important to successful project work — so subsequent experience has shown that these conditions in the wider health service are important for sustaining HIP as a whole. In particular the wider District Health Service still faces the problems of how a focus on services to particular client groups can be sustained within a set of management arrangements in which professional divisions can easily assume prominence; how the identity of particular institutions can be protected as hospitals are incorporated into much larger management structures; how decision making can be sufficiently decentralised to permit the necessary flexibility and opportunity for staff participation; and how all these conditions can help to restore staff confidence in their own capacity for informed change. Solving these problems can be seen as the central challenge now facing the psychiatric services.

7 LEADERSHIP, PARTICIPATION AND THE CLIMATE FOR INFORMED CHANGE

Maurice Fenn, Oliver Hodgson, Anne Long and
John Pushkin and Others

Intrinsic to the preceding analysis of the Hospital Innovation Project
has been a view of Fulbourn Hospital as a *social system* in which
different parts are closely related to each other and the wider environment. For example, the possibility of junior staff enlarging their
contribution to improving care has been seen to depend to some degree
on the willingness of senior staff to reconsider their approach to
management; the initiative of one profession in developing its role in
treatment has been seen to require collaborative responses from the
other professions also involved. To the extent that HIP has proved a
successful approach to informed innovation therefore, wider changes in
the organisation and culture of the hospital as a whole have been
necessary.

This analysis can be complemented and enriched through an
examination of HIP from the various perspectives represented among
those who participated. Contributions have been sought from senior
and junior staff, from different professions, and also from inside and
outside the hospital. Each contributor has tended to address different
questions which reflect their own roles and experiences. All however
help to illuminate aspects of this process of change in psychiatric care
and provide further data for an assessment of how HIP was experienced
by those involved.

The main focus here is on the developments in hospital organisation
and culture achieved by the end of the pilot stage of HIP in 1974.
This period can now be viewed to some extent in retrospect and there
is adequate material available from several sources to provide a quite
diverse commentary. Some of this material has been drawn from
observations prepared for other purposes. Most of this commentary
however comes from participants willing to volunteer a contribution,
who largely represent those who have taken a positive view of HIP.
In a critical assessment of the Project, therefore, this selectivity must be
borne in mind. Moreover, the account by Clive Harries (in Chapter 6)
of developments since 1974 suggests that later views would provide a
significantly changed picture.

This presentation of different perspectives begins at the 'top' of the organisation. The role of leadership in facilitating staff participation in HIP has been emphasised by the preceding analysis: this seems particularly important in the case of nursing, the largest and perhaps most hierarchically organised of the psychiatric professions. The strong commitment of many nursing staff to HIP can be related therefore to the role taken up by the principal nursing officer|during the pilot stage of the Project, Maurice Fenn. He describes the thinking which informed the development of his own approach to management during this period, and which was more widely influential throughout the nursing service in the hospital. This nursing view is followed by a note from Oliver Hodgson, the consultant psychiatrist with particular responsibilities for the psycho-geriatric units. He describes the kind of supportive medical leadership required to encourage innovative developments in long term care like those reported by the Denbigh Ward team in Chapter 3.

These views from senior staff are then complemented by a collection of contributions which reflect the experience of grass roots participants in the hospital. Particular attention is given to the views of trainee staff. A fortunate bonus here was the inclusion of Fulbourn within a comparative study of trainee nurses in six other hospitals, undertaken by an independent research team, Anne Long and John Pushkin. As the editorial commentary argues, their data permit a more systematic and quantitative assessment of the extent to which a distinctive organisational climate had developed at Fulbourn, consistent with the HIP approach to informed change. Drawing on some varied illustrative material, an attempt is then made to suggest the likelihood of some patterning in the relationships between these views of staff and those of other participants in the system of psychiatric care: patients, their relatives and the wider community.

Finally in Chapter 8, all these issues are located within a more explicit theoretical framework. Eric Miller provided external consultancy to the development of HIP. Reflecting on his experience of this and a wide range of other action research projects, he presents an illuminating analysis of the relationships between leadership, autonomy, dependence and innovation in institutions whose primary task involves the care or development of others.

A Senior Nursing View — Changing the Role of the Institution
Maurice Fenn

Circumstances today demand that 'established' give way to 'adaptive' patterns of organisation (Urwick, 1957). There is a clear need for changes in the health service and particularly for psychiatric services to adapt to meet modern needs and expectations. A nursing manager responsible for a traditional or 'established' institution is faced with the problem of the creation of conditions that will enable the 'established' to give way to the 'adaptive'. What are these conditions, and how can rapid response and innovation be facilitated? From my own experience of the organisation of nursing services, in addition to having a management structure based on effective delegation and strongly influenced from the 'bottom' upwards, the following seem to me to have particular importance.

First, the attitude and approach of formal leaders will decide whether the atmosphere is marked by 'This is how it must be done' or 'What needs to be done? How can it best be approached?' Second, nursing resources must be clearly divided and allocated, and the way the nursing cake is cut must be seen to be fair. Third, a style of day to day supervision must be developed, aimed at self development and the retention of the initiative for action by those supervised. Fourth, it must be recognised that every level in the organisation is a point of planning and policy interpretation in which the spirit is as important as the letter. Further, every level is an interface and communication point between planning and policy decisions coming down and the need for new plans and policies coming up. Fifth, an 'adaptive' organisation can only develop when change is 'built in'. This is unlikely to occur with tight central organisation. It is more likely to occur when a number of multi-disciplinary groups are focussing on special areas of need, functional or geographical, in an organisation in which these can be reconciled.

Leadership, Approach and Attitude

We underestimate the influence a leader with formal authority has in a hospital. Envisage the atmosphere produced by a senior nurse who regards those under his control as colleagues, stating, 'We are working with patients, families, doctors, administrators, occupational therapists, etc. to provide our area with a service.' Compare this with the atmosphere likely to result from a senior nurse's attitude which could be stated as 'I am the senior nurse and the nurses will be organised and work as follows . . .' If 'adaptive' processes are to continue to develop it is absolutely vital that those in senior positions should be willing to enter into situations and discussions from which they may not emerge 'on top'.

Such willingness will ultimately be reflected through the line organisation to have a significant effect on the attitude of staff to the patients with whom they are in contact and on the quality and effectiveness of this most crucial link between the service and its clients. McGhee (1961) identified barriers in this relationship, pointing out that patients identify themselves most closely with the junior nurse whom they see as the object of the same discipline and authority as themselves. Thus if patients are not to feel at the mercy of a mystery shrouded system, with their activities and destiny controlled by staff with defensively organised roles using information to which they have exclusive access, subjected to many pressures to comply with little right of challenge and the initiative for action being with someone else . . . then the staff next to the patients must not be subject to such conditions.

The extent to which staff and patients are subjected to these circumstances will depend upon the attitude of those at the top of the organisation. In organisations characterised by inertia, centralisation of decision making, predictability of routine and with the emphasis on compliance, it will be found that therapeutic opportunities are few as are opportunities for personal or professional development. Activities are directed to maintaining the approval of one's senior. In such institutions, senior staff maintain and underline their seniority by encouraging mystique, keeping information exclusive to themselves and making sure their permission has to be asked before anybody does anything.

Nothing is so destructive of initiative as the notions that, 'There are important things I don't know' or 'I would have to ask permission before I could depart from routine'. Even more harmful is to get on with something, then to be given a 'You are not here to think but to do as you are told' style of reprimand.

In such an institution it is understandable that professional training which would require a departure from the system in order to meet patient need is regarded as less important than experience of the system. 'You are not in the school now you know' is an example of encouragement to shelve professional approach and technique.

Students in such an atmosphere have little opportunity of reinforcing theory with practice. Therefore this theory with its potential for roles and skills remains undeveloped. This may explain in part the feeling of many trained nurses that training 'is all right, but not related to what I do'. 'What they do' is influenced more by the system than by their training. Indeed, the quality and spirit of their training is subverted by the system.

If such circumstances are to be avoided, those in senior positions must recognise that they will be poor judges of their own actions and talents. Success must be judged by the effectiveness with which patients' needs are met and in terms of the ideas, projects and initiatives produced by the patients and staff in an area, rather than by the individual who has overall responsibility for it.

Those in senior positions should, with developing insight and encouragement of honest feed back: attempt to eliminate ego massage from decision making; have a consultative questioning challenging approach; not assume that 'they know best'; create an atmosphere in which decisions, especially those that have to be made by senior or subordinate without consultation can be challenged and analysed without rancour for mutual learning and development; recognise that circumstances, client need and the means to meet this need are constantly changing; seek success rather than avoid failure; take the blame when things go wrong; and ensure that those with effort, energy, ideas and initiative have the freedom and knowledge to use them and receive full credit and recognition in the process.

Apportioning Nursing Resources

'Why should we slog our guts out when that other ward has more staff than we have and only half the work?'

'Everybody knows that what we need is more staff: it's no good thinking about *anything* until we get them.'

'Improvements? Yes, we could make them if "they" would give us the staff to do it with.'

' "They" could allocate more staff to us if they wanted to: we have told them we want them but we get no answer.'

'We have been waiting for five years, I expect we will have to wait another five.'

If the situation reflected by such comments is to be avoided the 'cake' representing the nursing resource must not only be fairly divided but the division must be *seen* to be fair. A position must be achieved such that staff will say, 'we can do with more but we have got our fair share of what is available: we must be able to make better use of our time.' When the credibility of such a belief has been sufficiently tested for it to be held by the majority, it will of course be part of the culture.

In these circumstances staff will take| a more quantitative approach
to the identification of need and use of resources, and will both look
for and welcome help to do this. Examples of this can be seen in
various HIP projects including the series of projects on the use of
nursing resources in psycho-geriatric care.

Supervision
In an 'established' organisation with centralised decision making and
activities directed by unchanging policies which are used as a power
source for the imposition of authority, development is the exception,
senior staff have little to contribute in real terms, and supervision
becomes negative. Delegation and decentralisation are important
foundations upon which to build a style of supervision and professional
counselling that will enable professional and personal development and
rapid responses in the field, sensitive to changing need and circumstance.

It is vital that staff do not have the problem they discuss with their
supervisor (line superior) snatched out of their hands, but that they are
helped to feel their way towards answers themselves; and that they do
not see this as an invitation to delegate the problem upwards. An
individual bringing an issue or problem to their supervisor may wish to
verbalise, clarify or test the soundness of their thoughts, explore constraints or political barriers, test validity of direction. It might well be
that the supervisor might say, 'Well, we are both at a loss with this one,
let's look at it again together.'

A simple example of such supervision and counselling is demonstrated
by the following conversation between a nursing officer and his supervisor:

Nursing Officer: 'The clinical team of an admission ward have been
    talking about coming out of uniform. Would they get permission
    to do this?'
Supervisor: 'What do you think about it?'
Nursing Officer: 'I feel rather uncertain about it.'
Supervisor: 'Why do they want to come out of uniform?'
Nursing Officer: 'It is thought there will be several benefits.'
Supervisor: 'It is interesting: articles I can remember on this subject
    are all rather emotive and heavily biased towards| the pros or the
    cons and it seems to me without any real attempt to look at it
    from the patient's point of view.'
Nursing Officer: 'I think it would be worth giving it a trial if the
    means could be established of verifying that the notional benefits
    are being obtained.'

Supervisor: 'Yes, we should establish just what these advantages are; also the disadvantages so that we can try and minimise those.'

This shortened version of one of several conversations was an important factor in the initiation of the series of projects on developing organisation and treatment in an admission ward.

Policy and Planning

Accepting that policy and planning can be substantially influenced and directed nationally and can be subject to change resulting from political or financial initiatives, it is an important principle of reorganisation that there should be local variation. There is in fact substantial freedom to meet the special needs of localities within existing guidance. In the country as a whole it is neither possible or desirable that developments should be strictly uniform in style or pace. Rather we should look for, encourage and use existing or developing islands of excellence and models of good practice.

Unfortunately it is far too often that we see examples of the letter of national guidance being used to defeat the spirit. Too often we see the letter being used to produce a result exactly opposite to that intended. Contrary to popular belief the DHSS does not wish guidance to be used as an excuse to depart from common sense. Nelson said, circumstances so often vary 'that an Officer has almost every moment to consider, "What would my superiors direct did they know what is passing under my nose?" ' Although it is expected that the annual planning cycle will be a means of programming action related to wide strategic policy choices and long-term aims, there still remains the opportunity to take account of local need, choice and points of emphasis.

Within a general strategy, both policies and courses of action requiring planning should arise from the selection of alternatives produced by an active, informed staff working to meet client need. As Dunning (1973) has said, 'It is in the selection from the alternatives and in the timing of letting that choice emerge, that competent managers and organisations reveal themselves.' The key to this is, with a decentralised approach, the creation of the conditions and atmosphere, marked by self-motivation and innovation, in which staff will produce these alternatives for selection in the development of an integrated service. These alternatives should be influenced by and influence district planning and area and regional strategy.

Built-In Change

Although in detail enormously complex, the key to institutional change is often to be found in the attitude of staff. Are they expected to take advantage of opportunities, are they expected to create opportunities for the improvement of a patient-centred service? As well as making logical requests for more resources, are they expected to continue the search for a better use of existing resources? A new dynamism has been added by change of attitude from, 'improve the service within the institution' to 'improve the service to the community'.

In this process of meeting changing needs staff must have the knowledge, freedom and support to take action and make appropriate decisions as near to the scene of the action as possible; this depends not only on sound delegation within a discipline but often on full co-operation within a multi-disciplinary team approach. This has served to underline the move from a centre-periphery model to a more amorphous sensitive structure. This concept, noted by Hunter (1973), requires peripheral focuses of multi-disciplinary organisation.

The Hospital Innovation Project has complemented and accelerated these developments and changing attitudes. We have not seen the development of a few sophisticated projects, but a spread of relatively unsophisticated but sound work. We have learnt that support for work at grass roots level is needed; mistakes are made, problems are caused, policy is stretched, awkward questions are asked, 'the system' is questioned and the organisation is often pulled from its sometimes uneasy ledge of compromise onto unfamiliar ground. But more importantly: success is sought rather than failure avoided; the development of a client-centred service is accelerated; an atmosphere increasing the potential of patient contribution is encouraged; the articulate, able, questioning people with ideas begin to be used; opportunities are created for personal and professional development of a sort that is lacking especially in the field of nursing . . . And more than this, experience has shown that self discipline is created at the business end of the organisation of a quality that could never be imposed.

The Consultant Role in Psycho-Geriatric Care

Oliver Hodgson

Psychiatry, like general medicine, has recently discovered that the problems of the elderly are no longer a side issue which can largely be ignored.

The chronic patients in a large mental hospital are no longer young and middle-aged schizophrenics; they are now elderly dements, most of whom have not grown old in hospital but have been admitted only a short time previously. The number of these patients is increasing; in addition to this their age of admission is also increasing, so that these elderly patients come into hospital not at 65 but at 75 and even 85. When they are admitted, therefore, they are often in a very frail condition. This means that they need more resources to care for them. These resources have never been very adequate and are not expanding fast enough. Because there is no cure for old age, traditional medical methods of treatment are not always very helpful. But if the hospital only phases out these traditional methods of treatment, then the staff are liable to become unhappy and frustrated.

This is one of the classical situations which can occur in any institution. With mounting frustration, morale will decline; this decline in morale will not long be confined to the old people's wards. It will spread throughout the hospital, and in the end will affect the treatment of all other types of psychiatric patients. It is therefore a problem for the psychiatric hospital as a whole, and the whole organisation must therefore be prepared to give the geriatric unit its help, support and understanding. It is only with this internal support that the geriatric units in a hospital can give their full attention to their proper tasks: namely helping the hospital to care for the elderly and supplementing the community services in providing a comprehensive service for the elderly mentally infirm.

All those working in the geriatric unit are part of a team: this team therefore consists of medical, paramedical staff, nurses and administrators; and each has of course a different role to play in the team. The purpose in this contribution is to consider what is the role of the senior doctor, the consultant psychiatrist, who has perforce a very important role to play, because he is the person legally responsible for all the patients under his care.

Very often he cannot give individual attention to every patient (often several hundreds) on the units. He must therefore delegate part of his responsibility to other medical staff and to the nursing staff. This will necessitate unit teams carefully analysing their work, and classifying this into nursing tasks, medical tasks or even the tasks that are best left to the administration. Even when the consultant understands clearly what is his primary medical task, the consultant will have to realise that he is, as his name implies, a consultant and therefore he must be freely available to be consulted by every member of the team, and he must not try to do the work of the whole team. He must

therefore satisfy himself that all members of the team are competent;
but once this is done he must trust the team to consult him; and to
make himself approachable in order that they may do this if they wish.

The geriatric team is there to aid the community services in dealing
with the difficult task of helping the elderly mentally infirm: the team
therefore must liaise with the community services and set up with them
common standards for the assessment of the need for inpatient treatment. Inpatient resources are bound to be stretched. They must
therefore be rationed out carefully, but even when this is done there
may still be friction and misunderstanding. It is in these areas in which
the consultant will be most needed. He will thus have to be approachable not only by the geriatric team but also by the community services,
and also be trusted by both.

He will have to defend the actions of his staff on the geriatric unit
to those working outside the hospital; he will have to respond
immediately to a crisis in the community and use his skills and
knowledge to solve it. This may even mean over-riding the decisions of
his own team; this will be his hardest task, to do this in such a way that
he does not forfeit the trust of his team; he must therefore be
consistent, and, when he has special knowledge and skills in directions
which the team does not cover, use this skill in a positive way in a
manner which is never demeaning to others.

Inside the unit he will have to set treatment goals and educate staff
as to what is possible, and what is not possible. Teaching the elderly
new skills is a well-nigh impossible task, but re-educating the elderly to
regain lost skills and interests is always possible, and sometimes the
most rewarding, as is helping them to feel that there is some purpose in
each day, and that their lives still have some dignity and meaning.

To achieve these goals means that on occasions the team may have
to admit that traditional medical treatments, such as the use of drugs,
are not of primary importance. The elderly need an opportunity to do
things. They want activity and work, and in many cases they value
these more highly than drugs and other complicated forms of treatment.
It is therefore important for the geriatric teams to be aware of this, so
that they can treat every patient in the unit all the time, and not just
the few who need the more traditional medical and psychiatric skills of
the team.

It is with these goals in mind that the geriatric unit at Fulbourn
has been trying to function. This unit cares for 300 patients all over
65 years of age. All the patients on the unit have been encouraged to
do something. Whenever possible patients have been sent to one of two

day-centres, one for the better-preserved, where they can do part-time
industrial work; packing plastic plugs, packing dressings for the local
general hospital, and spending the rest of the time in other activities
such as games, music, etc. The money that is earned is used to give all
the patients on the unit outings and other small luxuries, so that they
all benefit from the work performed in this day centre. The second
centre is for the less well-preserved; these patients play simple games,
perform physical activities, sing songs, go on outings, etc., which
enable them to keep active and stimulated. Disuse causes the atrophy
of mental functions just as surely as it does of physical powers.

When it is realised that 90 per cent of the patients on the unit can
benefit from these activities, the unit staff begin to realise that they
need not only their traditional medical and nursing skills, but also the
new skills of a specialised rehabilitator of the elderly; and that there is
just as much skill needed for the rehabilitation of the elderly as there
was in the rehabilitation of polio victims in pre-vaccine days.

With the need to liaise with the community services comes the need
for the hospital staff to go into the community; and by going into the
community the unit staff realise how valuable are those skills which
they have acquired inside the hospital; and how little do those outside
the hospital in the community know about the handling and the
rehabilitation of the elderly. Their skills, gained in hospital, can be used
to prevent admission, reduce tension in the home, solve family crises
and aid the return of patients into the community from hospital. With
these new abilities staff gain in morale and take pride in their work;
and enable student nurses to feel that the care of the elderly mentally
infirm is a worthwhile branch of psychiatry, in which there is still
much to be discovered.

Change never comes easily, it is almost always forced on us. The
changes which have just been outlined have happened in the geriatric
unit at Fulbourn Hospital in the last three to four years. They have
happened because the staff there were forced to examine why the
problems on the unit were growing and not diminishing. Four years ago
the unit was hospital oriented; admission to the unit almost invariably
meant long-term care. There was a long waiting list; the community
services seldom liaised in an effective way with the hospital staff, and
were mainly perceived by the hospital staff as people who were trying
to force old people into hospital and who did not care what happened
so long as they shed the burden.

In the last four years much of this has changed: community services
come into the hospital and they now have beds there which they can

use as they think best; the hospital staff now go regularly into the houses of ex- and prospective patients to offer help and advice; most patients are admitted for short-term care only. The waiting list has been reduced and the unit is able to meet more promptly some of the community's needs.

This does not mean that all the problems have been solved; the number of elderly patients is slowly and steadily rising. Resources in the NHS and the local authorities have been pruned because of recent economic difficulties. It is still difficult to meet all the needs for permanent day care, but something can now be done either by visiting, day-care in the new purpose-built day centre, or short-term care to meet some of the community's needs; and the situation today is better and the unit staff are happier because of these changes in methods.

The Experience of Grass Roots Participants

The extent to which the approaches advocated by senior staff like Maurice Fenn and Oliver Hodgson were in fact realised, needs of course to be tested against the experience of other participants in the hospital and the kind of innovative activity which was generated. Particularly important here are the views of junior staff. As Maurice Fenn has argued, these staff have the most sustained contact with patients. They may also share with patients similar experiences of the impact of the larger organisation on their own capacity for initiative and informed action.

This exploration of junior staff views begins with a vignette on his personal experience of nurse training on Denbigh Ward, supplied by Tony Widdowson (one of the contributors to Chapter 3). It can be anticipated that work on this ward would be influenced by the leadership offered by both the principal nursing officer and the responsible consultant psychiatrist. Tony recalls:

> When I was first told I was going to a psycho-geriatric ward I thought 'O Hell, give me a shovel and a bucket'. The thought of going around clearing up after grotty old senile girls did not appeal to me. It is a thought that does not appeal to many people.
>
> Most people, it seems, are under the impression that geriatric and psycho-geriatric nursing involves mainly boring, routine work. Fighting against something you cannot stop, that is, the onset of old age and death; working yourself to the bone and getting nowhere fast. How wrong can people be!
>
> During the first week I spent on Denbigh ward, my whole attitude

towards this type of nursing changed. On arriving on Denbigh ward, I found to my surprise, that the staff there were undertaking a project. They had just finished the first part, a time study on the staff, and were discussing how to tackle the second part, a patient assessment. This was entirely devised and carried out by the nursing staff on Denbigh ward, with some helpful advice and encouragement from Clive Harries, in the role of research adviser.

'Wow' I thought, 'we really are doing something for these people!' This must have been the first time I had ever thought of these people as being actual people.

It was then that my thoughts and attitudes towards psycho-geriatrics began to change. During my stay on Denbigh, being part of a team involved in changing the ward programme and helping to change the patients' way of life, gave me an incredible amount of personal satisfaction and pleasure. Seeing a patient lay the table or going to the toilet, dressing herself and washing herself, things that she would not have done on her own a few weeks ago. And to think that I helped her to achieve this.

I did not want to leave Denbigh when my time there had finished. Things were still happening there. We were talking about taking the assessment outside to prospective admissions. I still keep in contact with the ward, visiting whenever I can. The people there may not remember me, but the feeling I get when I see how much these ladies have improved, fills me with a great warmth. I shall look back on Denbigh as a time which was very enjoyable and gave me a great deal of insight into old age and its problems.

As Tony implies, the considerable difficulties associated with the care of the elderly, and prior stereotypes about what this is likely to entail are such that even modest opportunities for staff to do something positive can release quite substantial amounts of energy, initiative, and concern, to the extent perhaps of then obscuring the intractable nature of some of these problems.

Alongside the enthusiasm and stimulation which Tony and other junior staff experienced, there was also recognition of the important learning opportunities which participation in project activities offered, both in the sense of providing experiences which would not otherwise be available and also in giving junior staff the chance to contribute and test out their ideas in a practical context. As Felicity Matthews, the administrative trainee who made the main contribution to the project which investigated ward satisfaction with the supplies services, was

able to identify, this work had contributed to her own development as
a future manager in at least four ways:

> I learnt about the organisation of administrative work, through the
> need to work very closely to a brief, organise my methods of
> research, and act as secretary to the project committee. I gained a
> much greater awareness than is usually possible for administrative
> trainees of how a psychiatric hospital functions, particularly because
> the research allowed me to work directly with a wide range of ward
> staff. I learnt a lot about hospital organisation, including the
> significance of political factors, through seeing how my research was
> commissioned and the report acted upon. And most important of all,
> I learnt directly about human relations through the need as an out-
> sider to build up a feeling of trust with all the staff involved.

These and other vignettes supplied by junior staff provide one
source of information about the way HIP was experienced at the grass
roots of Fulbourn, and the view of this work held by some junior staff.
In testing out how far a 'culture of self-innovation' had really been
generated throughout the hospital however, a wider and more
representative sampling of views would have been helpful. Here it was
fortunate that during 1974 a large sample (58) of the trainee nurses
at Fulbourn were included within a comparative interview study of
similar numbers of such nurses in seven hospitals, being undertaken by
sociologists employed by another Health Authority. Anne Long and
John Pushkin (1976) have generously supplied the data from their
study, which show clear differences between the views of Fulbourn
trainees and those of the staff of most other hospitals in their set.
They report as follows:

'Data have been collected on staff responses to a number of key
issues affecting nurses in their work. This material has been analysed
to point up how views on these issues varied between hospitals. Thus
Table 7.1 shows the responses of trainee nurses to a question about
how well the work they do on the wards is related to the patients'
needs. In each table, the last column shows the distribution of responses
from Fulbourn nurses. It will be seen that eighty-eight per cent of
Fulbourn trainee nurses, compared with an average of seventy-eight
per cent at the other six hospitals, said that the work they did on the
wards related well or very well to the patients' needs. Table 7.2
similarly shows responses to a question about whose job it is to ensure

Table 7.1: Responses of Trainee Nurses (per cent) to Question of How Well the Work they do on the Wards is Related to the Patients' Needs

HOSPITAL	1	2	3	4	5	6	F
Very well	17.9	25.5	15.0	17.9	10.5	32.1	22.8
Well	60.7	54.5	60.0	58.9	64.9	50.9	64.9
Unsure	16.1	10.9	11.7	12.5	3.5	13.2	7.0
Badly	5.4	5.5	11.7	10.7	17.5	3.8	5.3
Very badly	0.0	3.6	1.7	0.0	3.5	0.0	0.0

Table 7.2: Responses of Trainee Nurses to Question of Whose Job it is to ensure Patients Receive the Best Possible Care

HOSPITAL	1	2	3	4	5	6	F
Self	16	22	21	18	19	19	22
Nursing staff	10	1	3	6	14	10	3
Nurse in charge	32	21	33	23	22	30	14
Teamwork	1	6	2	9	1	3	24
Senior staff	1	4	3	1	5	2	2
Doctors	2	1	6	3	5	6	5
Others	3	4	–	2	3	2	5
Total number of responses	65	59	68	62	69	72	75

Table 7.3: Responses of Trainee Nurses (per cent) to Question of How Well the Behaviour of Senior Nursing Staff is Related to the Position They Hold

HOSPITAL	1	2	3	4	5	6	F
Well related	9.3	21.1	15.3	19.6	21.1	31.5	34.5
Related	35.3	33.3	42.4	33.9	28.1	22.2	41.4
Unsure	27.8	33.3	20.3	23.2	5.3	35.2	13.8
Not well related	24.1	10.5	22.0	19.6	40.4	9.3	10.3
Not at all related	3.7	1.8	0.0	3.6	5.3	1.9	0.0

that patients receive the best possible care. Most striking here is the finding that while Fulbourn and other nurses are alike in emphasising their own responsibility for patient care, Fulbourn staff are notably more inclined to see 'teamwork' as significant, with apparently a correspondingly reduced dependence on the 'nurse in charge'.

Several questions explored junior staff views about their relationships with more senior nursing staff. As shown in Table 7.3, seventy-six per cent of trainees at Fulbourn felt that the behaviour of senior nursing staff was appropriate to the positions they hold, compared with an average of fifty-two per cent of trainees at the other hospitals. In discussion, nurses at Fulbourn also indicated their favourable attitudes towards senior nursing staff and were much less likely than staff elsewhere to complain about the hierarchical nature of nursing. These differences between hospitals were evident in relation to responses on three other questions, shown in Tables 7.4, 7.5 and 7.6. Thus from Table 7.4, it will be seen that sixty-one per cent of nurses at Fulbourn felt that senior nursing staff were concerned a lot about their welfare, compared with an average of only twenty-one per cent at the other hospitals. Similar differences emerged on questions about how easy it was to talk to senior staff (Table 7.5) and how satisfactory they were in responding to work problems (Table 7.6).

Tables 7.7 and 7.8 show responses to two further questions in which substantial differences between hospitals again are evident. Thus, eighty-five per cent of trainee nurses at Fulbourn compared with an average forty-four per cent at the other hospitals, thought that the channels of communication open to nurses for the expression of grievances were adequate or very adequate (Table 7.7). Equally striking, ninety-one per cent of Fulbourn nurses compared with an average of fifty-nine per cent of the nurses at other hospitals, considered that senior nurses would sometimes or always act upon their suggestions (Table 7.8).

In addition, nurses in the different hospitals responded to a Likert job satisfaction scale. Fulbourn nurses gave scores totalling 63 out of a possible (high satisfaction) 80, suggesting a high degree of satisfaction with their work, and certainly significantly higher (t test, $p < .05$) than nurses at any of the six other hospitals.

Finally, those trainees who said they planned to continue in psychiatric nursing after qualification, were asked whether they intended to nurse in their training hospital. Table 7.9 shows that at Fulbourn twenty-seven nurses had this intention, while only four responded in the negative.

In interpreting these interesting comparative findings it is necessary to keep in mind that Long and Pushkin's independent study was concerned with morale and communication structure, rather than with a direct assessment of HIP. Moreover these data provide a 1974 snapshot

Table 7.4: Responses of Trainee Nurses (per cent) to Question about How Much Concern Senior Staff Show for their Welfare

HOSPITAL	1	2	3	4	5	6	F
A lot	19.6	19.6	18.3	27.8	15.8	23.1	61.1
A little	23.2	25.0	51.7	37.0	45.6	28.8	22.2
Unsure	14.3	37.5	10.0	9.3	7.0	21.2	9.3
Not a lot	17.9	12.5	13.3	9.3	15.8	21.2	5.6
Not at all	25.0	5.4	6.7	16.7	15.8	5.8	1.9

Table 7.5: Responses of Trainee Nurses (per cent) to Question about How Easy it is to Talk to Senior Nursing Staff

HOSPITAL	1	2	3	4	5	6	F
Very easy	15.8	29.8	25.0	23.2	12.3	37.0	54.5
Easy	42.1	47.4	38.3	64.3	54.4	40.7	40.4
Unsure	21.2	17.5	20.0	5.4	5.3	7.4	3.5
Not very easy	19.3	3.5	16.7	3.6	21.1	14.8	1.8
Not at all easy	1.8	1.8	0.0	3.6	7.0	0.0	0.0

Table 7.6: Responses of Trainee Nurses (per cent) to Question about the Kind of Answers Senior Staff give in relation to Work Problems

HOSPITAL	1	2	3	4	5	6	F
Very satisfactory	18.5	17.9	10.2	9.3	3.6	29.6	19.3
Satisfactory	44.4	46.4	47.5	53.7	58.2	38.9	66.7
Unsure	18.5	19.6	25.4	22.2	12.7	13.0	5.3
Unsatisfactory	14.8	16.1	13.6	13.0	25.5	14.8	8.8
Very unsatisfactory	3.7	0.0	3.4	1.9	0.0	3.7	0.0

Table 7.7: Responses of Trainee Nurses (per cent) to Question about the Adequacy of Channels that Allow Trainees to Express Grievances

HOSPITAL	1	2	3	4	5	6	F
Very adequate	3.8	4.1	3.4	3.6	2.0	9.6	32.1
Adequate	37.7	40.8	37.3	44.6	34.7	42.3	52.8
Unsure	17.0	18.4	18.6	23.2	10.2	21.2	3.8
Not very adequate	22.6	32.7	27.1	17.9	36.7	13.5	11.3
Not at all adequate	18.9	4.1	13.6	10.7	16.3	13.5	0.0

Table 7.8: Responses of Trainee Nurses (per cent) to Question about Senior Staff Reactions to Suggestions made by Trainees

HOSPITAL	1	2	3	4	5	6	F
Always act upon them	0.0	10.9	0.0	3.6	1.8	5.7	12.3
Sometimes act upon them	62.5	52.7	50.0	58.9	53.6	56.6	78.9
Unsure	8.9	18.2	23.3	14.3	1.8	18.9	3.5
Rarely act upon them	19.6	9.1	18.3	14.3	37.5	15.1	5.3
Never act upon them	8.9	9.1	8.3	8.9	5.4	3.8	0.0

Table 7.9: Responses of Trainee Nurses to Question of Whether They Intend to Continue Psychiatric Nursing in their Training Hospital

HOSPITAL	1	2	3	4	5	6	F
Yes	12	21	20	19	8	28	27
No	18	10	13	17	20	7	4
Unsure	12	4	18	18	4	8	13
Total	52	35	51	54	32	43	44

of the views of staff, most of whom would have joined Fulbourn during the pilot stage of HIP; it does not show how far the culture at Fulbourn had changed during that period. Neither does it show of course, how junior staff views have changed in the subsequent three years of post-reorganisation difficulty described by Clive Harries in the preceding chapter.

Even with these reservations, however, the data reported here do appear to provide significant and unsolicited evidence of the existence by the end of the pilot stage of HIP of a set of approaches and attitudes at ward level which were demonstrably different from those in many other hospitals. Summarised briefly and without inferring too much, trainee nursing staff at Fulbourn were more likely than similar staff elsewhere to regard themselves or their staff team as responsible for patient care; to take a favourable view of the roles assumed and concern shown by senior nursing staff, along a number of dimensions including their openness of communication, their responsiveness to junior staff suggestions, and their helpfulness with work problems; and perhaps as a consequence of all these points, to have high job satisfaction and see their own work as well related to the needs of patients.

In short, the views of junior nurses about work and relationships at Fulbourn were fully consistent on this evidence with the key aspects of hospital organisation and culture which David Towell's analysis in Chapter 6 suggested as important achievements of the pilot stage.

Two further observations are pertinent here. Three senior staff from other hospitals who attended the King's Fund Conference on HIP in 1973 commented in their published report (Sutherland, J.G. et al, 1974):

> In the course of discussion on the Project, conference participants were continually reminded of the importance of people in an organisational structure, especially where change was desired. What the Project at Fulbourn has achieved is to provide the means for meaningful involvement of staff at various levels in the decision-making processes which will have direct effect upon their primary work goals and, by changing staff attitudes to their roles, has introduced a dynamism unachievable in a traditional 'top-down' management structure.

At around the same time, two members of the Hospital Advisory Service team which had originally suggested the HIP experiment, made a return visit to Fulbourn to assess progress and the value of this approach more widely in improving standards of care. Dr Tom Riordan recorded this view:

> The main value of the Project appears to lie in the experience and skills acquired by the staff in the process of participation . . . While it is not likely to have direct application in other hospitals unless the hospitals have well established multidisciplinary treatment teams and a top management supportive to the Project, it has a lesson for the less well endowed hospitals which, in the first instance, must concentrate on developing satisfactory multidisciplinary treatment teams as being the quickest and most effective way of having attention drawn to problems of patient care . . . The general principle of seeking to create conditions of work in which staff were encouraged to accept responsibility for drawing attention to problems and difficulties, to be able to get help and, if necessary, participate in defining and clarifying problems and indeed of solving them, should have application in all hospitals, even those less well endowed and less receptive than Fulbourn.

However, it may be realistic to approach these observations and findings with some capacity for continuing scepticism. The views of staff and other professionals need to be tempered through attention to the views of other parties to the system of psychiatric care: directly or vicariously, patients, relatives and the wider community, can each be regarded as grass roots participants in this system. Indeed, it may be helpful to locate staff attitudes in the context of a larger pattern, in which related but not necessarily similar feelings about care are distributed among these various parties. Thus, returning for example to services for the elderly, we have seen how the Denbigh project mobilised positive aspects of staff attitudes towards old people in seeking to develop more appropriate forms of care. Outside hospital too there is public ambivalence towards the elderly: there is evidence that old people are neglected and rejected; there is guilt about this failure of support; and there is also much genuine care provided.

In this light, it was possible to identify some vicarious involvement in the Denbigh project from a wider public reaction, which seemed to embody a strong desire to perceive these worthwhile efforts as something truly remarkable. As the *Cambridge News* reported under the heading 'Fulbourn: old people learn to live again':

A unique staff-management project at Fulbourn Hospital is keeping many old people out of the hospital who would otherwise have been admitted as 'psychogeriatric' patients. The project could revolutionise the care of the old and mentally ill.

The results of the two-year-old experiment have astonished staff. They have found that many patients previously written off, now find themselves making tea, washing their smalls, making their beds and doing the bits and pieces they would normally have done at home . . .

The response from the patients has led staff to wonder how many patients in the past have been written off as 'psychogeriatric' when in fact their 'senility' was nothing more than a symptom of their rejection by families, a gradual withdrawal by the old person from the hurt of his or her surroundings.

While one of the paper's readers in similar vein responded:

The article was wonderful. I only hope the whole of Cambridge residents will take the matter to heart. I have taken the opportunity of posting a copy to Mrs. Barbara Castle and other members of

Parliament whom I trust will see the necessity of a grand and quick
end to the awful plight of our own elderly sick (parents?) and/or
neighbours.

But even where substantial improvements have been made in
standards of care, it is as well to be reminded of the relativity of these
standards, and the very different perceptions which patients and their
relatives may have. In a letter to 'Mind Out', the husband of a woman
who was cared for and died on this ward, described the great
difficulties he saw in providing adequate care, particularly when the
ward was not fully staffed:

Let me say that the food at Fulbourn is excellent and in abundance:
the accommodation more than adequate and the care (what there is
of it) dedicated and compassionate. In retrospect, had I had £500
per week to spend on her at a private nursing home, I would far and
away rather have had her a patient at this fine institution . . . [But]
after several visits to the long stay ward which was in the charge of
a truly dedicated and highly competent qualified young man, one
fact was obvious to the meanest intelligence – namely the appalling
shortage of nursing and domestic staff . . . Are those in authority
going to continue to sit with their heads in the ground, waiting for
the inevitable major catastrophe to occur? Can there be any shadow
of doubt that the imperative need of additional nursing and domestic
staff at all our psychiatric hospitals is number A1 priority?

In different vein, but further illuminating the links between the
experience of clients and the social structure of the hospital, the final
word here on Fulbourn in this period comes from the published
account (Crockett, 1974) of a patient's perspective on life in an
admission ward. She writes:

Getting better was a slow process but one which was based on
individual and communal efforts between both sick patients and
caring staff. The modern admission unit to which I had been
assigned, was set a little apart from the main group of buildings.
Here patients entered a ward and became part of a small community
linked through group activities to the other three wards. It was a
unit designed to help reintegrate people back into society and,
therefore, the running of the ward was geared to the needs of the
patients rather than the other way about. The result was an apparent

lack of order, a freedom to do as one pleased, which must have seemed to a stranger's eyes a little bewildering and in marked contrast to other types of hospitals . . .

Some people dressed more or less soberly, according to their taste; others remained in night attire or in a dressing-gown. Nobody was told to get dressed but eventually the desire to build up self respect provided the momentum to do so. In this way a step forward was made on the road to recovery through no prompting from the staff. True, this was only a beginning, but it was the way back to the shining light of reality.

Movement towards this goal was slow and uneven but contact with the community was essential and involved the whole of one's personality . . . Through the breakdown of the power of coherent thought, through depression and anxiety, a better perspective on the balance of the human mind could grow into the future and flourish in helpful and meaningful relationships.

8 AUTONOMY, DEPENDENCY AND ORGANISATIONAL CHANGE

Eric J. Miller

My experience of the Hospital Innovation Project at Fulbourn has been part-time and largely second-hand. I helped David Towell to formulate the original proposal; I acted as consultant to him in his role of social research adviser, especially in the earlier stages when he was trying to forge a role that would enable him to work both with the overt needs of his client groups and with some of the more covert demands they were making on him; and I was an adviser to the Steering Committee for the first three years. Meanwhile I have continued other consultancy and research. Some of it has been in the health services, with a particular focus on long-stay hospitals; some in industry and some in government. Much of the work in this last category has been in Third World countries, where one pressing interest has been in government programmes for rural development. Alongside these activities has been an involvement at the Tavistock Institute with a particular approach to group relations training, in which we try to help participants to explore in depth the interplay between individuality and membership of a group or organisation.

Practically all this work, HIP included, relates to the problem that organisations have in using and developing the resources and potentialities of people. But it is people who make organisations. Hence I see my concern in terms of helping individuals and groups to discover and use their authority. Thus a central — perhaps *the* central — message of HIP is that the group of staff actually working on a job have the requisite knowledge and authority themselves to examine it critically and to seek new and more effective ways of performing the task; and they may indeed question the accepted definition of the task itself.

One major theme of this chapter, therefore, is 'autonomy'. I shall be expanding on the meaning of that term; but for the moment let me express it in the form of a simple hypothesis:

> The greater the control that the worker himself exerts over the productive process, the greater his job satisfaction and the better his performance.

172

This is no new discovery and the evidence for it is overwhelming. Recently for example, an American team analysed the findings of about 600 research studies conducted over the previous 15 years on organisational factors affecting job satisfaction and productivity. To quote from their summary of findings:

> the theme of *autonomy* emerges as a significant organisational factor related to both satisfaction and productivity. The concept of autonomy appears as an important aspect of the work itself, the nature of superior-subordinate relations, and the organisational climate of work.

With proper scientific caution they point out that 'correlational results do not demonstrate causality', but nevertheless:

> the predominance of autonomy over many of the studies suggests that it is a potentially effective action lever for improving productivity and the quality of working life (Srivastva et al, 1975, p. xvi).

So we have here a conception that seems to have everything on its side. There is the immediate pragmatic argument: organisations that make better use of their human resources tend to carry out their tasks more effectively. There is the wider social justification: organisational misuse of people and consequent alienation incur a high social cost. And more generally this is in tune with contemporary values: people matter; human dignity and rights must be respected; older notions of boss-worker relations are exploitative. On this basis one might expect sweeping changes to be taking place in a whole range of organisations. Reality, however, as the reader will know, does not support that expectation. First, successful experiments like HIP are rare. Second, the changes achieved, notwithstanding their evident benefits, often remain precarious — and, in this, HIP is not exempt. Third, there seems to be immense difficulty in disseminating innovations.

Why should this be so? Why should this 'potentially effective action lever' be so little used? One factor is that it poses managers, whether in industry or in the health service, with a discomfiting paradox. Their wish, understandably, is to maximise their control over their subordinates' activities — for example, what the factory worker does to the product or what the nurse does to the patient. This leads to a mechanistic and hierarchical model of management, in which each action is precisely controlled and monitored. The idea that *loosening* of control may enhance performance seems to fly in the face of common sense. So even where there are signs of willingness to permit autonomy there is usually also a wish to limit its influence. Thus a question that I and fellow social scientists are often asked runs like this: 'How can the people under me be motivated to change their attitudes/behave more responsibly/increase their productivity . . .?' Nearly always there is an unspoken qualifying clause: '. . . without my having to consider any changes in my own attitudes or behaviour.' My response is to try to help the enquirer examine the total system of behaviour, including his own contribution to it. If he persists in defending his own role as inviolable, I send him elsewhere.

So this is a second theme that I shall be considering in this chapter — the need to make a more rigorous analysis of existing systems than is usually undertaken. Local innovations can seldom, if ever, be sustained unless there are also consistent changes, structural and cultural, in the wider system. Let me give one illustration. A rehabilitative strategy for geriatric patients — as we saw in the case of Denbigh Ward at Fulbourn Hospital — leads to a questioning of comfortingly familiar routines and to a ward that does not live up to conventional standards of tidiness. Risks are also involved: a frail patient encouraged to walk may fall and break a limb, which can lead to complaints from relatives; if she is tucked dependently and safely into bed, there is no such danger. How many hospitals ostensibly pursue a strategy of rehabilitation and at the same time use tidy wards and absence of complaints as criteria of good nursing?

Inconsistencies of this kind in different parts of a system can be seen as reflecting ambivalence towards change. I have been emphasising managers' hesitations about the consequences of 'autonomy' for conventional superior-subordinate relations; but the managed too may find such changes disconcerting. A particular aspect of organisational systems that needs examination is the way in which they cater for quite basic dependency needs of those involved. A system of activities set up to perform a task also provides a system of defences for those who perform it; and if, as in many health care systems, the task itself is painful, dependency relationships are a significant part of the defensive structure.

This leads then to my third theme. Since an innovation geared towards autonomy is highly likely to threaten established dependency structures, what steps can we take to look after the dependency that gets dislodged, as it were, during the transitional period, while both the task system and the defensive system are being re-formed? This problem is insufficiently appreciated; and I shall be suggesting that we have to think specifically about providing roles for this purpose during a process of change.

In the rest of this chapter, therefore, I shall first expand on the meaning of 'autonomy', drawing on experience from widely different contexts. I shall then discuss particular aspects of systems engaged in patient care which pose problems of securing and maintaining changes. Thirdly, I shall say something about leadership and consultancy in change processes. I hope in this way to illuminate the conditions for success in sustaining the HIP and for approaches like this to be developed in other settings.

The Meaning of 'Autonomy'

A pioneering experiment in forming autonomous work-groups was conducted in India by a late colleague of mine, A.K. Rice, in 1953-4. This illustrates what is involved in re-designing systems of work organisation and at the same time highlights difficulties that arise in trying to transfer an innovation.

> The original experimental site was a textile company in Ahmedabad, where automatic looms had been introduced into a weaving shed. Output was much lower and damage much higher than had been hoped. Rice found that the weaving process had been broken down into component elements assigned to nine grades of workers, who were individually accountable to two shed supervisors. Rice proposed the idea of a group of workers taking responsibility for all the weaving tasks on a group of looms and having authority as a group to manage themselves. The nine grades would be reduced to three and a form of group payment introduced. Shed supervisors and workers grabbed the idea and spontaneously formed four experimental groups. These quickly reached a higher level of performance and new groups were formed with similar success. After six months, however, there was a sharp decline. Investigation showed that the groups had been faced with a combination of adverse factors — for example, an excessive range of different cloths in any one group and the induction of untrained workers — as a result of which they had regressed to individual modes of working. Once corrective measures had been taken, output and quality quickly recovered, and so also did job satisfaction; and the new high norms of performance were sustained over several years. An experiment on non-automatic looms achieved comparable success.

Accounts of the experiments were published (Rice, 1953, 1955a, 1955b, 1958, 1963) and became widely known, both locally and internationally. Locally, some other mills in Ahmedabad instituted similar forms of group working, but failed to achieve the expected results.

Much later, in 1970, another colleague and I returned to the original company to assess the long-term outcomes. We found that, even within the company, later attempts to extend the 'group system', as it was called, had either achieved only mediocre results or failed entirely. In one of the original experimental loom-sheds, the form of group working had remained unaltered over the 16 years and performance was as high as ever; in the other, some degradation had occurred (Miller 1975). One reason for lack of success in spreading this innovation was undoubtedly the fact that attempts were made to transplant the *form* of group working, without sufficient regard to the *processes* involved in the original experiments.

Essentially, Rice had put forward working hypotheses, indicating a possible alternative form of organisation that would satisfy the needs of both task and people; workers and supervisors themselves, through experimentation and discussion, had played an active part in design and development of the group system. It was a process that recognised from the outset the *authority* of the workers to take such a role, and this in itself was a significant innovation in the hierarchical culture of Indian industrial organisations (and indeed of most work organisations elsewhere). A second, related factor was that the conception of the form to be transplanted was almost certainly too narrow.

Given that internal management of the system was now vested in the group of workers, the role of the supervisor had to be reconceptualised. It was no longer appropriate to think of him as telling individuals what to do and making sure that they did it. His job was to provide the *boundary conditions* within which the group could manage itself. That is to say, he had to ensure that the group was equipped with the necessary resources to perform its task: trained workers, spare parts for the looms, yarn in the right quality and quantity for weaving, and so on. Management of progressively wider systems was conceived in the same way. In such a conception, if performance declines and/or the group reverts to a more rigid internal division of labour, this is taken as presumptive evidence that the necessary boundary conditions are not being sustained. When such symptoms are observed, the sophisticated managerial response is to reduce the sources of disturbances imported

across the boundary of the system — for example, poor quality or
excessive variability of inputs — and to reinforce the internal resources
of the system — for example, by attending to training of personnel and
maintenance of machinery.

This is precisely what happened when the first experiment had been
running for six months, and as a result of that regression and
subsequent investigation it became possible to specify much more
accurately the boundary conditions within which the groups could
be expected to retain their resilience. When my colleague and I looked
at the degradation that had occurred in this same loom-shed by 1970,
it became apparent that the requisite boundary conditions had not
been sustained — for example, sub-standard spare parts were being
supplied — and also that the supervisory role had shifted. Instead of
transmitting pressure through their superiors to the suppliers, the
supervisors intervened within the groups to try to get individuals to
work harder. By doing this, they further helped to destroy the
resilience of the groups as self-managing systems and made it inevitable
that norms of performance would drop (Miller 1975).

Rice's experiments in 1953-4 therefore implied a re-thinking of the
meaning of 'management' which in some ears still sounds radical more
than 20 years later. Management as an activity is not the preserve of an
elite with the title and status of managers. Every individual employee
may be conceived as being a 'manager' in two senses. First, he manages
the boundary between himself as a person and his role: he determines
what skills, attitudes, feelings and other internal resources he will devote
to the role and what he will withhold. Secondly, he manages his
activities within the role and his transactions with other role-holders.
In practice the individual will act as a manager in both these senses:
the issue is whether space will be made for him to do so in the service
of the task of the enterprise by giving him a role which has attached to
it a sufficient range of discretion within which he can legitimately
exercise his authority. Paradoxical though it may seem, the wide range
of discretion, as opposed to tight definition of roles in a mechanistic
framework, is likely to *increase* the viability of the system and the
predictability of outcomes: if the role is closely circumscribed, the
individual is more likely to impose his own range of discretion on it
and therefore act in 'illegitimate' ways.

If everyone is a manager, then the role that we more conventionally
think of as managerial changes its meaning. Instead of vague notions
of man-management, with its heroic or manipulative connotations —
depending on one's point of view — we have to conceive of system

management. The managerial role is located on the boundary of a
system or sub-system and is concerned with regulating the linkages
between the internal activities of the system and its external environment. It is then the job of the manager to establish the task of the
system and to provide the boundary conditions within which members
working in it can manage their own roles and relationships in such a
way as to produce effective performance of the task. His authority,
like the authority of people within the system, is derived not from
status and power but from the task itself.

Rice's early experiments therefore give some practical and
operational meaning to the notion of autonomy and make it clear that
a group of weavers (or, for that matter, a group of nurses) cannot
extend their authority to manage themselves in their own roles without
consequential changes for managerial roles in the wider system of which
they are a part. Both structural and cultural changes are involved, each
needing the other.

I can perhaps illustrate this from much more recent work on rural
development in Latin America — an experience which is not quite so
remote and irrelevant as it might appear at first sight. I have found it
useful to define 'under-development' as: 'relative lack of control over
relations with one's environment'. Most development projects concen-
trate on helping the peasant community to extend its control over
recognised and unrecognised resources in its internal environment.
Health schemes and adult literacy programmes are designed to enhance
the human resources of the community; agricultural extension services
introduce new seeds, use of fertilisers and pesticides, and new methods
of cultivation in general; and investment may be made in irrigation
schemes or soil conservation projects. Outcomes, however, seldom live
up to expectations. One common reason for failure is lack of
community participation in selection and design of projects. However,
even when the community has participated in this way, the enthusiasm
generated at the beginning for a project that will manifestly benefit the
community seems nevertheless in many instances to evaporate quite
quickly and the innovation is aborted.

My own observations and analysis of a number of cases in Mexico
have led me to the tentative hypothesis that changes will not take root
within a community unless they are also accompanied and reinforced
by changes in the external relations of the community with the wider
social, economic and political system. At the simplest level, new
agricultural practices or new crops do not appear very attractive if
there is no market for the products or if the added proceeds are largely

swallowed up by rapacious middlemen. On the other hand, if a community succeeds in breaking that pattern — for example, by buying a truck that will take the produce to the market and so becoming independent of the middleman — the consequent benefits are not only economic: what seems to happen is that the community acquires a new self-image of greater potency, which is confirmed by a changed external image of the community. So along with the structural changes there is a resurgence of confidence, which reverses the typical pattern of so many backward communities in which the peasants, who have in fact been subjected to a long history of exploitation, display symptoms of apathy, impotence and self-depreciation. In the case of rural development, therefore, I am now arguing that the primary task of a development agency is to help its client system — the rural community — to acquire greater control in its relations with its external environment, and that the conventional development projects must be conceived not as ends in themselves but as means to that end (Miller 1976b, 1977).

This view fits with the conclusions that a colleague and I drew from a study — much nearer home — of residential institutions for the · younger physically handicapped and chronic sick (Miller and Gwynne, 1972, 1973). We found it useful to compare institutions in terms of the kinds of roles that inmates occupied. Adults in ordinary life occupy many roles — in the family, at work, in leisure pursuits, and so on — and move from one to another. Some roles provide for the individual's needs to be dependent and looked after; others for his drives towards self-assertion and autonomy. Even within a single relationship, such as marriage, the individual shifts between varying 'sub-roles', as it were, in some of which he is more autonomous and in others more dependent.

In many of these residential establishments, however, the individual has only dependent roles open to him. In the course of his day, he is got up, washed, dressed, fed, dosed, toiletted and put to bed, and in between he lapses into a kind of limbo of rolelessness, while he waits for a staff member to take the next initiative. The inevitability of a degree of physical and emotional dependency made it seem to us the more important to make room also for 'independent' roles which catered for drives towards autonomy. In this way, the inmate could come closer to the ordinary adult experience of moving between multiple roles. In the few institutions which provided these opportunities, inmates were characterised by a much greater aliveness, especially where they were involved in transactions across the boundary of the institution and so relating to the external environment. In this way, they were taking over responsibility for transactions normally handled by staff or 'management'; and indeed the logical conclusion, which we helped one voluntary home to implement, was full inmate participation in management. Like the Mexican peasants, therefore, they were extending their control over their environment, instead of being passive victims of external forces.

The Lure of Dependency

Creation of multiple roles in residential institutions is a specific solution to a problem that has been arousing more and more public concern over the last decade: the problem of institutionalisation, depersonalisation and more overt ill-treatment in hospitals providing long-stay care for the old, the mentally ill and the mentally handicapped. Indeed, this concern dates back at least to the 'fifties and contributed to the passing of the 1959 Mental Health Act. My impression, however, is that Barbara Robb's *Sans Everything*, published in 1967, was significant in making it an issue for the public and not just for the professionals. Since then, we have had a succession of committees of enquiry, each evoking a new surge of public indignation. At first the emphasis was the neglect or sadism of individual nurses; this was then linked to gross under-provision of resources; and it is only in the reports of more recent enquiries, such as South Ockenden (1974) and St Augustine's (1976), that — without denying deficiencies of individual staff and of resources — accountability has been more directly attributed to organisational and managerial shortcomings. In my terminology, the organs of hospital management stand accused of failing to provide the boundary conditions within which ward staff can properly manage their own roles.

   To put it another way, the kind of role that Gwynne and I proposed for inmates and, more generally, the kind of treatment that it is now more widely felt should be accorded to long-stay patients, inescapably calls for a different role on the part of nurses and other caring staff. My argument would suggest, there is little possibility of nurses acquiring and sustaining such an alternative role unless there is also a change in their relationship with the wider system within which they operate, and which defines the task they are there to perform. Patients cannot exercise more autonomy unless nurses exercise more autonomy; but there are powerful forces holding patients in a dependency relationship on nurses and holding nurses in a similar relationship to doctors.

   I will first examine dependency in the patient-nurse relationship. We can make a rough distinction between mature and immature dependency relationships. In the mature relationship, I as patient or client confer my authority on a professional, whom I judge to be competent, to take care of something on my behalf. It is a form of delegation which I continue to have authority to withdraw. In the immature relationship, this may still be the formal situation; but *de facto* I surrender my authority and the professional takes me over. This is closely akin to the 'basic assumption' behaviour in groups that was identified by Bion (1961). He observed that at times groups operate as if they are seeking dependency upon an omniscient and omnipotent leader, who will satisfy all the needs of every member. This can be seen as expressing a wish for return to the security of the womb or of early infancy. It is then very tempting for the leader to fall in with this demand and so to behave as if he is more knowledgeable and more powerful than he actually is; hence a reciprocal relationship is established which confirms the inadequacy of the one party and the superiority of the other.

Many of the residential institutions we visited in the course of our study exhibited this phenomenon in a striking way. The mothering, and thus the infantilisation, of inmates by caring staff was not simply one aspect of a relationship that at other times made room for individuality and autonomy: it was the totality of the relationship. Inmates had in effect lost their boundaries as individuals and surrendered their ego functions to staff, who would typically say: 'We have to do their thinking for them.' Listless and withdrawn for much of the time, they lacked any identity of their own; they had only the identity conferred on them, as it were, by staff. Similar patterns are familiar, of course, in the back wards of many hospitals.

Now it is very easy to say that this should not happen, that it is antithetic to rehabilitative objectives or ordinary human dignity, and that nurses should be more mature; but it is by no means so easy to bring about a change. Exhortation is usually fruitless. More helpful may be an attempt to understand what it is about the system that sustains the culture of dependency. Thus as we discovered in our study of residential care it is only part of the reality to say that cripples are admitted to these institutions because they are too disabled to look after themselves or be looked after in the community. In fact they are no more handicapped, and sometimes less so, than many who remain outside. What those inside more significantly have in common is that they have been rejected. They have for the most part been rejected as individuals, in that their families are no longer willing or able to look after them. More importantly, by crossing the boundary into the institution, whether voluntarily or not, they fall into a rejected category of non-contributors to and non-participants in society' (Miller and Gwynne, 1972, p. 73).

Goffman made a similar point about psychiatric hospitals: 'the society's official view is that inmates of mental hospitals are there primarily because they are suffering from mental illness', and this provides the rationale for staff behaviour; but, he asserts, 'mental patients distinctively suffer not from mental illness but from contingencies' (Goffman, 1968, p. 126). He analyses in some depth the processes of *extrusion* from family and community and the patient's corresponding experience of *betrayal*. Inmates of these residential institutions are unlikely ever to be rehabilitated: for most of them the prognosis is progressive deterioration and death. The realities of the disabilities, the rejection and the future are almost too painful to bear, either for staff or for inmates.

So what we came to call a 'warehousing' culture of dependency, with its infantilisation and dehumanisation, provided a re-definition of reality which was less intolerable for staff to cope with. Possibly it was less intolerable too for inmates to regress to a childlike position than to come to terms with depression at the loss of ordinary adult experience. Related to this, dependency serves a function in keeping at bay emotions of anger and aggression: instead of being directed outwards against, for example, staff, these emotions are turned inwards in destruction of the self. We have here, therefore, an example of what Isabel Menzies called 'the functioning of social systems as a defence against anxiety' (Menzies, 1960). By examining the dynamics in this way, one can grasp the obstacles to change in such a setting. It is highly improbable that staff would take steps to alter their posture without external support; and even if they did so, the inmates for their part, far from welcoming liberation, can be expected to suck staff back into the *status quo*.

A study that colleagues and I made of geriatric hospital care disclosed a slightly different dynamic. Again, the manifest input into the system is an elderly person needing treatment. Arriving with the patient, however, are various and conflicting expectations from family and community. Indeed, the family's feelings are often ambivalent: it wants the hospital to cure, to rehabilitate and, at a less conscious level, to postpone death indefinitely, and it wants the hospital to take over the problems and provide terminal care. One way in which the hospital, as a system, may cope with this ambivalence is through an emotional division of labour. Both doctors and nurses respond to the family's rejection of the patient: the doctor, defending his limited beds from becoming clogged by long-stay patients, adopts a rigorous rehabilitative policy which compels the family or community 'to look after its own'; the nurse, empathising with the rejected patient, responds to the pressures for dependency, wishing to become the good caring person whom the patient has lacked, and in doing so tacitly opts for custodial treatment, in opposition to the more austere regime that the doctor's rehabilitative strategy demands.

Obviously I have over-simplified. What I am concerned to illustrate, however, is the nature — and intransigence — of dependency in such health care systems. The geriatric example also further illustrates the point that change within the nurse-patient relationship is improbable unless there are also other changes, which must, in the hospital, minimally include a change in the relationship with the doctor.

Both patient and nurse invest much dependence in the doctor, especially the consultant. At least titularly, he is the leader of the treatment enterprise: he controls admissions and discharges; and he is also the carrier of the medical mystique. Notwithstanding my earlier comments, a degree of less than mature dependency in the relationship may be therapeutically necessary. With him I cannot be quite so objective about delegating my authority as I can, say, with a lawyer: faith that he can make me better may be an important ingredient in successful treatment. These little bits of faith are the building blocks of the massive dependency culture. It is epitomised in the ritual of the full-scale ward round, with the god-like consultant at the head, followed by his hierarchy of white-robed angels in descending order of rank. Most consultants are aware of the processes of deification and try to mitigate its worst effects; on the other hand, it is almost impossible to be the linchpin of a dependency structure without being seduced at times into illusions of omnipotence and omniscience.

One can put forward a number of hypotheses about nurses' needs for defences which are satisfied by this type of dependency structure. Menzies did this in the case of general hospitals. She showed that responsibility for intimate care of sick and dying patients resonated painfully with the nurse's unconscious anxieties; this made her individual defences precarious; various mechanisms in the social system of the hospital could be seen as providing supplementary shared defences against these anxieties (Menzies, 1960). The phenomena that she described are widely prevalent in other types of hospital, though each may have certain specific characteristics as well. Thus one can postulate that, inasmuch as the geriatric hospital is tacitly asked to solve, or at least to bear, the insoluble problems of ageing, death and bereavement, nurses are subjected to a heavy burden of demands for dependency, some of which they then shift onto the shoulders of the consultant. The powerful structures I have described may well appear to be intractable. Is there really any hope that nurses or patients can escape from the toils of dependency and acquire autonomy? Menzies suggests that defensive systems lead to less than optimum performance of the primary task of patient care; that this intensifies the use of the defensive systems, leading to further decline in task performance; and so on, in a deteriorating cycle. Perversely this offers a ray of hope: the situation may become so intolerable that something has to be done about it. And one thing that can be done, in my view, is to make more explicit the problems and processes of the kind that I have been discussing. The stress and pain of caring for the crippled, the old, the mad or the dying cannot be made to go away; but if they are articulated, then at least the burden can be distributed more widely. In this way the need for defensive structures, though not eliminated, may be reduced, and alternative systems may be found which, while catering for defensive needs, do so in a way that is less destructive of the autonomy of the parties concerned.

Leadership and Consultancy in Change

Let me first consider the role of the medical consultant in change. It is probably fair to say that most innovations in patient care in hospitals have come from the initiative of consultants. I have called the consultant the linchpin of the defensive dependency structure, and the metaphor is an apt one, because it is the linchpin that keeps the chariot-wheel on its axle. Unless he changes, it seems, nothing else can; but the positive side of this is that when he makes use of his charisma to introduce something new he is in a strong position to get it implemented within his system.

Paradoxically, however, while it is this charisma that makes change possible, it also makes it precarious. Although methods of working and even staff roles and relationships may have been altered, the new pattern continues to be sustained by the shared dependence of the system on the consultant. In other words, the basic dependency structure persists, and indeed the dependence on him is likely to be magnified during the uncertainties of the transition; and the consequence is that the continuance of the pattern relies on his presence. All too often, then, such innovations evaporate when the initiating consultant departs; and even when he is absent for relatively short periods regression is often observable. As I have indicated, to occupy the apex of a dependency structure is a heady and seductive experience, so that the consultant needs rigorous and continuing self-discipline to distinguish between the authority that rightly belongs to his actual competence and the fantasied powers that are imputed to him. It is a rare consultant who does this thoroughly enough to enable the nurses and patients around him to acquire and retain their own individual authority. And, even if he does so, the chances are that his less conscientious and sophisticated successor will only re-mobilise the latent pull towards dependency.

From this it follows that sustained change in the direction of autonomy cannot be localised within the system most directly affected: changes must also be brought about in the relationship between the system and the environment in which it operates. Indian weavers could not sustain their new way of working without concomitant changes in the relationships with supervisors and managers. Mexican peasants cannot establish new agricultural techniques unless they also bypass exploitative middlemen and discover a new sense of potency in their external transactions. Crippled inmates of residential establishments cannot win independent roles only by striking a new bargain with caring staff; they need to express such roles through exercising authority in relationships across the boundary with the environment; and this development will not survive unless the roles and role-relationships of caring staff are also re-cast. And correspondingly nurses in psychiatric, mental subnormality or geriatric hospitals cannot be expected to extricate themselves from immature dependency and to make room for the individuality of their patients unless they themselves not only acquire a new relationship with the consultant but also exercise greater authority across the boundaries of the system as a whole.

In order to achieve such transformations, one or preferably both of two conditions seem to be necessary. The first is the operation of a sanctioning authority which straddles both the system concerned and the relevant environment. The second I shall call 'consultancy'. These can be illustrated by going back over the examples I have used.

In the case of the weaving innovation, the boundary that I have identified as crucial was that between the new type of work-group and the supervisor. Rice's description of the original experiment in 1953 and 1954 makes it plain that he was in effect acting in a consultancy relationship with a 'vertical slice' of the organisation, from the company chairman and senior manufacturing management through to the weaving supervisors and operatives directly involved (Rice, 1958). The chairman was committed to the innovation and kept himself closely informed of progress; and in addition to the developments at shop-floor level, Rice and I helped with a wider management reorganisation of the

company, through which boundaries of organisational systems were
re-drawn and a somewhat different conception of the managerial role —
in line with my definition earlier in this chapter — began to be introduced (Rice, 1958, 1963). Hence the changes in management helped to
reinforce the 'group system'; and, as is often the case, an element of
organisational 'conscience' was vested in the consultancy role, so that
even the intermittent presence of outside consultants over several years
also reinforced both the group system and the reorganisation of management. By 1960, the consultancy had ended; the chairman, now involved
in direction of an expanded group of companies, was seldom seen inside
the mill; and the new ethos of management, which had supported the
autonomous work-groups, was gradually eroded (Miller, 1975).

The rural development scene is much more complex. In the case of
Mexico, for example, the Federal Government, in making large sums
available for rural investment, aims to remedy a history of neglect and
injustice. Thus it is providing an overall sanction for change, and it is
making new resources available for the poorer peasants; but it is not
intervening in local exploitative systems that perpetuate the poverty.
Significant change does not therefore occur unless more local leadership/
consultancy is available to help a client community acquire a greater
control over its environment. As I have written elsewhere:

> There is a need to help them discover an identity as a client
> system. One approach is through political education: they learn
> that their condition is not the result of inherent inferiority but
> the consequence of perhaps generations of oppression and
> exploitation. Dependency gets transformed into fight. However,
> this needs to be accompanied by improved social and economic
> capability. A community that relies too much on fight as its basis
> of identity and organisation is placed at risk not only by defeat
> but by victory. The other approach is the transfer of dependency
> to the benign leadership of the 'developer'. He guides his protégés
> along new paths of economic development and secures their
> commitment to new activities and methods. Here the risk is that
> the client system will not have been allowed to learn through
> making mistakes and it will have been protected from adjusting
> and developing its internal organisation to cope with the changes.
> Hence, if the benign leadership disappears, the system is likely to
> collapse. Very few development efforts in Third World countries
> have been able to to navigate a course between this Scylla and
> Charybdis (Miller, 1977, pp. 41-2).

In the residential institution where my colleague and I had a consultancy role, leadership in change (which had originally been initiated by a small group of inmates) had been taken up by the chairman of the management committee, thus embracing a system that included both inmates and staff plus relevant elements of the environment. Our consultancy was with the three groups: inmates, staff and the committee itself. Our main function was to identify underlying issues and processes, so that they could become available for examination, and to provide help and support while the three parties struggled to reach agreement on a philosophy, policy and organisation that legitimated inmates' participation in management. One thing we helped to do, for example, was to draft a job specification for the role of warden when it became vacant and to help devise mechanisms through which inmates took part in the selection procedure (Miller and Gwynne, 1972). The consultancy ended in 1967 and my evidence at the time of writing (1976) is that innovations that were controversial ten years ago have become firmly established as a taken-for-granted part of institutional life.

My conclusion from these and other experiences is that over and above the specific leadership towards innovation that may come from the sanctioning authority or the specific advice that may be given in the consultancy relationship, one or both of these roles has to have a major function as a receptacle for dependency. Although the culture of dependency and associated defensive structures are especially pervasive in 'people-processing institutions', such as hospitals, they are present in all organisations. The importance of this for the consultancy role in change was recognised by my Tavistock Institute colleagues 25 years ago:

There was a shared recognition that both individuals and groups develop mechanisms to give meaning to their existence and to defend themselves from fear and uncertainty; that these defences, often unconscious and deeply rooted, are threatened by change; and that consequently it is an important aspect of the professional role to serve as a container during the 'working through' of change, so as to tackle not only the overt problem but also the underlying difficulties (Miller, 1976a, p.48; cf. Wilson, 1951).

Less recognition, however, has been given to the role of superordinate leadership as a repository for what I have called elsewhere 'dislodged dependency' during transactions (Miller, 1977). The kinds of transitions we have been examining dislodge prevailing defensive structures not simply within the system (e.g. a group of weavers) that is acquiring autonomy, but in at least one other system with which its relationship is changed. In organisations this is usually the next higher-order system within which it operates (e.g. the weaving department). I would postulate that leadership that can give sanction and carry dependency is required at least at the level of the next wider system (e.g. the factory, or the company). My reasoning is that individuals and groups most directly affected by the change need temporarily to deposit dependency in a leadership that encompasses both the pre-change and post-change configurations. This is not to suggest that the superordinate leadership itself remains unchanged: in the shifts towards autonomy the operation of that role too will be subject to modification if the revised system is to survive. Insecurity at this level, however, should be less.

In the case of change through conflict, which I mentioned briefly in reference to rural development, an oppressed group usually receives consultancy/leadership from outside — e.g. from a political activist — to fight for a new deal that will give it greater autonomy. He has the same function of carrying the group's dependency during the transition.

I am not suggesting, therefore, that both internal sanctioning leadership and external consultancy are necessary. Whilst, obviously, my own experience has been of the consultancy role, many transformations occur without such external help. I would expect to find in such cases, however, an internal leadership that has been strong enough and resilient enough to contain the dislodged dependency, and at the same time sophisticated enough to relinquish it again as the new system became established.

Some support of a consultancy type may also be drawn from an internally created group, such as the innovation forum which emerged at Fulbourn. Such a body, however, is likely to be a weak container of dependency if, as in that instance, its membership is only very part-time: the pull of ongoing working relationships is correspondingly powerful. It would therefore thrive only in the context of the wider sanctioning mechanisms that would be provided by a fully developed and institutionally secure 'HIP'.

Implications for HIP

If in conclusion, then, we turn back to the emergence of HIP at Fulbourn, we can see that both conditions that I mentioned have been present. In relation to the specific projects undertaken, the Steering Committee, which included the senior members of the nursing and administrative hierarchies and the most influential consultant in the hospital, has operated as a sanctioning authority above the level of the systems most directly affected by the changes; the social research adviser has provided the consultancy; both roles have carried dependency; and the Project as a whole has been successful in fostering an ethos of questioning past ways of doing things and of seeking more effective approaches.

One project in particular — Denbigh Ward — nicely illustrates my proposition that a significant and sustained change is unlikely to occur only within a system: reinforcing change is also required in the relationship between the system and its environment. In this particular case my hypothesis is that the new treatment strategy within the ward is reinforced by the enlarged role of the nurses in relation to the external Social Services Department, including some relocation of authority for admission. This innovation was greatly facilitated by the geriatric consultant, who, while recognising the symbolic importance of his role, was alert to the negative aspects of the dependency culture and who therefore made ample room for the nurses to take authority in developing their new roles.

None the less, the success in Denbigh Ward, as in HIP as a whole, remains precarious. A potentially major weakness — of which I was not fully aware until I put my thoughts together to write this chapter — is that the Steering Committee and the social research adviser have been primarily devoted to encouraging innovations rather than with sustaining them. The latter has been left to the discretion of individual Steering Committee members in their managerial roles. Now if a new method of working affects staff only within one discipline, such as nursing, then it is possible — and, given the present incumbent, quite probable — that the senior nursing officer who is a member of the HIP Steering Committee will also concern himself as a manager to safeguard the boundary conditions for sustaining the innovation. But in this he has no accountability to the Steering Committee. An innovation straddling disciplinary boundaries is even more vulnerable to the vagaries of a new nursing officer or a new consultant. As has been mentioned elsewhere in this book, the 1974 NHS reorganisation has dispensed with the old Hospital Management Committee and left a vacuum at that level; and the disciplines in the hospital have still to come together and form an authoritative management group of their own. Such a body is required to confirm that the philosophy and concepts of self-management that are inherent in HIP are an integral part of hospital policy and to ensure that they are implemented and maintained. That body will also need to defend Fulbourn's innovations against the creeping bureaucratisation of the NHS hierarchies. By my definition every employee is a manager and at least some of the staff at Fulbourn have acquired the requisite authority to manage their roles. The notion that groups of staff have the capability and authority to take initiatives and that it is the task of managers of wider systems to provide the boundary conditions within which nurses and other staff can perform their task more effectively seems, however, to be at odds with the culture of prescriptive superior-subordinate relationships that prevails in the NHS generally. Until, therefore, such a hospital management has come into being and taken on this task, the long-term future of HIP and of the specific innovations that have been introduced must remain in doubt.

CONCLUSION: IMPLICATIONS FOR DEVELOPING BETTER CARING SERVICES

David Towell and Clive Harries

We began this account of the Hospital Innovation Project by recognising the widespread concern which exists about the standards of provision in the more deprived sectors of the health and welfare services. The quality of life available to substantial numbers of the mentally ill, mentally handicapped and dependent elderly, both in institutions and through 'community' care, is far below what we believe should be acceptable in 1978. These are still 'Cinderella' services, for which the annual reports of the Health Advisory Service constitute a regular reminder of the gap between aspirations and the often depressing reality.

Moreover, while all these 'client groups' have been assigned priority in Government planning for the future and declared policies for 'Better Services' contain much to be welcomed, all past experience would justify considerable scepticism about how far these desirable aims are likely to be achieved. Indeed, the prospect of prolonged economic constraints in the public sector must make it doubtful whether extra resources to these services will even be sufficient to keep pace with the growing needs of the aged.

Clearly it would be unwise to underestimate the magnitude of the problems which are faced: concerted action will be required through many professional, administrative, community and political channels, if significant changes are to be achieved. Within the health and welfare services, widespread development programmes are needed to mobilise staff in the struggle to overcome existing difficulties. As we have already emphasised, for the foreseeable future these efforts to improve patient care and develop better services are likely to rely heavily on the ability of staff to transform existing practices and make the very best use of available resources.

In this context, we hope the HIP experiment at Fulbourn may have more general relevance. This book provides others with the opportunity to test this proposition. We believe that HIP has demonstrated the possibility of more fully utilising the potential contribution of staff at all levels in achieving informed innovation. At the same time, the oscillating fortunes of this work have underlined how even under favourable circumstances, securing change can be a complex, lengthy

191

and difficult process.

From the outset, we invited readers critically to examine their own experiences in the light of those reported here, with a view to evaluating the possible application elsewhere of what has been learnt from this work. Consistent with the HIP approach, we believe that potential users must themselves accept responsibility for deciding what might be the implications of this analysis for the particular problems faced in their own roles and organisations. In this way we hope our final chapter will become not a conclusion but rather a further step in the wider process of achieving innovation in patient care.

With these wider applications in mind, we examine here our own experiences to date of utilising aspects of the HIP approach in new situations and draw some *general lessons* for strategies of service development. We also outline how this approach might prove relevant to other key issues confronting the health and welfare services.

HIP: Dissemination and Utilisation

It will already be evident that Fulbourn staff have generally been very prepared to share their experiences of HIP with interested people from other places. We noted earlier how through conferences, published articles, many visitors and in other ways, aspects of this work have become quite widely known.

The impact of these different methods of dissemination has naturally been difficult to assess. In the case of the working conferences however (see for example Harries, 1974), some inferences can be drawn. Reflecting the organisation of Fulbourn itself, these conferences typically invited participation by multi-disciplinary teams having responsibilty in their own hospitals for the issues being examined (for example, the provision of psycho-geriatric services; the care of disturbed patients). The format then sought to provide opportunities for participants to exchange experiences and learn from each other. Evidence from the evaluation of these conferences showed that the capacity of different staff to make use of these opportunities varied quite considerably according to the extent to which these hospitals had established similar organisational conditions, the freedom with which staff felt able to question their own practices, and the authority they possessed to apply new ideas back in their own situations.

More directly, we have ourselves been involved in a number of efforts, both successful and unsuccessful, to apply aspects of the HIP approach elsewhere. Each of these initiatives has permitted further learning about the process by which a Project of this kind can be more fully utilised.

During 1974, the social research adviser undertook explorations to test out interest in HIP in three other kinds of health care institution. In each case, factors could be identified which suggested that with the limited resources available for disseminating this work, new projects modelled on the development af HIP at Fulbourn were unlikely to be productive in these new settings.

One example was provided by the experiment in developing experiential learning groups for nurses on a ward of the nearby general hospital, which arose from the project on the secondment of general nurses to Fulbourn. Through the strong support of the ward sister, this experiment lasted until she left the hospital. It became clear through this experience however, that the high degree of anxiety within the general nursing service, the tendency to deny problems, and the lack of confidence between levels in the management hierarchy, were all likely to make an extension of the HIP approach within this hospital very difficult. The possibility of extension in this case was also reduced by the start of this work near the junior end of the organisation and within a single discipline.

In another exploration, this time with a hospital for the mentally handicapped, interest in HIP was first expressed by the most senior nurse. Here again, while some conditions were more favourable, a highly centralised nursing administration in which the managerial climate gave little support to initiative or questioning by more junior staff, seemed less than conducive to a concern with self-innovation.

In the third case, a small psycho-analytically oriented psychiatric institution had already established a senior nurse in a 'project officer' post. However, it proved difficult to develop this role as an effective support to change activities: the senior management group was reluctant to fully sanction problem-centred work which crossed existing disciplinary boundaries; the emphasis in the treatment culture on here-and-now interpretation of events displaced staff attention from any systematic longer-term examination of institutional functioning. As a consequence, in this instance the new post was discontinued when its first occupant moved elsewhere.

Subsequently, the opportunity has arisen for one or both of us to contribute to three more successful programmes to develop psychiatric services in different parts of the country: each programme employing strategies specifically designed for the situation in question.

In a region containing several large hospitals, one of which had been the subject of a critical enquiry, we have provided some help to the Regional Health Authority's officers in instituting a programme to develop services for the mentally ill and mentally handicapped throughout their region. The initial step here was for these officers to convene a three-day seminar for management teams from regional down to hospital level, in which the problems facing these services could be examined in detail from the different perspectives of the tiers and professions involved; and where work could begin on a joint strategy for change. Over the following two years, there have been further meetings of this seminar at six monthly intervals, supplemented by a range of supporting activities. Emerging from these joint activities, a development group for the psychiatric and mental handicap services seems to have been superimposed onto the previously disparate components of these services within the region's total health organisation.

In another programme, a small group (psychiatrist, nurse, social worker and social scientist, all independent of the Health Authority involved) has been assembled to provide part-time help to the staff of a very large psychiatric hospital and the main health and social services agencies in the hospital's catchment area. The aim here is both to improve in-patient care and encourage the development of new patterns of local services. By defining its role as being to provide assistance to staff in their own efforts to tackle problems and improve services, this group has gained sanction for its work from senior hospital staff and higher tier authorities. Although resembling in some respects an HAS team, this 'assistance group' has emphasised its commitment to working directly with staff on issues of concern rather than writing reports for subsequent action; in this way the professional experience of its members is being made available to any staff prepared to use their own initiative in seeking change.

Over the first eighteen months of its work although not without considerable difficulty, this assistance group has shown the capacity to work simultaneously with different professions, different agencies and at different levels in the complex system of provision drawing on this large hospital: thus it has demonstrated the potential of this approach for stimulating and supporting a wide range of interlocking improvements, both in the delivery of services and in the way these services are managed and planned.

In these two programmes, experience is suggesting that the working hypotheses emerging from the analysis of HIP have relevance on a considerably wider scale to achieving innovation in psychiatric care. The needs of large hospitals relating to complex catchment areas are such that the regional tier is having to exercise a leadership role in developing the strategy for the future pattern of these services: at the same time helping to give stronger identity to the total psychiatric service in the face of cross-cutting administrative and professional distinctions. It is evident from this approach that the problems of the large hospitals cannot be solved only within these institutions: change must be focussed on this total system of care.

Throughout this system, much effort is required to clarify organisation and management so as to provide the boundary conditions within which developments in services can be encouraged. Particularly important is the establishment of authoritative management arrangements for the large hospitals themselves.

In turn these institutions are requiring sub-division into smaller units for service development, most commonly by bringing together multi-disciplinary groups of staff responsible for services to patients from defined parts of the hospital's catchment area. This is then providing the basis for better joint planning and operational co-ordination between parts of the hospital and the local health and welfare services relating to the same population. Thus representatives of parts of the hospital and local agencies are considering together the needs of this population and how these needs can best be met through joint action; and such groups are contributing to the planning process an informed assessment of problems, opportunities and requirements as seen locally. Through negotiation at the interface between such local service development groups and the leadership on strategy from higher tier authorities, it is also proving possible to combine 'top down' and 'bottom up' approaches to planning in a way which fosters integrated movement towards new patterns of services.

Moreover as at Fulbourn, decentralisation in management, more effective collaboration between the professions, and the opportunity for widespread staff participation, are proving to be additional requirements for improving patient care. Both these programmes are further demonstrating that to the extent these conditions can be established and a framework provided for action, then with appropriate support many staff can themselves be mobilised to examine existing practices and initiate valued changes.

In a third piece of work focussed more directly on the level where clients meet service providers, one of us is helping staff of a medium-sized mental handicap hospital in their efforts to achieve greater integration in care and training activities. In this example, the hospital management team has set up an internal 'development and liaison group' to stimulate, support and co-ordinate a programme of change beginning from the wards. Thus the first nine months of this programme have attended particularly to the introduction of multi-disciplinary assessment procedures for all patients, establishing ward and departmental policies, and through both these activities, developing more decentralised patterns of team work.

Further Action Research Strategies

Clearly there is much still to be learnt from these new programmes. However reviewing these various experiences has helped us to develop an understanding of appropriate strategies through which the lessons from action research projects like HIP can be more widely utilised.

It will be recalled that the instigation of the Project at Fulbourn itself depended on a combination of fortunate events which gave the idea momentum. Continuation of HIP in the second stage used the experience of this pilot experiment, while exploiting fresh opportunities: giving the second social research adviser the chance to make something new from this role at the same time as building on what was established. Diffusion of knowledge about this work and a variety of linkages which could not be anticipated later provided the impetus for our involvement in the three current programmes: each permitting further testing of aspects of the HIP approach as these are being adapted according to the requirements of these different situations.

In the light of these applications of HIP, we have come to regard a pre-determined and centrally controlled dissemination strategy as inappropriate for action research of this kind. As others have found (see particularly Thorsrud, 1976), real diffusion occurs in unexpected ways, which can be encouraged but must necessarily remain responsive to naturally occurring contingencies in the new centres of development. Moreover, these experiences underline how just as in individual projects at Fulbourn, new applications of HIP need to start from how relevant staff define their own situation and help them to discover for themselves their capacity to bring about change. An approach which genuinely seeks to mobilise staff participation cannot be 'pre-packaged'. Each new group must make and accept responsibility for their own development programme.

However three general conditions can be identified which seem likely to be necessary for further applications of the HIP approach. First, there is the need for some pre-existing motivation towards change among at least some key role occupants; second, the possibility must exist therefore of generating authoritative sanction on a multi-disciplinary basis for staff participation in a programme across the organisational systems of relevance; and third, either internally or externally some staff resources should be available to support development.

HIP and other current work has also suggested a number of alternative strategies which in different circumstances can provide this support: we have described the social research advisory role, the innovation forum, the 'development and liaison group' in the mental handicap hospital, the regional seminar, and the large hospital 'assistance group'. Each of these instruments has served the functions of stimulating staff to examine their own work; mediating relevant experience from elsewhere; carrying on a transitional basis some of the uncertainty generated by change; and helping staff work through the problems involved in achieving innovation.

It follows that the design of future programmes of this kind should desirably be a collaborative process: aiming in the light of local conditions, available resources and previous experiences, to create the optimum development strategy for each particular situation. As this implies, the most distinctive feature of the Fulbourn Project – the institutionalisation of the social research advisory role, may seldom be appropriate elsewhere. Relevant conditions in this case included the favourable precedents for the growth of this initiative at Fulbourn, the relative intensity of investment in the experimental phase, the quite long period of external support for the Project, and the scope thus provided for developing a wide-ranging and original approach to the examination and resolution of problems.

Two other lessons emerge from this experience. Where projects begin through the involvement of external social scientists, it is clearly important for any longer term or larger scale utilisation of such work that appropriate arrangements are made to develop resources internal to the systems in question, capable of continuing these programmes. As the Fulbourn example suggests, succession to the social research advisory role requires that any new role occupant be provided with relevant training and ongoing support. In multi-site programmes, this is likely to entail creating a network of relationships through which those involved can share experiences with others in similar positions. In this way too, experiments like HIP can take their place among a range of related initiatives, with mutual enrichment through the cross-fertilisation of different approaches.

Further inferences can be drawn about the institutional arrangements required for the future promotion of action research. We have seen from our own experience that there is considerable potential value to be gained from social scientists and the people directly concerned, collaborating in work designed both to increase understanding of health and welfare issues and contribute to informed change. If this potential is to be fully realised however, the dissemination strategy commended here strongly suggests the need for a firmer institutional base and longer term support for work of this kind than can typically be provided through research project funding. Rather, a small number of centres are required where groups of staff are able to mobilise a range of disciplinary and other skills in such a way as to respond creatively to emerging problems, with programmatic support from funding agencies sympathetic to the special difficulties that action research necessarily encounters. Thus the cumulative learning from such work should also become more readily available for application to new challenges.

Wider Implications

In conclusion, we should like to outline what we believe are some of the wider implications of this work for future developments in health and welfare services.

The HIP approach is in many ways the antithesis of the way change was managed in reorganising the NHS, at least as this change was perceived by many of those primarily affected. As the example of Fulbourn suggests, the national imposition of a blueprint for the new structure, extensive and continuing departmental guidance, increasing centralisation at district level, and frequent disruption through staff movement, have each encouraged passive accommodation by managers and acceptance of the idea that all authority comes down from above. The subsequent complaints of staff that team management and elaborate consultative processes produce a sense that no one is responsible, while the attention required to the weight of guidance leaves little time for one's own work, can in turn be traced back to the reorganisation experience.

Perhaps the time has come when merely complaining about these difficulties and hoping for salvation from some new structural blueprint with less tiers or whatever, is less than appropriate. Even worse is the quite widespread tendency to assume that the only way change can be generated is through the painful and costly mechanism of external enquiries.

Rather, our experience would suggest the need now for staff at all levels to take back the authority for clarifying their own roles and working to establish the conditions required for effective task performance by themselves and others. It is in this sense that we would support the common dictum 'managers must manage'. In these circumstances too, we would expect that any further central guidance would become a valued stimulus to thought and hence a resource to be used, not a set of injunctions to be obeyed.

Further lessons follow about the emerging requirements for managerial and professional development. Working with and for change has been seen as intrinsic to everyday management and professional practice. In a complex field of action, the need for managers to exercise initiative within and across existing bureaucratic divisions in analysing problems and mobilising the social processes required for their resolution, has become increasingly evident. In the NHS at least, management training has to date relied heavily on off-the-job courses. Instead, we would suggest the importance of a change of emphasis towards practice-based approaches to management development: approaches which essentially involve learning in and through action relating to real problems — most usefully those arising in the manager's own organisation. In this way, management development opportunities might become a more central element in wider strategies which increase recognition of the scope which exists for managerial initiative and support staff in becoming their own agents of informed change.

New opportunities for professional development are equally required. In the past there has been some tendency for the extension of professional roles to be seen as a 'zero sum game': more for one has been perceived as less for another, with consequent battles over the defence of traditional territory. More consistent with the needs of current practice would be approaches to professional training which from the outset stress the role of each profession as a component in a necessarily collaborative service. Greater attention to how putative team members can learn together in seeking mutual development would also be helpful.

In addition, on the basis of our experience we can identify the desirability of extending the functions of agencies like the Health Advisory Service and the National Development Group for the mentally handicapped. Currently, multi-disciplinary teams of professional staff working from these agencies are available to monitor services and provide advice to their colleagues in different localities, often through short visits followed by written reports. The lack of impact of much of this advice suggests the need however for these agencies also to provide rather more sustained support to staff in the field as efforts are made to bring about improvements in services.

Another significant influence affecting the wider climate for change, has been the growing role of professional associations and trade unions, particularly marked by increasing militancy in the period since 1973.

With the pressures arising from external inflation, it has often seemed that each group's pursuit of their own economic interests has been split off from, and sometimes expressed in opposition to, the concern with the quality of services which members share with those in other representative groups and relevant policy makers. Without underplaying the realistic basis for many conflicts, we would hypothesise that to the extent genuine participation of all staff in the struggle for better services is sought, then the substantial positive contribution of professional associations and trade unions in support of this shared concern is more likely to be realised.

Meanwhile the Royal Commission is re-examining the whole pattern of health care provision, with growing speculation about what new 'solutions' will be advanced. While radical changes in the NHS may still be necessary, it should be clear that we would have substantial reservations were their deliberations to result in another completed blueprint. Rather, HIP has given us more confidence in arguing the desirability of future changes proceeding on a more experimental and incremental basis — albeit with signposts for the 'right' directions — leaving wide scope for variability in relation to local perceptions of how the tasks of the caring services can best be accomplished.

In these evolutionary processes, some experience suggests that the recent introduction of more systematic planning activities into the NHS and the incentives to joint planning with local authority services, could if used creatively, contribute usefully to more informed choices about future patterns of provision. We would argue that this is more probable to the extent that the planning cycle facilitates close interaction between staff involved in service provision and those at 'higher' levels in a relationship characterised by reciprocal problem-solving: that is, with staff at different levels learning from each other in negotiations about appropriate strategies and proposals. It is even more important that the potential for enriching these problem-solving processes through appropriate client and community participation (most obviously by involving Community Health Councils) should be fully exploited.

As we have implied in discussing the need for better collaboration between health and local authority services, it is increasingly the case that the quality of care received by particular sets of clients depends on effective co-ordination and complementarity in the services provided by different agencies. This principle can be extended into a more wide-ranging concern with the development of joint approaches to social policy which focus not just on the provision of integrated services, but also on the scope that exists for more radical interventions designed to reduce the need for these services. To return to the theme with which this book began, this attention to prevention would necessarily raise more basic questions about the capacity which existing political institutions provide for more purposive control over the social changes which affect health and welfare.

Our final suggestion about application of the HIP approach is therefore more fundamental. In discussion of the state of the 'Cinderella' services, we have held in mind that ultimately these services and their clients are part of a much bigger system — our society — in which clearly we are all deeply implicated. The harsh truth to be faced here is that while standards of provision may often be unacceptable, we do in fact accept these standards.

Our ambivalence towards the mentally ill, mentally handicapped and dependent elderly, can be closely related to social values and the supporting power relationships which favour private production over public services, consumption of goods over contributions to the community, and dependence on professional agencies over personal autonomy. While there are still very substantial efforts made by ordinary people to care for themselves and provide care for others, these efforts receive little support and are indeed handicapped by many aspects of contemporary life styles and their social determinants.

We believe that against this background, what Fulbourn staff have demonstrated in their professional roles has some lessons for all of us in our roles as citizens in a democracy. Specifically, we all have the authority, through reflection and action on our own situation, to seek to contribute to the development of a different society — a society in which the interests of disadvantaged groups and our own potential for caring would be much better realised; a society indeed where improved health in its widest sense for all the community would be a primary goal.

APPENDIX A: ANNOTATED LIST OF MAJOR PROJECTS UNDERTAKEN 1972–1977

1.   Series of projects on the development of new approaches to treatment in an admission ward, including exploratory survey of problems (arising out of disagreements about nursing uniform); introduction of counselling groups for staff; review of ward organisation and management; examination of ways of improving links with extra-hospital services; and study of patients' experiences in hospital. A detailed account of these projects in presented in Chapter 2.

2.   Evaluation and improvement to the training of student general nurses seconded to Fulbourn for three months. A detailed account of this project is presented in Chapter 4.

3.   Survey on the use made of volunteers within the hospital. Fulbourn Hospital pioneered the introduction of voluntary service organisers into hospitals and now makes extensive use of volunteers in a variety of roles. At the instigation of the voluntary services organiser and with support from a hospital-wide staff meeting, a survey was commissioned to examine the views of both staff and volunteers about the current uses being made of volunteers, the problems being encountered, and possible new ways in which volunteers might contribute to the work of the hospital. This survey was undertaken by three cadet nurses, with some support from the social research adviser, and involved interviews with a cross-section of staff and volunteers across the hospital.

The report on this survey, which was widely circulated in the hospital, contributed to a clarification of the roles assumed by volunteers, indicated the need for better training for both the volunteers and staff who worked with them, and identified a number of areas in which volunteers could make an increased contribution. The cadets undertaking this survey found it a valuable means of getting to know more staff in the hospital and learning about small scale social research, including the difficulties of encouraging effective use of their findings. Although the information generated in the survey proved useful in planning developments in voluntary services, it did not lead to much further work on the problems involved in making more effective use of volunteers.

4.   *Examination of the work of Unit Nursing Officers and the functions of a Central Nursing Office, and efforts to develop new role for Nursing Officers.* A detailed account of this project is presented in Chapter 4.

5.   *Study of the problems experienced by wards and departments in relation to the services provided by the Area Supplies Department, and introduction of improved procedures.* The manager of the Area Supplies Department serving Fulbourn Hospital was interested to learn more about the problems experienced by staff using these services, as a basis for making improvements. With support from the heads of departments meeting, a small project committee consisting of this manager together with administrative and nursing representatives, was set up to direct a survey on these issues.

With advice from the social research adviser, the main research was undertaken by an administrative trainee, working in all the hospital's wards and departments for short periods and using this as an opportunity to explore problems with staff in situ. Substantial information was thereby generated and reported back in detail to the officers concerned. As well as numerous particular complaints or difficulties, it was possible to identify more systematic deficiencies relating, for example, to requisitioning and condemning procedures, the need for launderette services, and the way priorities for new equipment were determined.

Attention to these issues by hospital officers led to some procedural changes, although other problems proved more difficult to tackle because of the complexity of the inter-connected issues involved and the limited commitment of other senior departmental heads whose interest would also have been required. Direct engagement with both ward and senior staff in the attempt to understand and resolve real problems, made this exercise a valuable contribution to the training of the administrative trainee concerned.

6.   *Study group to examine the training arrangements through which nurses acquire professional attitudes.* At the invitation of the General Nursing Council, hospitals were asked to contribute suggestions from qualified staff on the most effective means of providing opportunities for the learning of acceptable professional attitudes. The nursing administration at Fulbourn set up a study group, comprising a small

cross-section of (mainly nursing) staff, to respond to this invitation, and this group asked the help of the social research adviser in this task.

The study group was able to provide a forum for the exchange of views and experiences, out of which the meaning of the questions (particularly what was to be understood by 'professional attitudes') raised by the GNC was clarified, and progress was made both in conceptualising the processes through which attitudes are acquired and also in identifying good practices in this area. As well as providing an opportunity for learning within the study group, the results of this work were distilled into a pamphlet for submission to the GNC. The social research adviser was also able to help the group examine how the dissemination of this pamphlet throughout the hospital, could provide the basis for the more effective use of their work in improving aspects of nurse training more locally.

7.   *Review of treatment needs and improvement of rehabilitative facilities for long-stay patients.* Arising from the belief among staff of the long stay (Social Therapy) area of the hospital and the Occupational Therapy Department that the needs of long stay patients for rehabilitative activity were not being adequately met, while existing facilities for occupational therapy were not being optimally used, the area meeting invited the help of the social research adviser in examining these problems. Although there was considerable conflict between OT and ward staff, it proved possible with the adviser's assistance to establish a multi-disciplinary working party with representatives of the main staff groups concerned, to undertake this work on behalf of the Social Therapy Area.

The working party constructed a questionnaire covering the current and likely future needs of patients (as seen by staff and patients themselves), and encouraged the formation of multi-disciplinary treatment teams (including an occupational therapist) on each ward to fill out the questionnaire for every patient through an assessment process. At the same time the working party divided into sub-groups to examine whether existing rehabilitative facilities could be better used, and what further resources and facilities might be required to meet the needs identified in the patient survey.

Linking these two aspects of the review together, the working party was able to identify a substantial number of proposals for improvements in relation to industrial and occupational therapy, domestic rehabilitation, and ward-based group activities. Acceptance of the working party's report by the Social Therapy Area meeting as a whole led to the establishment of a group to monitor and encourage progress in the implementation of these proposals. More fundamentally, the model of multi-disciplinary working provided by the working party, and the sustained efforts made over a year to work through the emotional issues which had led to conflict between different professional groups, provided a significant input to the wider development of a new culture in the area, more conducive to collaborative work between the professions and the facilitation of effective social therapy.

8.   *Series of projects on the use of nursing resources in psychogeriatric care, including time study of nursing activity; assessment of patient needs; and development of new patterns of liaison with community services.* A detailed account of these projects in presented in Chapter 3.

9.   *Organisation and assessment of a working conference on the management of disturbed behaviour.* In response to widespread concern about the management of disturbed behaviour in psychiatric hospitals and the interest of visitors to the 'disturbed' ward at Fulbourn, the staff in the long stay area of care arranged a national conference on this topic in July 1973. A small multi-disciplinary planning committee was formed, which invited the social research adviser to help them organise the event. The complexities of the problems of managing 'disturbed' behaviour were recognised at the outset, and the organisers felt that a participative form of conference was desirable, and that multi-disciplinary attendance was a pre-requisite for participation to be a profitable experience. A conference was designed to enable participants to raise questions and problems, in groups of their own discipline and grade, which then formed the basis for a problem-solving session by multi-disciplinary groups. The planning committee was able to identify staff from different disciplines willing to take the role of group conveners in the working conference, and the social research adviser also contributed to the training of staff for these roles.

The conference proved to be successful to the extent that the day was oversubscribed, a high degree of participation was achieved, and there was a wide sharing of relevant experience among attenders. Subsequently an evaluation of what had been learnt from this experience was undertaken, and an account of this work prepared for publication (Harries, 1974).

10.   *Experiment in helping to provide experiential learning groups for*

nurses in a nearby general hospital. An earlier project on improving the value of general nurse training by psychiatric secondment, involving collaboration between staff from Fulbourn and the nearby general hospital, had led to some clarification both of what general nurses were learning from this secondment experience, and also of the difficulties these nurses experienced in applying this learning back in the general hospital situation. Discussion of these issues with ward sisters and nursing officers in the general hospital focussed particularly on the problems general nurses experience in giving adequate attention to the psychological care of patients there.

In the light of this discussion, one sister volunteered her ward as the site for an experiment in which nursing staff would make use of the skills of an experienced psychiatric nurse in developing group meetings designed to help them learn from their experiences of working with patients and provide support for them in coping with the problems which can arise in this work. This was a radiotherapy ward where particular difficulties for nurses could be expected, located in a new hospital where the design of wards was already requiring patterns of relationships between the sister and her staff different from the traditional 'control by observation' possible in open-plan wards.

The experiment involved the introduction of experiential learning groups on this ward, modelled on the innovation in nurse training already established in an admission ward at Fulbourn and with the ward sister from that ward initially taking the main counselling role.

The social research adviser provided support to the staff involved in this experiment and helped in monitoring its value. After nine months general hospital staff were able to continue this experiment without outside support but this innovation did not survive a change in ward sister, for while trainee nurses reported the groups to be of considerable value, it did not prove possible to establish wider support within the nursing administration for this new approach to nurse training.

11. Working group to review interprofessional co-ordination arrangements at hospital level. This project originated in an increasing awareness among the 'tri-partite heads' in the hospital (hospital secretary, principal nursing officer, and chairman of the division of psychiatry), particularly after the demise of the Hospital Management Committee with reorganisation in 1974, that there were deficiencies in the existing arrangements for management and interprofessional co-ordination at hospital level. A basic problem here was seen to be the reluctance of the doctors to be involved in any body with management responsibilities.

A working group was set up, composed of the tri-partite heads, with the social research adviser available as consultant to help the group examine the deficiencies in existing arrangements on the basis of their joint experience, and explore new organisational arrangements which might better serve the management and co-ordination requirements identified at hospital level. In addition, the adviser was able to assist the three officers in working through previous difficulties they had experienced in working together, and finding mutually agreed strategies for future joint working.

Supported by a new conception of their meetings as a 'centre for reticulation' in the complex organisational structure of the new Health Service, the outcome of this work was agreement among the three officers that they would meet weekly in future, with the purpose of facilitating the exchange of information and increasing co-ordination between different professions, and where necessary in the light of this, convening meetings between other officers to tackle problems which were emerging. Subsequent changes of staff disrupted these arrangements however, and it was not until 1977 that a firmer hospital management system began to be established.

12.   Improving the nursing care of patients in a long-stay ward through staff examination of patients' own views about life on the ward. A detailed account of this project is presented in Chapter 2.

13.   Assessment of patients' performance at work as an indicator of successful occupational resettlement, leading to a reappraisal of industrial rehabilitation services. Occupational therapy staff approached the social research adviser and described a number of inter-related problems. The difficulties of formulating a more definitive work assessment for patients seemed particularly important in relation to the problems of resettling often quite psychiatrically disabled patients in work outside the hospital.

A small project group was formed, led by the head occupational therapist and including another occupational therapist with industrial workshop responsibilities and the workshop manager. The group began by reviewing patients recently resettled in work, and identifying from their own knowledge of the patients those factors which seemed to be relevant to their being successfully employed. Wider discussions enabled the criteria for successful occupational resettlement to be more fully clarified. These results were then compared with recent research publications on this topic and an assessment schedule compiled; together with a guide to how this should be completed. The schedule was used both in preparing patients for resettlement and as an assessment for outside employment. Later work has examined more widely the appropriate organisation of Industrial Unit staff.

14.   Series of projects in the area of psycho-geriatric care. Following the innovations in collaboration between ward and social service staff in an earlier project (reported in Chapter 3), other psycho-geriatric wards were 'zonally linked' with particular social services teams. Reorganisation of social services at the end of 1975 threatened to disrupt these working relationships and necessitated the staff in the psycho-geriatric area reconsidering this form of organisation. With the help of the social research adviser, a working group examined the patterning of the area's main work in the previous year, and tried to see what effect the social services reorganisation would have had, if it had happened twelve months earlier. This provided the basis for considering options for re-zoning the work within the psycho-geriatric area – so that decentralised collaboration could continue with the new social service teams.

Discussions of problems arising out of the re-zoning project, led to further work to find ways of improving the assessment of prospective clients in their homes. A ward sister made a comparative analysis of various assessment formats in current use, and the working group were able to agree an improved assessment format for use by the whole area. The working group also recognised the need for improving the training of staff to undertake assessments and produced a videotape training film for this purpose.

Subsequently the staff of the psycho-geriatric area organised a national conference, in which their experiences of changing roles and developing services over the previous four years were exchanged with those of multi-disciplinary teams from several other hospitals where efforts to improve psycho-geriatric care were being made.

15.   Improving the statistical information system relating to the patient workload of the hospital. In response to questions raised by medical staff regarding the distribution of work between them, a working party was established which comprised three consultant psychiatrists, the medical records officer and a nursing officer. In the background there seemed to be a more general need for information

on the way in which the shape of the service provided by the hospital
was changing with an increasing number of day patients and with the
increasing amount of community work undertaken out of clinical
teams. At the same time the resources available to the hospital in the
medical records office were unable to meet the new demands for
information.

At the outset the group, with assistance from the social research
adviser, tried to answer the question 'What information is required by
whom, and for what purpose?' This led the working group to ask
medical and other staff in the hospital to suggest what items of
information they would find useful if incorporated into a regular
information service. This enabled the working group to obtain a
realistic grasp of the range of data being requested, to consider its
usefulness, and at the same time to highlight afresh the inadequacies
of existing information services. Exploration of alternative resources
for managing an information system led then to a feasibility study
being undertaken in collaboration with officers from the computer
staff of the RHA. As a result of this study, a computerised information
system has been designed.

16.   *Preparation of ward policy on a long-stay ward, and training a*
ward team to present this process at a national conference. A multi-
disciplinary team from the 'disturbed' ward at Fulbourn who were
commencing the process of revising their ward policy, were invited
to make a contribution to a day conference at the King's Fund Centre
by describing how this was being done and the advantages and
disadvantages involved in their approach.

The social research adviser was asked by the staff to help in the
preparation of the team's presentation. The problems perceived by
the staff group included, first, understanding more fully how their
roles interlocked and influenced the way each saw the importance
of a ward policy, and the way each contributed to its formulation;
and second, their inexperience of talking in public, and particularly
in front of more senior officers in the Health Service.

The social research adviser suggested the formation of a work group
to examine the roles of team members, and at the same time to review
each individual's draft contributions for the presentation. Through
this process the roles of different individuals on the team became more
consciously recognised by the others, and the work group was able
to tease out those aspects of the ward policy which held special
significance for them in relation to problems encountered in exercising

their obligations within the wider team. In preparation for the conference, the team also tested out their presentation at a social therapy area meeting and videotaped this performance. This presentation raised issues about ward policies more widely in the long-stay area of care.

17.   Describing and measuring aspects of the psychiatric service to the community provided by the hospital's nursing staff. 'Community nursing' had evolved at Fulbourn largely through the nursing members of clinical teams providing both in-patient care and a service to the team's clients 'in the community', although there were also four nurses 'outposted' to distant parts of the catchment area. The senior nursing officer initiated a project to review these developments, establish more clearly the nature of the service being provided, and seek improvements.

With the assistance of the social research adviser, the first step in organising this project was taken by inviting representatives of the various clinical teams to meet and to discuss these issues. From this was created an inter-team project committee. In initial discussions the large differences between the work undertaken out of the various clinical teams was recognised, and factors were suggested which could form the basis for a more systematic collection of information about these services. A 'community contact' form was devised for systematic recording of each nursing contact outside the hospital's boundary, and this was used in a month's census of all such work. Analysis of this census showed the nature of the differences between the services provided by the specialised units, and permitted clarification of some of the problems encountered. Among other things, this work also demonstrated the need to develop improved methods for assessing the 'community' workload.

18.   Appraising the work of a hospital chaplain. After three years in post, and having settled into a relatively stable pattern of work, the anglican chaplain raised questions regarding the adequacy of the service he provided, in the context of a changed organisational climate in the hospital. A three-pronged approach to reviewing the work of a lone professional was evolved: a simple survey amongst ward and other staff, to try to determine how they saw the service provided; a commentary from an outside clergyman who was invited to join the chaplain's scheduled work; and the analysis of a special sixteen week diary of unscheduled events in the chaplain's work, to throw some light on his wider religious and pastoral activities.

The results of the methods employed were considered by the chaplain and an interested multi-disciplinary group. Some new areas of work for the chaplain resulted from the process of undertaking the survey, and he devised new strategies for allocating time for his scheduled work. In addition, the project shed some light on the organisational constraints affecting a member of the clergy working in a psychiatric hospital, and the ways in which fuller use could be made of the pastoral skills which may be possessed by modern clergy.

19. Assessing the amount of nursing time required to meet the needs of psycho-geriatric patients. Following a demand from district level for a more rational assessment of the number of nursing staff required in psycho-geriatric care, at a time when the hospital felt itself to be short of staff, a ward group offered to try to assess needs more clearly, aiming to achieve this in a way which might be later applied to other wards in the hospital. On the suggestion of the adviser, the staff group reviewed a list of nursing activities from earlier psycho-geriatric projects and updated it as a starting point to assess workload. Taking one category of activity at a time (for example, feeding, bathing, etc.) they identified four sample groups of patients of differing dependency, and measured the amount of nursing time required to accomplish satisfactorily various activities with each group. In the light of their experience of doing this, they also attempted to evolve clear definitions of dependency for each dimension measured, for wider application. (This project is continuing.)

20. Retrospective review of a cohort of patients referred for long-stay care. Arising from doubts about the efficiency of their work, a multi-disciplinary team assessing patients' suitability for long-stay care decided to undertake a detailed review of 60 patients referred for such care between March 1974 and October 1975. The team assisted by the social research adviser, evolved a schedule of questions for completion and a student social worker assumed the role of research assistant, gathering the data on each patient and reporting back weekly to the assessment group.

Drawing on the systematic data, the experience of undertaking assessments, and some of the difficulties encountered by the student social worker in collecting data, areas of improvement for the assessment process and of subsequent patient management were readily identified. This led the assessment team to set up a discussion forum with representatives from the admission wards in an attempt to ensure that prospective patients were prepared better for assessment, and to the team itself experimenting with new ways of making their assessments and recording information. This work has also led to attention to the form of management needed to support new developments in long-stay care, and an examination of how resettlement can be encouraged. (This project is continuing.)

APPENDIX B: SCHEMA FOR PROJECT ANALYSIS

For Each Project:

1.   Background to the Issues

* What were the wider influences and local developments which led to the issues to be considered?

2.   The Experience of the Problem

* What was the origin of the problem, and how did it come to be experienced as such?
* How was the problem initially being defined by the various people involved?

3.   Responses to This Experience

* What kind of search procedures did this experience lead to?
* What kind of things happened and what options were considered?
* How did staff come to approach the social research adviser?
* Whose idea was this and what role did sponsorship play in it?

4.   The First Steps

* What took place in the initial discussions with the social research adviser?
* What were staff expectations about the project, and what strategies did the adviser adopt?
* Who was involved in the project at this stage?
* Was a project committee composed and what was its membership?
* What contract was established with the adviser, and what degree of sanction did this initial contract have?
* What were the collaborative characteristics of the project in regard to how much influence the adviser and others had in shaping its initial definition and so forth?

5.   Identifying the Problems

* What diagnostic activities were undertaken and by whom?
* How was the project now defined and did this involve any reconceptualisation?
* What was the source of any such changes in conceptualisation?

214 Schema for Project Analysis

6. *The Investigations Undertaken*
* What was the nature of any investigations into these problems?
* Who undertook this investigation? What did this involve?

7. *Working Through the Implications*
* What were the findings from the investigation, and how were these presented?
* What conclusions were drawn from these findings?

8. *The Use of Project Work*
* What types of innovation/outcome arose from the project? (Distinguish changes in practices, policy, organisation and roles, training and other.)
* What was the extent of these changes?
* What assessment could be made of these changes?
  Were they beneficial –
  (i)   according to subjective evaluations?
  (ii)   according to objective indicators on intervening or ultimate measures?
  (iii)   were there any side benefits?
* What contribution did the project make to these changes?

9. *Institutionalisation*
* Did these innovations persist?
* Did these innovations diffuse to other situations?
* Did the process of self-examination reflected in the project continue on to new issues?

10. *The Social Research Adviser*
This should be implicit in all the earlier questions, but distinctive points may be drawn together here on the types of input and intervention made by the adviser, their rationale and appropriateness, the conceptions which underlay them, and the impact they had particularly on the participants' definitions of the situation; also points about the role played by the social research adviser at different stages.

11. *Interpretation of the Change Processes*
* How did change come (or not come) about? What explains this?
* What conditions were relevant?
* What influences were significant?
* What interventions, strategies were useful?

* What functions did the investigation perform?
* What contribution did the adviser make? And what problems were encountered?

12. *Concluding Summary*

* Draw together a summary of the significance of the problem, the nature of the innovation achieved, the resources required to accomplish this, the processes by which it occurred, and any other particular insights drawn from this project.

BIBLIOGRAPHY

Aitken, J., Harries, C.J., Lloyd, A., McRae, I., Murrell, J. and Towell, D. 'Improving General Nurse Training by Psychiatric Secondment', *Nursing Times* (Occasional Paper), 27 June 1974, pp. 29-32.

Barton, R. *Institutional Neurosis* (Wright, Bristol, 1959).

Bion, W.R. *Experience in Groups and Other Papers* (Tavistock, London, 1961).

Brown, G.W. 'The Mental Hospital as an Institution', *Social Science and Medicine*, 7, 1973, pp. 407-24.

Caudill, W. *The Psychiatric Hospital as a Small Society* (Harvard University Press, Cambridge, Mass., 1958).

Cherns, A.B. 'The Use of the Social Sciences', *Human Relations*, 21, 4 (1968), pp. 313-25.

Clark, D.H. *Administrative Therapy* (Tavistock, London, 1964).

Clark, D.H. *Social Therapy in Psychiatry* (Penguin, London, 1974).

Clark, D.H., Hooper, D. and Oram, E. 'Creating a Therapeutic Community in a Psychiatric Ward', *Human Relations*, 15 (1962), pp. 123-49.

Clark, D.H. and Myers, K. 'Themes in a Therapeutic Community', *British Journal of Psychiatry*, 117 (1970), pp. 389-95.

Clark, D.H. and Oram, E. 'Reform in the Mental Hospital: An Eight Year Follow-Up', *International Journal of Social Psychiatry*, 12 (1966), pp. 997-1005.

Clark, P. *Organisational Design: Theory and Practice* (Tavistock, London, 1972a).

Clark, P. *Action Research and Organisational Change* (Harper & Row, London, 1972b).

Crockett, H. 'Fulbourn Hospital: A Patient's View', *Nursing Times* (18 April 1974), pp. 603-4.

Department of Health and Social Security. *National Health Service Reorganisation: England*, Cmnd. 5055 (HMSO, London, 1972).

Department of Health and Social Security. *Report of the Committee on Nursing* (Chairman: Professor Asa Briggs), (HMSO, London, 1972).

Department of Health and Social Security. *Progress on Salmon* (HMSO, London, 1972).

Department of Health and Social Security. *Report of Committee of*

Enquiry: South Ockenden Hospital (HMSO, London, 1974).

Department of Health and Social Security. *Better Services for the Mentally Ill* (HMSO, London, 1975).

Dunning, G. 'Policy-Fallacy', *Health and Social Services Journal* (22 December 1973), pp. 300-1.

Dykens, J.W., Hyde, R.W., Orzack, L.H. and York, R.H. *Strategies of Mental Hospital Change* (Department of Mental Health, Mass., 1964).

Fenn, M., Mungovan, R. and Towell, D. 'Developing the Role of the Unit Nursing Officer', *Nursing Times* (13 February 1975), pp. 262-4.

Ford, J. and Plumb, B. *Bibliography on the Utilisation of Social Science Research* (Centre for Utilisation of Social Science Research, Loughborough University, 1970).

Goffman, E. *Asylums* (Doubleday, New York, 1961, and Penguin Books, 1968).

Greenblatt, M., Levinson, D.J. and Williams, R.N. *The Patient and the Mental Hospital* (Free Press, Glencoe, Ill., 1957).

Harries, C.J. (ed.). 'Disturbed Behaviour: Report of a Day Symposium at Fulbourn Hospital', *Nursing Times*, 68 (1974), pp. 748-50.

Havelock, R.G. *Planning for Innovation through the Dissemination and Utilisation of Knowledge* (Institute of Social Research, University of Michigan, 1969).

Havelock, R.G. *A Guide to Innovation in Education* (Institute of Social Research, University of Michigan, 1970).

Heyworth Committee. *Report of the Committee on Social Studies*, Cmnd. 2660 (HMSO, London, 1965).

Higgin, G. and Bridger, H. 'The Psychodynamics of an Inter-Group Experience', *Human Relations*, 19 (1964), pp. 391-446.

Hooper, D. 'Changing the Milieu in a Psychiatric Ward', *Human Relations*, 15 (1962), pp. 111-22.

Hospital Advisory Service. *National Health Service Hospital Advisory Service Report 1969-70* (HMSO, London, 1970).

Hospital Advisory Service. *Report of the Hospital Advisory Service for 1973* (HMSO, London, 1974).

Hunter, T.D. 'The Last Round-Up', *Health and Social Services Journal* (16 June 1973).

Jones, M. *Social Psychiatry* (Tavistock, London, 1952).

Jones, M. *Beyond the Therapeutic Community* (Yale University Press, London, 1968).

King, R., Raynes, N. and Tizard, J. *Patterns of Residential Care*

(Routledge & Kegan Paul, London, 1971).

Klein, L. 'The Hospital Innovation Project: A Study of the Process of Social Science Utilisation' (Tavistock Institute of Human Relations, London, 1974).

Lawrence, G. and Robinson, P. 'An Innovation and Its Implementation: Issues of Evaluation' (Tavistock Institute of Human Relations, London, 1975).

Long, A. and Pushkin, J. 'Comparative Study of Trainee Nurses in Psychiatric Hospitals', North East Thames RHA, Management Services Division, St Faith's Hospital, Brentwood, Essex (1976).

McGhee. *The Patient's Attitude to Nursing Care* (E. & S. Livingstone, London, 1961).

Marris, P. and Rein, M. *Dilemmas of Social Reform* (Penguin, Middlesex, 1972).

Menzies, I.E.P. 'A Case Study in the Functioning of Social Systems as a Defence Against Anxiety', *Human Relations*, 13 (1960), pp. 95-121.

Miller, E.J. 'Socio-Technical Systems in Weaving 1953-1970: A Follow-Up Study', *Human Relations*, 28 (1975), pp. 348-86.

Miller, E.J. 'The Open-System Approach to Organisational Analysis, With Special Reference to the Work of A.K. Rice', in Hofstede, G. and Sami Kassem, M. (eds.), *European Contributions to Organisation Theory* (Van Gorcum, Amsterdam, 1976a).

Miller, E.J. *Desarrollo integral del medio rural: un experimento en Mexico* (Mexico, D.F.: Fordo de Cultura Economica, 1976b).

Miller, E.J. 'Organisational Development and Industrial Democracy: A Current Case Study', in Cooper, C. (ed.), *Organisational Development in the UK and USA: A Joint Evaluation* (Macmillan, London, 1977), pp. 31-63.

Miller, E.J. and Gwynne, G.V. *A Life Apart: A Pilot Study of Residential Institutions for the Physically Handicapped and the Young Chronic Sick* (Tavistock, London, 1972).

Miller, E.J. and Gwynne, G.V. 'Dependence, Interdependence, and Counter-Dependence in Residential Institutions for Incurables', in Gosling, R. (ed.), *Support, Innovation and Autonomy: Tavistock Clinic Golden Jubilee Papers* (Tavistock, London, 1973).

Miller, E.J. and Rice, A.K. *Systems of Organisation* (Tavistock, London, 1967).

Ministry of Health, Scottish Home and Health Department. *Report of the Committee on Senior Nursing Staff Structure* (Chairman: Brian Salmon), (HMSO, London, 1966).

Ministry of Health. *Committee of Enquiry into Allegations of Ill-Treatment of Patients and other Irregularities at the Ely Hospital, Cardiff,* Cmnd. 3975 (HMSO), London, 1969).

Ministry of Health. *Committee of Enquiry into Conditions at Farleigh Hospital,* Cmnd. 4557 (HMSO, London, 1971).

Ministry of Health. *Committee of Enquiry into Conditions at Whittingham Hospital,* Cmnd. 4861 (HMSO, London, 1972).

Morgan, R. 'The Work of a Junior Doctor in a Psychiatric Hospital', in Freeman, H. and Farndale, J. (eds.), *New Aspects of the Mental Health Services* (Pergamon Press, London, 1967).

Mungovan, R. 'Evolution of a Therapeutic Community', *Nursing Times* (15 March 1968), pp. 365-6.

Myers, K. and Clark, D.H. 'Results in a Therapeutic Community', *British Journal of Psychiatry,* 120 (1972), pp. 51-8.

Pantall, J. and Elliot, J. 'Can Research Aid Hospital Management', *The Hospital* (June, July and August 1965 and September, October and December 1967).

Parlett, M. and Hamilton, D. 'Evaluation as Illumination: A New Approach to the Study of Innovatory Process' (Centre for Research in the Educational Sciences, University of Edinburgh, 1972).

Pattemore, J. 'The Development of a Disturbed Ward', *Nursing Times* (18 January 1957), pp. 73-5.

Revans, R.W. (ed.). *Hospitals: Communication, Choice and Change* (Tavistock, London, 1972).

Rice, A.K. 'Productivity and Social Organisation in an Indian Weaving Shed', *Human Relations,* 6 (1953), pp. 296-329.

Rice, A.K. 'The Experimental Reorganisation of Non-automatic Weaving in an Indian Mill', *Human Relations,* 8 (1955a), pp. 199-249.

Rice, A.K. 'Productivity and Social Organisation in an Indian Weaving Mill. II: A follow-up Study of the Experimental Reorganisation of Automatic Weaving', *Human Relations,* 8 (1955b), pp. 399-428.

Rice, A.K. *Productivity and Social Organisation: the Ahmedabad Experiment* (Tavistock, London, 1958).

Rice, A.K. *The Enterprise and its Environment: a System Theory of Management Organisation* (Tavistock, London, 1963).

Robb, B. *Sans Everything: a Case to Answer* (Nelson, London, 1967).

Rowbottom, R. et al. *Hospital Organisation* (Heinemann, London, 1973).

Savage, B. and Widdowson, T. 'Revising the Use of Nursing Resources in the Care of the Elderly', *Nursing Times* (5 September and 12

September 1974), pp. 1372-4 and pp. 1424-7.

Savage, B. and Wright, T. 'Shared Care of the Elderly', *Health and Social Service Journal*, (8 May 1976), pp. 840-1.

Sofer, C. *The Organisation from Within* (Tavistock, London, 1961).

South East Thames Regional Health Authority. *Report of Committee of Enquiry, St. Augustine's Hospital, Chartham, Canterbury* (Croydon, Surrey, 1976).

Srivastva, S. et al. *Job Satisfaction and Productivity. An Evaluation of Policy Related Research on Productivity, Industrial Organisation and Job Satisfaction: Policy Development and Implementation* (Cleveland, Ohio: Case Western Reserve University, Department of Organisational Behaviour, 1975).

Stanton, A. and Schwartz, M. *The Mental Hospital* (Basic Books, New York, 1954).

Strauss, A., Schatzman, L., Ehrlich, D., Bucher, R. and Sabshin, M. 'The Hospital and its Negotiated Order', in Friedson, E. (ed.), *The Hospital in Modern Society* (Free Press, Glencoe, Ill., 1963).

Strauss, A., Schatzman, L., Ehrlich, D., Bucher, R. and Sabshin, M. *Psychiatric Ideologies and Institutions* (Free Press, Glencoe, Ill., 1964).

Sutherland, J.G., Sharpe, J.G. and Clark, A. 'The Hospital Innovation Project', *Health and Social Service Journal* (26 January 1974), p. 172.

Suzuki, J. 'Socio-Psychological Dynamics of Becoming a Long Stay Patient in a Mental Hospital' (Fulbourn Hospital, Cambridge, 1974).

Thorsrud, E. 'Democratisation of Work as a Process of Change Towards Non-bureaucratic Types of Organisation', in Hofstede, G. and Sami Kassem, M. (eds.), *European Contributions to Organisation Theory* (Van Gorcum, Amsterdam, 1976).

Towell, D. *Understanding Psychiatric Nursing* (Royal College of Nursing, London, 1975).

Towell, D. 'Making Reorganisation Work: Challenges and Dilemmas in the Development of Community Medicine', in Barnard, K. and Lee, K. (eds.), *Conflicts in the NHS* (Croom Helm, London, 1977).

Town, S.W. 'Action Research and Social Policy: Some Recent British Experience', *Sociological Review*, 21, 4 (1973), pp. 573-98.

Urwick, L.F. *Leadership in the Twentieth Century* (Sir Isaac Pitman, London, 1957).

Wieland, G. and Leigh, H. *Changing Hospitals* (Tavistock, London, 1971).

Wilson, A.T.M. 'Some Aspects of Social Process', *Journal of Social*

Issues, Supplementary series, No. 5 (1951).
Wing, J.K. and Brown, G.W. *Institutionalism and Schizophrenia* (Cambridge University Press, 1970).
Zaltman, G., Duncan, R. and Holbeck, J. *Innovations and Organisations* (Wiley, London, 1973).

NOTES ON CONTRIBUTORS

Jim Aitken, SRN, is Senior Nursing Officer (Personnel) with Southend Health District. Between 1972 and 1976 he was Nursing Officer to the Medical Unit at Addenbrookes Hospital, Cambridge.

Lalchan Bhim, RMN, RNMS, is Charge Nurse of a long-stay ward at Fulbourn and is concerned with rehabilitation and the development of social approaches to psychiatric care.

John Burgess, RMN, SRN, is Charge Nurse of a long-stay ward at Fulbourn where he has encouraged fresh thinking about living in hospital.

David H. Clark, MD, PhD, FRC Psych., is a Consultant Psychiatrist at Fulbourn Hospital. He was Medical Superintendent (1953-71) and was involved in opening ward doors and developing therapeutic communities; he is now concerned with developing new social treatment techniques. He is the author of *Administrative Therapy* and *Social Therapy in Psychiatry*.

Maurice Fenn, RMN, SRN, was formerly Principal Nursing Officer at Fulbourn Hospital, and now holds the Divisional Nursing Officer's post, responsible for all nursing, midwifery and health visiting services in the south-western half of the Bury St Edmunds Health District in Suffolk.

Clive Harries, RMN, SRN, was Senior Nursing Officer at Fulbourn Hospital until taking up the role of Social Research Adviser to the Hospital Innovation Project. Previously he worked with the Hospital Advisory Service and has undertaken research on community psychiatric nursing.

Oliver Hodgson, MA, MB, FRC Psych., is a Consultant Psychiatrist in Cambridge where he has worked for 18 years, taking a special interest in old people.

Aggie Lloyd, RMN, SRN, is engaged in family care work as a local

222

authority social worker. She previously held the posts of Ward Sister and Unit Nursing Officer at Fulbourn Hospital, and contributed to the development of more social psychiatric approaches to acute care.

Anne Long and *John Pushkin* work as social scientists for the North East Thames Regional Health Authority. Their main area of interest is the patterning of communication within and between organisations in the health and other allied services.

Ian McRae, RMN, SRN, is now a Nurse Tutor at Hellesdon Hospital, Norwich. Most of his experience in psychiatric nursing has been gained at Fulbourn Hospital, where he was previously a Charge Nurse.

Eric J. Miller, MA, PhD, joined the Tavistock Institute of Human Relations in 1958, where he has developed a systemic approach to studies of group and organisational behaviour through a wide variety of research and consultancy. He has published several papers and four books, including (with G.V. Gwynne) *A Life Apart*.

Ruby Mungovan, RMN, RMPA, has most recently been concerned with establishing group homes, and rehabilitation programmes for long stay patients, as a Nursing Officer, at Fulbourn Hospital. She was previously involved in the development of therapeutic communities at Fulbourn.

Joan Murrell, SRN, RNT, is a Nurse Tutor at Addenbrookes Hospital, where her interests have included the benefits to trainee nurses of psychiatric secondment.

Bev Savage, RMN, is now a Nursing Officer in the Psycho-geriatric Area at Fulbourn Hospital, having previously been Charge Nurse on one of the wards in this area.

David Towell, MA, PhD, was the first Social Research Adviser to the Hospital Innovation Project. He is now involved in a wider programme of action research on developing the 'Cinderella' services, based at the King's Fund Centre and the School for Advanced Urban Studies, University of Bristol. He is author of *Understanding Psychiatric Nursing* and a contributor to *Conflicts in the National Health Service*.

Tony Widdowson, RMN, is a Deputy Charge Nurse at Fulbourn Hospital, where he has worked since leaving school.

Anthony L. Wright is a Senior Social Worker based at the City Division of Cambridgeshire Social Services Department, from where he has taken a direct interest in improving psycho-geriatric care with Fulbourn Hospital.

INDEX

226   *Index*

supervision 155-6, 176
supplies 203

Tavistock Institute of Human
  Relations 15, 18, 32, 37, 127,
  172, 187
therapeutic community 17, 28-9,
  31, 51, 131
Towell, David 15, 17, 26, 31, 32, 40,
  83, 94, 105, 127, 131, 191, 223
trade unions 199-200
trainee nurses: views of 163-8
treatment: medical approach 44;
  social psychiatric approach 39,

treatment—*cont.*
  41, 44, 48

values 19
volunteers 202

ward policy 57, 209
ward sister 45, 49, 101
wards: admission 40-9; long stay
  50-60; psychogeriatric 61-81
Widdowson, Tony 61, 161, 223
Wieland and Leigh 17, 109
Wright, Tony 61, 224